EDDIE GARTH

THE BOOK OF ROMANS

the Smart Guide to the Bible™ series

BE SMART · BE INSPIRED ™

Gib Martin

Larry Richards, General Editor

THIS IS A COMMENTARY BOOK

THOMAS NELSON
Since 1798

NASHVILLE   DALLAS   MEXICO CITY   RIO DE JANEIRO   BEIJING

The Book of Romans
The Smart Guide to the Bible™ series
© 2007 by GRQ, Inc.

Published by Nelson Reference, a Division of Thomas Nelson, Inc., P.O. Box 141000, Nashville, Tennessee 37214.

Originally published by Starburst Publishers under the title *Romans: God's Word for the Biblically-Inept*. Now revised and updated.

Scripture quotations are taken from The New King James Version® (NKJV), copyright 1979, 1980, 1982, 1992 Thomas Nelson, Inc., Publishers.

To the best of its ability, GRQ, Inc., has strived to find the source of all material. If there has been an oversight, please contact us, and we will make any correction deemed necessary in future printings. We also declare that to the best of our knowledge all material (quoted or not) contained herein is accurate, and we shall not be held liable for the same.

General Editor: Larry Richards
Managing Editor: Lila Empson
Associate Editor: W. Mark Whitlock
Scripture Editor: Deborah Wiseman
Assistant Editor: Amy Clark
Design: Diane Whisner

ISBN 978-1-4185-0992-7

Printed in the United States of America
10 11 12 13   9 8 7 6 5 4

Introduction

Welcome to *Romans—The Smart Guide to the Bible*™. This volume is part of a series that takes the Bible as it is—the Word of God—and makes it both entertaining and enlightening. If you want learning to be an adventure, you'll appreciate this approach to study. If you have a thirst for the truth, you've just found a cool drink. If you've been looking for a way to enrich your knowledge of God's Word, studying the apostle Paul's letter to the Romans is a great way to start.

To Gain Your Confidence

Romans—The Smart Guide to the Bible™ keeps God's Word clear and simple and at the same time accurate, thorough, and interesting. It will take us to new spiritual heights in our journey with God. In the thin air of the climb, one's spiritual vision is sharpened, and at the summit we can see more clearly what it means to be a follower of Jesus. So strap on your climbing gear and get ready for this delightful adventure into God's truth!

Why Study Romans?

Romans is a book that helps us understand who God is and who we are in relation to God. If we have a right understanding of these two things, we will know better how to live in such a way that pleases God, brings us fulfillment, and makes a difference in the world around us.

How to Study Romans

Paul's Letter to the Romans is widely recognized by every class of people, common folk and scholar alike, as the single most influential document within the Scriptures. This book effectively speaks to all the key issues of the Christian faith as pertaining to the Gospel; it presents the whole counsel of God.

In carrying out this remarkable mission, we are also given a demanding presentation of Paul the apostle. In an unquestionable way, we hear the voice of Paul, "a servant of Christ Jesus," and simultaneously we are confronted with the "voice of the Holy Spirit." Paul is a premier theologian, and when we take time to listen carefully to the wisdom he brings to this writing, we are enriched spiritually and intellectually.

As you begin this study in Romans, you will become increasingly aware that this is a great theological treatise that carefully explains the dynamic nature of God's righteousness as it is revealed in the person and the purpose of Jesus. Humankind is in need of righteousness if we are to be able to fellowship with our Creator God. Paul carefully explains that neither Jew nor Gentile is righteous; so God acted in Christ Jesus, providing righteousness as a gift to all who believe in the Lord Jesus Christ.

I would like to suggest, even recommend, an approach to your study of this extraordinary writing, an approach to the study of Scripture that has helped many whom I have mentored over the years:

1. Get acquainted with the apostle Paul, the author of this book. His insights, his unique ability to express truth in understandable ways, will encourage your heart and equip you for your ministry.

2. Familiarize yourself with Paul's other letters: 1 and 2 Corinthians, Galatians, Ephesians, Philippians, Colossians, 1 and 2 Thessalonians, 1 and 2 Timothy, Titus, Philemon, and Hebrews.

3. Read through Romans at least once before you begin your study in *Romans—The Smart Guide to the Bible*™.

4. Take time to pray. Invited the Holy Spirit to be your teacher and guide. Jesus taught that the Spirit "will guide you into all truth" (John 16:13 NKJV). What a great promise!

5. If possible, develop the habit of journal writing. This helps us remember the truth that the Spirit is bringing to light. A few journaling techniques that I have found helpful:

6. Write out questions that come to mind as you read and study. For example: the meaning of words with which you are becoming familiar; names of people and places you might want to study in your research later on.

7. When you discover an answer to a question you have been pondering or discussing with a friend, write it down.

8. When the Holy Spirit addresses a personal need, take time to note it and write down this new insight; then take a moment to thank God for speaking his will into your heart and mind.

9. Be creative! When something you read inspires you, take a moment to write a prayer or a poem. A letter to a special friend—sharing your adventure in God's Word—is a thoughtful way of sharing God's grace with others. Remember, God sent this letter you are studying to the church as a gift of his love.

How to Use *Romans—The Smart Guide to the Bible*™

Sit down with this book and your Bible.

- Start the book at chapter 1.
- As you work through each chapter, read the accompanying verses in your Bible.
- Use the sidebars loaded with icons and helpful information to give you a knowledge boost.
- Answer the Study Questions and review with the Chapter Wrap-Up.
- Then go on to the next chapter. It's simple!

One Final Tip

Knowledge of the Bible is not meant to be an end in itself. God wants us to know his Word, but he also wants us to know him. In the same way, Paul wanted his readers to understand what he said, but he also wanted them to have a personal relationship with his Lord.

God, who gave us the Bible, is present with us when we read it. As you read Romans, ask him to help you understand his Word. Ask him to show you his wonderful grace and to help you put your faith in him. You'll be surprised and delighted as he answers your prayer. The Bible will enrich your life!

A Word About Words

There are several interchangeable terms in this book: *Scripture, Scriptures, Word, Word of God,* and *God's Word.* All of these mean the same thing and come under the broad heading of the Bible. The Bible is divided into two sections: the Old Testament and the New Testament. Throughout this commentary I use the terms *Old Covenant* and *Old Testament* to mean the same thing, and I use *New Covenant* and *New Testament* to mean the same thing as well. The word *LORD* in the Old Testament refers to Yahweh, God, whereas in the New Testament it refers to God's Son, Jesus Christ.

About the Author

The Reverend Gib Martin grew up in a family of twelve children in the township of Leroy in northeast Ohio. After he finished college and completed his military obligation, Gib was converted to faith in Jesus Christ. He studied Bible and theology for four years in Dallas and was with the Jesuit School of Theology in Berkeley for three years. For forty-three years he has been pastor-teacher of the Trinity Church in Seattle. His gifts have led him into a ministry of discipleship, counseling, and mentoring in the States and in a number of other countries. He served eight years with Arrow Leadership Ministry International, twenty-five years on the Board of Missions to Unreached Peoples, and is past NW regional chairman of the Billy Graham Phone Centers. Gib and his wife, Linda, have three daughters, three sons-in-law, and six grandchildren.

About the General Editor

Dr. Larry Richards is a native of Michigan who now lives in Raleigh, North Carolina. He was converted while in the Navy in the 1950s. Larry has taught and written Sunday school curriculum for every age group, from nursery through adult. He has published more than two hundred books that have been translated into twenty-six languages. His wife, Sue, is also an author. They both enjoy teaching Bible studies as well as fishing and playing golf.

Understanding the Bible Is Easy with These Tools

To understand God's Word you need easy-to-use study tools right where you need them—at your fingertips. The Smart Guide to the Bible™ series puts valuable resources adjacent to the text to save you both time and effort.

Every page features handy sidebars filled with icons and helpful information: cross references for additional insights, definitions of key words and concepts, brief commentaries from experts on the topic, points to ponder, evidence of God at work, the big picture of how passages fit into the context of the entire Bible, practical tips for applying biblical truths to every area of your life, and plenty of maps, charts, and illustrations. A wrap-up of each passage, combined with study questions, concludes each chapter.

These helpful tools show you what to watch for. Look them over to become familiar with them, and then turn to Chapter 1 with complete confidence: You are about to increase your knowledge of God's Word!

Study Helps

The thought-bubble icon alerts you to commentary you might find particularly thought-provoking, challenging, or encouraging. You'll want to take a moment to reflect on it and consider the implications for your life.

Don't miss this point! The exclamation-point icon draws your attention to a key point in the text and emphasizes important biblical truths and facts.

go to

death on the cross
Colossians 1:21–22

Many see Boaz as a type of Jesus Christ. To win back what we human beings lost through sin and spiritual death, Jesus had to become human (i.e., he had to become a true kinsman), and he had to be willing to pay the penalty for our sins. With his <u>death on the cross</u>, Jesus paid the penalty and won freedom and eternal life for us.

The additional Bible verses add scriptural support for the passage you just read and help you better understand the <u>underlined text</u>. (Think of it as an instant reference resource!)

How does what you just read apply to your life? The heart icon indicates that you're about to find out! These practical tips speak to your mind, heart, body, and soul, and offer clear guidelines for living a righteous and joy-filled life, establishing priorities, maintaining healthy relationships, persevering through challenges, and more.

This icon reveals how God is truly all-knowing and all-powerful. The hourglass icon points to a specific example of the prediction of an event or the fulfillment of a prediction. See how some of what God has said would come to pass already has!

What are some of the great things God has done? The traffic-sign icon shows you how God has used miracles, special acts, promises, and covenants throughout history to draw people to him.

Does the story or event you just read about appear elsewhere in the Gospels? The cross icon points you to those instances where the same story appears in other Gospel locations—further proof of the accuracy and truth of Jesus' life, death, and resurrection.

Since God created marriage, there's no better person to turn to for advice. The double-ring icon points out biblical insights and tips for strengthening your marriage.

The Bible is filled with wisdom about raising a godly family and enjoying your spiritual family in Christ. The family icon gives you ideas for building up your home and helping your family grow close and strong.

something significant had occurred, he wrote down the substance of what he saw. This is the practice John followed when he recorded Revelation on the **Isle of Patmos.**

What does that word really mean, especially as it relates to this passage? Important, misunderstood, or infrequently used words are set in **bold type** in your text so you can immediately glance at the margin for definitions. This valuable feature lets you better understand the meaning of the entire passage without having to stop to check other references.

the big picture

Joshua
Led by Joshua, the Israelites crossed the Jordan River and invaded Canaan (see Illustration #8). In a series of military campaigns the Israelites defeated several coalition armies raised by the inhabitants of Canaan. With organized resistance put down, Joshua divided the land among the twelve Israelite

How does what you read fit in with the greater biblical story? The highlighted big picture summarizes the passage under discussion.

what others say

David Breese
Nothing is clearer in the Word of God than the fact that God wants us to understand himself and his working in the lives of men.[5]

It can be helpful to know what others say on the topic, and the highlighted quotation introduces another voice in the discussion. This resource enables you to read other opinions and perspectives.

Maps, charts, and illustrations pictorially represent ancient artifacts and show where and how stories and events took place. They enable you to better understand important empires, learn your way around villages and temples, see where major battles occurred, and follow the journeys of God's people. You'll find these graphics let you do more than study God's Word—they let you *experience* it.

Chapters at a Glance

PART THREE: Experiencing Grace

PART FOUR: Jews and Gentiles

PART FIVE: A Grace-Filled Church

Part One
THE NECESSITY OF FAITH

Romans 1 A Servant's Longing

Chapter Highlights:
- A Divine Appointment
- A Commitment and Prayer
- A Holy Declaration
- The Human Condition

Let's Get Started

The apostle Paul wrote the book of Romans in the first century, which was a time of rapid growth for Christianity. Good roads and internal political peace made for swift evangelism throughout the Roman Empire (see Illustration #1). New churches were founded regularly.

Both biblical and nonreligious history report that many of the founders of the church in the city of Rome were **Jewish Christians**. Sometime around AD 45 the emperors (first Tiberius and then Claudius) announced an **edict** to expel Jews from **Rome** so the only people left in the Roman church were **Gentiles**. When the edict against the Jews was repealed at the time of Claudius's death, many of the Jews who loved their Roman heritage returned to the city.

When they came back, Jewish believers experienced a form of culture shock. The Gentiles gave little regard to many of the traditions and beliefs that the Jews dearly loved. The Roman church, therefore, was in tremendous tension. Paul, a seasoned saint and an expert on church growth, felt their concerns. He knew the Gospel could empower people to stick together despite their <u>differences</u>.

go to

differences
Ephesians 2:14–17;
Colossians 3:8–11

Christian church
Acts 7:54–60;
1 Corinthians 15:9;
Philippians 3:6

Jewish Christians
Jews who believed in Jesus

edict
edict a royal command binding on everyone

Rome
the capital of the Roman Empire

Gentiles
non-Jews, whatever their race or religion

Paul: Mr. About-Face

As a Pharisee, Paul, whose first name was Saul, believed in the Old Testament prophecies about a Messiah, a great leader who would emerge from the family line of King David. He, like most Jews, believed the Messiah would dethrone Roman rule, impose Old Testament law as national law, and usher in God's new kingdom.

One of Saul's duties as a member of the Sanhedrin was to travel around the country and arrest Christians because they were thought to be a serious threat to Judaism. Saul zealously sought to put an end to the exploding work of the <u>Christian church</u> in Jerusalem and all

go to

three
Acts 9:1–31;
22:5–21; 26:9–20

prison
Acts 28:17–31

Damascus
a city in Syria

Ephesian
of the city of
Ephesus, in modern
Turkey

of Judah. We have no record that Paul actually killed Christians, but in Acts 8 we do see him approving of the execution of the Christian disciple, Stephen. The text reveals, "Saul was consenting to [Stephen's] death" (Acts 8:1 NKJV.)

Not long afterwards Saul was on his way to **Damascus** to imprison Christians when "suddenly a light shone around him from heaven. Then he fell to the ground, and heard a voice saying to him, 'Saul, Saul, why are you persecuting Me?' And he said, 'Who are You, Lord?' Then the Lord said, 'I am Jesus, whom you are persecuting'" (Acts 9:3–5 NKJV). This encounter with the risen Christ changed Saul forever. His testimony is recorded <u>three</u> times in the book of Acts.

Paul spent the rest of his life traveling from city to city spreading the good news that God forgives. At the end of his life he is faithfully serving his Lord in a Roman <u>prison</u>.

In Acts 20 we gain some insight into how Paul arrived at his understanding of truth. The apostle had been in active ministry for a number of years. Prepared to depart from Asia for the next stage of his ministry, he gathered the elders of the **Ephesian** church, men whom Paul had trained for ministry, so that he could encourage and advise them one last time.

Illustration #1
Map of Roman Empire—The dashed lines show the boundaries of the eastern half of the Roman Empire about the time Paul wrote Romans in AD 57. The believers who lived in Rome were the recipients of Paul's letter.

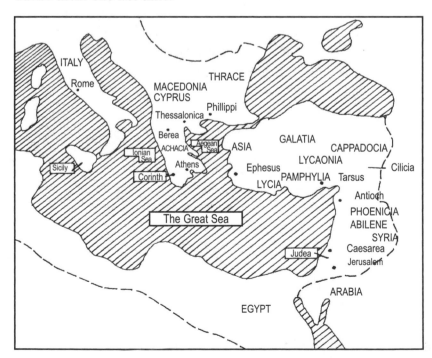

"You know, from the first day that I came to Asia, in what manner I always lived among you," Paul declared, "serving the Lord with all humility, with many tears and trials . . . For I have not shunned to declare to you the whole counsel of God" (Acts 20:18–19, 27 NKJV). The phrase "the whole counsel of God" is very important. It probably refers in part to the incompleteness of the Old Testament, foreshadowing what the New Testament reveals in full-orbed beauty. Paul is also pointing out that his <u>teaching</u> is not unbalanced. He doesn't, for instance, emphasize grace at the expense of responsibility.

Israel emphasized carrying out every detail of the law while neglecting what Jesus thought were the weightier matters (things like caring for sick people and nurturing good heart attitudes). This unbalanced perspective led the Jews to lose sight of God's purposes entirely and drift into legalism, satisfied with externals and unaware that their hearts were far from God. Paul is providing a balanced picture of God's plans and purposes, in which no aspect is emphasized at the expense of another, and with such harmony that the whole can be seen and understood by Jesus' people.

go to

teaching
1 Timothy 4:9–16;
2 Timothy 4:1–8;
Titus 3:1–10

title
Galatians 1:10;
Titus 1:1

kingdom
the rule of God

> **what others say**
>
> ### D. Martyn Lloyd-Jones
>
> [Romans] was written as a letter by a great pastor. . . . It is a letter written to a church, and like all New Testament literature it had a very practical aim and end in view. The apostle was concerned to help these Christians in Rome, to build them up and establish them in their most holy faith.[1]

Paul@servingJesus.com

ROMANS 1:1 *Paul, a bondservant of Jesus Christ, called to be an apostle, separated to the gospel of God (NKJV)*

Paul built his identity on being a servant of Jesus. The word *bondservant* is literally the word for *slave* in that culture, and it means "one who completely belongs to his owner and has no freedom to leave," not that Paul would want to leave. He wore this <u>title</u> gladly.

Once Paul was free, God commissioned him personally to be an apostle in the work of the **kingdom** of God. Paul told the Corinthian church, "I am the least of the apostles, who am not worthy to be called an apostle, because I persecuted the church of God. But by the grace of God I am what I am, and His grace toward me

go to

Ananias
Acts 1

vessel
Acts 22:3–16;
26:9–18

epistle
letter

was not in vain" (1 Corinthians 15:9–10 NKJV).

The word *apostle* comes from a Greek word meaning "one sent forth." In the historical sense, to be an apostle meant to be sent forth by Jesus Christ to build the church.

Years before Paul penned his letter to the Romans, God gave a man named <u>Ananias</u> a tough assignment. God told Ananias to go see Paul, who was staying in the home of a man named Judas, and pray for him. All Ananias knew about Paul was that he hated Christians, and Ananias wasn't prepared to be Paul's next victim! But God's command to Ananias was clear: "Go! For he is a chosen <u>vessel</u> to bear My name before Gentiles, kings, and the children of Israel. For I will show him how many things he must suffer for My name's sake" (Acts 9:15–16 NKJV). It's possible Paul learned his first lesson in servanthood from this good man.

John Chrysostom (AD 347–407), a patriarch of Constantinople (AD 398–404), was a man of great influence as a preacher, author, and leader. It was reported that he had failing eyesight, so to stay active and theologically accurate, he had Romans read to him twice a week.

Centuries later, John Wesley felt his heart strangely warmed in a little London prayer meeting in Aldersgate where the truths of Romans were being set forth. This experience set Wesley on a path that was to reach out to all of England and across the ocean to America.

---

what others say

Samuel Taylor Coleridge

[Romans is] the profoundest [sic] book in existence.[2]

Martin Luther

The **Epistle** to the Romans is the true masterpiece of the New Testament and the very purest Gospel, which is well worth and deserving that a Christian should not only learn it by heart, word for word, but also that he should daily deal with it as the daily bread of men's souls. It can never be too much or too well read and studied, and the more it is handled the more precious it becomes, and the better it tastes.[3]

---

what others say

F. L. Godet

The Reformation was certainly the work of the epistle to the Romans and that to the Galatians, and it is probable that every great spiritual renovation in the church will always be linked, both in cause and in effect, to a deeper knowledge of this book.[4]

Paul's Pocket-Sized Guide to Jesus

ROMANS 1:2–4 *which He promised before through His prophets in the Holy Scriptures, concerning His Son Jesus Christ our Lord, who was born of the seed of David according to the flesh, and declared to be the Son of God with power according to the Spirit of holiness, by the resurrection from the dead. (NKJV)*

Paul began his letter with a brief, yet very complete, account of who Jesus was. He sees an understanding of Christ, as presented in the Bible and revealed through Jesus himself, as the only truth broad enough to consolidate and unify the heart of God's message to humankind. This is why Paul's compact statement of Christ—about his nature, his **lineage**, his **Sonship**, and his resurrection—is Paul's point of departure.

On the human side Jesus came through the line of **David**. He was also "declared to be the Son of God with power" (Romans 1:4 NKJV). In this context, declared means "to be determined, to be marked out" with certainty as the Son of God. His divine nature was clearly demonstrated "by the resurrection from the dead" (verse 4 NKJV). He was indeed the long-awaited Messiah of Israel and the Savior of humankind (Luke 24:25–27, 45–47).

After years of ministering, Paul told the Philippians his reason for living: "to me, to live is Christ" (Philippians 1:21 NKJV). The essence of Paul's life was Christ. His motivation for doing what he did, his goals, the way he treated people around him, everything about him revolved around the person of Jesus. His life was completely wrapped up in the purposes of Christ.

Paul's servant heart inspired him to live submissively under his Lord's authority.

The promise God made to David in the **Davidic Covenant** was an unconditional promise. David would be in the bloodline of the

life
Acts 26

Old Testament
the first thirty-nine books of the Bible, all written before Christ's birth

eunuch
by the first century, the title of a high government official

Philip
a leader of the first Christians in Jerusalem

baptism
sacred ritual involving water, symbolizing membership in God's family and purification from sin

the Incarnation
doctrine that the Son of God became a true human

grace of God
kindness and love shown by God to people who do not deserve it

Mosaic law
the Ten Commandments and the other laws that God gave to Moses as standards of righteousness

Messiah. The Christ child was a descendant of Nathan, one of David's sons, so the unconditional promise was fulfilled (Luke 1:26–37; 2 Samuel 7:16).

A good example of an **Old Testament** prophecy of the Gospel is found in Acts 8:30–35 where an Ethiopian **eunuch** asks **Philip** who is being referred to in Isaiah 53:7–8. Philip "preached Jesus to him." The eunuch believes immediately and seeks **baptism**.

> **what others say**
>
> **Francis A. Schaeffer**
>
> Paul shows both the human and the divine side of **the Incarnation**. He certainly believed in Christ's deity, but the fact of His being truly divine does not change the fact that Christ was also a true man and came down through the natural line of David.[5]

Called to Christ

ROMANS 1:5–6 *Through Him we have received grace and apostleship for obedience to the faith among all nations for His name, among whom you also are the called of Jesus Christ;* (NKJV)

The church at Rome was a body of believers made up of both Jews and Gentiles, and Paul's mission was to all nations: "Through Him we have received grace and apostleship for obedience to the faith among all nations for His name." Romans is for everyone.

The Gospel was the apostle Paul's introduction to grace. In Paul's theological development as a follower of Christ, there was nothing more important to grasp than an understanding of the **grace of God**. He wrote to the Corinthian church, "But by the grace of God I am what I am, and His grace toward me was not in vain; but I labored more abundantly than they all, yet not I, but the grace of God which was with me" (1 Corinthians 15:10 NKJV). The message of God's grace permeated every aspect of Paul's <u>life</u> and every letter he penned to the churches.

Romans is about something the Bible calls the "New Covenant." Through Moses God had made an agreement—a contract or promise—with the Jewish people. This contract, also called the **Mosaic law**, was the "Old Covenant." Through Moses God promised to bless his people if they obeyed him, and to punish them if they disobeyed. Jesus introduced a "New Covenant." The New Covenant was predicted by the prophet Jeremiah, who said it would not be like the Old Covenant. God's people had not been able to keep the Old Covenant, and suffered many troubles. With the New Covenant God said he would change people from within, to make them truly good. Romans is about the New Covenant, and key words are *righteousness* and *grace*.

go to

sainthood
1 Peter 1:15–16;
Ephesians 1:1–2

Spain
Romans 15:24, 28

saints
people who trust in
Jesus as their Savior

From a God's-Eye View

ROMANS 1:7 *To all who are in Rome, beloved of God, called to be **saints**: Grace to you and peace from God our Father and the Lord Jesus Christ.* (NKJV)

As the epistle opens, we are introduced to God's view of the believers in Rome. Paul begins with a greeting, which acknowledges that these people have a special place in God's heart. Paul's Roman brothers and sisters were not called to be apostles, as he had been called, but to be *saints*, a word that was commonly used for believers back then. The words *apostle* and *saint* both carry the idea of being "set apart," or called to holiness.

Linguistic scholar W. E. Vine says, "This sainthood is not an attainment, it is a state into which God in grace calls men."[6] Saints are deeply loved and share in God's life and mission. Paul's greeting demonstrates his recognition that all believers are members of one body, God's family.

Prior to this, Paul had completed a number of missionary journeys in the eastern Mediterranean region, quite a distance from Rome. He had been planting churches in a number of major metropolitan centers throughout southern and western Asia Minor (present-day Turkey, Greece, and Albania). The Roman Empire indirectly helped to spread the Gospel. Travel throughout the region was fairly easy by the day's standards. Roads were good, language was unified, and people were free to travel without fear (see Illustration #1).

Rome was heavy on Paul's heart, but he wouldn't be able to visit the city until the second stage of his church-planting agenda. Though Paul deeply wanted to spend time with these believers, he planned to do so later on his way to Spain.

Illustration #2
Symbol of the
Roman Empire—
Among other ways
they unified the
region, the Romans
used an eagle,
shown here on a
ball, as a symbol for
the Roman Empire.

finished work
salvation through
Christ's death on
the cross

Lamb of God
Jesus, referring to
his death as a sacri-
fice for our sins

Paul longed to go to Rome both to meet the saints there and to minister to them, but due to other responsibilities, he was prevented from doing so. This letter was his way of serving the believers in Rome even while he was physically absent from them. A letter is still a wonderful way to encourage a friend, build a relationship, and serve the kingdom of God.

Dr. Francis A. Schaeffer thoughtfully reminds us, "Everything depends upon the **finished work** of Jesus Christ."[7] This is the divine power behind God's work of grace. God has no alternative plan. The Gospel of Jesus Christ is God's concluding message to a needy, sinful world. Paul discerned that his major mission was to plant the seeds of the Gospel as far and wide as the Spirit would lead him. He saw it as God's answer to our enslavement to sin, to self, and to Satan. In Christ Jesus, God had entered history as "the **Lamb of God**, who takes away the sin of the world" (John 1:29 NKJV).

what others say

Saint Augustine

Here again [in Romans 1:7] Paul has emphasized God's grace rather than the saint's merit, for he does not say "to those loving God" but rather "to God's beloved."[8]

The First Item on Paul's Agenda

ROMANS 1:8a *First, I thank my God through Jesus Christ for you all,* (NKJV)

Having taken care of the "From" and "To" parts of his letter, Paul lingers for a while in introductory matters before getting into his main concern. Why? It appears Paul just couldn't help but express how much he cared about his listeners. Like a boy who can't wait to show his mother the finger painting he did in school, Paul can't resist showing his gratitude. "I thank God for you!" he says.

The Bible tells us we ought always to pray and not lose heart. The disciples asked Jesus to teach them to pray because they saw how much he valued prayer. We too ought to ask God to teach us how to pray.

One of the best signs of a right understanding of grace is a desire to pray—not prayer on the run, but deep, thoughtful prayer on your knees, in your bedroom, in your study, or with a few close friends. It is a privilege we are to take advantage of daily.

Paul wanted to rescue the Romans from their bondage to the <u>law</u> and lead them into an understanding of grace through **faith**. Paul's prayers were not performances of **piety** to impress people; they were evidence of the fire in his soul.

go to

law
Galatians 4:1–7;
Romans 6:14

faith
trust in and reliance on God and his Word

piety
devoutness

key point

what others say

Adolf Schlatter

For Paul all that God does obligates him to give thanks, because God is "his God" . . . his capacity to give thanks is the work of Jesus in him; he is giving thanks "through him."[9]

World-Class Faith

ROMANS 1:8b *that your faith is spoken of throughout the whole world.* (NKJV)

Here we see the object of Paul's passion: spreading the Gospel. He doesn't say, "I thank God for you because of all the nice stuff you sent me last Christmas," or anything like that. He thanks God for them because he was thrilled that word of their faith was spreading. He goes so far as to use the exaggeration, "throughout the whole world." When we consider how much of "the world" was unknown to Paul, a contemporary equivalent to this statement might be, "I thank God for you because your faith is spreading all over the universe!" He was exaggerating, of course, much like the fisherman who gets really excited about his catch and says, "It was the size of Texas!"

There are those who worry about the use of hyperbole, feeling it discredits the integrity of the communicator. For those who have been privileged to read broadly, or even travel in other cultures, they are aware that it is a common way to express what one feels deeply. Yes, it can be misused, but it is my conviction it was simply Paul's way of encouraging the believers in Rome, for they indeed had a worldwide reputation as a Christian community.

Paul also thanks God for the faith of "all" the Christians in Rome. This is not just some expansive gesture. That would be out of character with Paul. Rather, it was an attempt to forge a single unit, or audience, out of groups of believers that were used to meeting in separate homes called "house churches" historically (Romans 16:5, 10–11, 14–15).

"That I may be encouraged together with you by the mutual truth" (Romans 1:12 NKJV) gives us a picture of the heart of this faithful servant of our Lord. It reminds me of another of God's great servants, Dietrich Bonhoeffer, who always found ways to encourage his fellow prisoners, in spite of his own needs. An English officer, Payne Best, a fellow prisoner, wrote of Dietrich: "He always seemed to me to diffuse an atmosphere of happiness, of joy in every smallest event in life, and of deep gratitude for the mere fact that he was alive." In suffering, Bonhoeffer, like Paul, still had the grace to encourage others and point them to Jesus.[10]

> **what others say**
>
> **John F. Walvoord and Roy B. Zuck**
>
> Paul made a practice of beginning his letters with a word of thanks to God, a specific prayer, and a personal message to the recipients. For the Romans he rejoiced that news of their faith had spread all over the world, a hyperbole, meaning throughout the Roman Empire.[11]

Don't Doubt

ROMANS 1:9–10 *For God is my witness, whom I serve with my spirit in the gospel of His Son, that without ceasing I make mention of you always in my prayers, making request if, by some means, now at last I may find a way in the will of God to come to you. (NKJV)*

The only time Paul used the phrase "God is my witness" was when there might have been some reason for his listeners to doubt him.

So, why wouldn't the Romans have believed that Paul prayed fervently for them? Well, if an acquaintance wrote you a Christmas card that said, "I pray for you always," wouldn't you assume they were just being nice and didn't really expect to be taken literally? Most of the Roman Christians did not even know Paul, so hearing him say he prayed for them all the time would have been odd to them. Now, imagine if the above-mentioned acquaintance said this instead: "I pray for you all the time, and I'm not just saying that. I really mean it!" You might be a little more convinced. This is similar to what Paul was doing with his "God is my witness" statement.

Also, Paul was about to leave for Jerusalem when he wrote this letter, but had not yet visited Rome. He may have thought the Roman Christians would think he didn't care as much about them as he did about the Christians in Jerusalem. He was doing his best to quell such suspicions.

He then told the Roman Christians that he was praying God would open the way for him to visit them. Paul did not rely on his own will but on God, "both to will and to do for His good pleasure" (Philippians 2:13 NKJV). Fortunately, God eventually answered Paul's prayer in the affirmative. Acts 18–28 gives an account of how Paul made it to Rome.

propitious
favorable

vouchsafes
grants

Temple
where Jews went to pray, worship, and offer sacrifices

what others say

Pelagius

Paul does not find the way **propitious** unless the will of God who knows all things has directed him to a place where he might reap some fruit. For example, we read in Acts that, although he wanted to go to one place, he was directed to another.[12]

William S. Plumer

Like other things, journeys are prosperous or adverse, as the Lord **vouchsafes** or withholds his favor and blessing. . . . And we should acknowledge his hand in the [most common] affairs of life.[13]

What Paul says concerning his prayer life is evidence of his religious roots. As a former Pharisee, Paul would have been used to a prayer ritual. As a devout Jew, he might have spent several hours a day in prayer, as many did in conjunction with the morning and evening offerings in the **Temple**.

high priest
Hebrews 4:14–16;
Hebrews 2:17

Psalms
Romans 3:9–18;
Romans 15:9, 11

high priest
chief person who
represents believers
before God

Illustration #3
High Priest—A high
priest such as this
one performed tem-
ple sacrifices and
was the mediator
between God and
people during Old
Testament times.
When Christ died
and rose again, he
became the only
mediator necessary.

Prayer

Prayer is learned, just as speaking is learned. We learn a few words and our parents praise us, even applaud us. Then we begin to build sentences. So it is with prayer.

Prayer is our method of communication with God. Jesus, our **high priest** (see Illustration #3) and mediator, hears the prayers of all believers and delivers them to the Father. We pray because we have a Father who will consider our requests and answer them according to his divine will.

The Holy Spirit empowers the believer's prayer life. When the Word of God exhorts us to pray "always with all prayer and supplication in the Spirit" (Ephesians 6:18 NKJV), it points us to the reality that God's Spirit lives in us and prays through us.

God helps us further by providing the Psalms as our prayer book. The Psalms act as a tutorial, showing us the purpose of prayer, the intimacy of prayer, and the potential of a life bathed in prayer. Paul often quoted the <u>Psalms</u> in his letters.

It's Been Way Too Long

pagans
those who believed
in many nature gods
and goddesses

ROMANS 1:11–13 *For I long to see you, that I may impart to you some spiritual gift, so that you may be established—that is, that I may be encouraged together with you by the mutual faith both of you and me. Now I do not want you to be unaware, brethren, that I often planned to come to you (but was hindered until now), that I might have some fruit among you also, just as among the other Gentiles. (NKJV)*

In order to interpret this passage accurately, we need to step out of our technological age, with its ability to provide up-to-the-second worldwide communication, and into the apostle's sandals. When Paul wrote, "I long to see you" (Romans 1:11 NKJV), he meant he had a yearning that could not be fully satisfied apart from a face-to-face visit. He tells them he wants to give them "some spiritual gift" (verse 11 NKJV), but as soon as he says this he humbly asserts that encouragement would flow in both directions. ✸

Jesus taught his disciples, "For everyone to whom much is given, from him much will be required; and to whom much has been committed, of him they will ask the more" (Luke 12:48 NKJV). Paul had been given much. The apostle held himself accountable to share his spiritual wealth with the people of God as well as with the **pagans**—an expression of humility, not pride.

Joseph Shulam, in his commentary on Romans, writes, "Paul specifies the reason for his desire to visit the congregation in Rome as mutual spiritual edification. As the apostle to the Gentiles he apparently feels some responsibility for a community which he himself did not found, at the same time as he does not want to encroach on another evangelist's territory (see Romans 15:20–22). He immediately modifies his apostolic authority by saying that his intention is to 'establish' (build up or edify) the congregation, and explains that intention by indicating that he is seeking *mutual* encouragement."[14]

what others say

Mother Teresa

Give the world the best you have, and it may never be enough; Give the world the best you've got anyway. You see, in the final analysis, it is between you and God; it was never between you and them anyway.[15]

go to

all people
1 Corinthians
9:19–27

good
2 Corinthians
10:31–32;
1 Peter 4:11

hostility
2 Corinthians 6:3–10

covenant
formal, binding
agreement or
promise

reconciled
restored to harmony
with God

---

what others say

Francis A. Schaeffer

Paul is not distant or aloof from the people he writes to. . . . He knows that such maturity will bring sweet and wonderful fellowship between himself and the Romans. He expects to receive a blessing from them as well as giving one to them. This is surely true among Christians always . . . the blessings run in both directions.[16]

Paul, the Eager Beaver

ROMANS 1:14–15 *I am a debtor both to Greeks and to barbarians, both to wise and to unwise. So, as much as is in me, I am ready to preach the gospel to you who are in Rome also. (NKJV)*

Paul explains his **covenant** responsibilities: "I am a debtor," or as it is translated in the New International Version, "I am obligated." A debtor is a person under obligation. Why does Paul consider himself a debtor? For the same reason all Christians are debtors. When we were saved, we were simultaneously called to be "ambassadors for Christ, as though God were pleading through us" (2 Corinthians 5:20 NKJV). Having been **reconciled** to God, God is calling each one of us to be ministers of reconciliation.

Paul's calling, like ours, was universal. He was indeed obligated to Greeks and to non-Greeks (non-Jewish people), to the wise and the foolish. He was, as are we, called by God to lay aside all prejudices, all judgments, and all slander. He is boldly affirming that God is for all people, everywhere, regardless of gender, race, or nationality.

Like fish that swim upstream, Paul went against a culture that was full of prejudice, hatred, and abuse. The Greeks considered themselves wise and the world foolish barbarians. The Jews looked upon the Gentiles as unclean and therefore dangerous.

Paul considered himself a debtor to both Jews and Greeks. He thought of himself as obligated to do good to all people, which eventually brought hostility from many directions.

Paul was eager to preach the Gospel in Rome or wherever else the Lord took him, regardless of the cost. He was ready to mobilize, to do whatever was required to accomplish God's bidding in this world-famous city, but neither fame nor money motivated Paul; his central concern was always the glory of God.

When you give your life to the Lord, there is a cost. Jesus warned his **disciples**, "If the **world** hates you, you know that it hated Me before it hated you. If you were of the world, the world would love its own. Yet because you are not of the world, but I chose you out of the world, therefore the world hates you. Remember the word that I said to you, 'A servant is not greater than his master'" (John 15:18–20 NKJV). We ought to remember and be encouraged by the truth that if the world hates us, it is because the world is ignorant of Christ's love.

Shout It from the Housetops

ROMANS 1:16 *For I am not **ashamed** of the gospel of Christ, for it is the power of God to salvation for everyone who believes, for the Jew first and also for the Greek.* (NKJV)

Paul wants to establish clearly in the hearts of his recipients that he is not in any way "ashamed of the gospel" (Romans 1:16 NKJV), not even in the capital city of the Roman Empire.

He explains why: "for it is the power of God to salvation for everyone who believes" (1:16 NKJV). The word *power* speaks of God's quenchless energy to transform all believing human beings into citizens of the kingdom of Christ. This transformation begins with the new birth and continues day after day, year after year until we finally meet Jesus face-to-face.

Note also that Paul says "for the Jew first then also for the Greek" (Romans 1:16 NKJV). This statement reflects Paul's basic strategy in all of his missionary journeys. When Paul arrived in a new city, he went first to the Jewish synagogues. He did this not only because Jews were there, but because God-fearing Gentiles were there, people who were interested in the Jewish view of God and in Jewish moral teachings. Out of this group he formed a core of leaders around whom he would build a church.

Locating True North

A compass is an instrument used for showing direction. Its swinging magnetic needle, which always points north, can keep you from going in the wrong direction. A compass is an excellent tool when you're lost.

apply it

go to

transformation
2 Corinthians
3:17–18;
John 14:1–7;
Revelation 21:1–4;
1 John 3:1–3

new birth
John 3

disciples
committed first followers of Jesus

world
society, culture

ashamed
concerned others will think less of me

go to

the Fall
Genesis 1:3

faith
trust in God's
promise of
salvation

the Fall
Adam and Eve's dis-
obedience, which
corrupted human
nature

mercy
compassion for the
needy that moves
one to help

The Gospel is the Christian's compass. If we live the Gospel, if we love the Gospel, if we continue to trust the Gospel, it will eventually lead us home. That is God's New Covenant promise: "I will never leave you nor forsake you" (Hebrews 13:5 NKJV). Now that is Good News.

Return to this starting point frequently, letting it do the work of a compass, pointing you to the true "North."

what others say

Apollinaris of Laodicea

Paul says that even if, in the very largest cities, the preacher of the cross of Christ will be mocked by the ignorant, he is not to be ashamed. For if the Son of God bore the shame of the cross on our behalf, how could it not be out of place for us to be ashamed at the Lord's suffering for us?[17]

Karl Barth

The Gospel is not a truth among other truths. Rather, it sets a question-mark against all truths. . . . Anxiety concerning the victory of the Gospel—that is, Christian Apologetics—is meaningless, because the Gospel is the victory by which the world is overcome. By the Gospel the whole concrete world is dissolved and established. . . . God does not need us. Indeed, if He were not God, He would be ashamed of us. We, at any rate, cannot be ashamed of Him.[18]

Righteousness from God

ROMANS 1:17 *For in it the righteousness of God is revealed from faith to faith; as it is written, "The just shall live by faith." (NKJV)*

Here we are brought to our predicament. Because of **the Fall**, our relationship with God has been fatally damaged and needs to be reconciled. The Gospel is God's way of extending his grace, love, and **mercy**—his only way of restoring our souls. It is through this restoration that we receive absolute righteousness from God.

Because we do not deserve this wonderful gift, and can do nothing to earn it, God elects to offer it to his fallen creation through the gift of <u>faith</u>, hence the phrase, "from faith to faith" (Romans 1:17 NKJV). We gain eternal life and a relationship with our Creator, and it costs us nothing.

To show the Christians in Rome that this is not some new, upstart doctrine, Paul quotes a famous Old Testament passage from Habakkuk 2:4: "The just shall live by his <u>faith</u>" (NKJV). Note the unity of the message between the Old and New Testaments.

go to

faith
Galatians 3:11;
Hebrews 10:38

suppress
to push down in
one's consciousness,
to ignore

what others say

D. Martyn Lloyd-Jones

"The just shall live by faith" . . . is the theme of this Epistle to the Romans; it says that God in His infinite wisdom, and in His infinite love and mercy and compassion, has found a way to save the unrighteous and to make them righteous, and the way is that He gives to us, that He imputes to us, the righteousness of His own Son, our blessed Lord and Saviour Jesus Christ. Now that is the heart of the Gospel.[19]

N. T. Wright

Paul's doctrine of justification is completely dependent upon his gospel, which as we have seen is the proclamation of Jesus as Lord. Allegiance to this Jesus must be total. One of Paul's key phrases is "obedience of faith." Faith and obedience are not antithetical. They belong exactly together. Indeed, very often the word "faith" itself could be properly translated as "faithfulness," which make the point just as well. Nor, of course, does this then compromise the gospel or justification, smuggling in "works" by a back door.[20]

The Great Devastation

ROMANS 1:18–20 *For the wrath of God is revealed from heaven against all ungodliness and unrighteousness of men, who **suppress** the truth in unrighteousness, because what may be known of God is manifest in them, for God has shown it to them. For since the creation of the world His invisible attributes are clearly seen, being understood by the things that are made, even His eternal power and Godhead, so that they are without excuse,* (NKJV)

Paul moves in verse 18 to a point that is critical to understanding his argument. He is making a historical statement, referring back to what happened in Genesis when humankind fell, but what he says is true on a psychological level as well so it is certainly relevant today.

He uses the word *suppress* to describe what people in their wickedness do with truth. If people suppress the truth, obviously they have some knowledge of the truth. We know about truth because God has built within us a recognition of himself. That's why Paul says, "God has shown it to them" (Romans 1:19 NKJV).

How do we recognize God? Through creation. Psalm 19 says, "The heavens declare the glory of God; and the firmament shows his handiwork. Day unto day utters speech, and night unto night reveals knowledge" (verses 1–2 NKJV). The psalmist is expressing in poetry the same truth that Paul expressed in his letter to the Romans. Creation shouts to us that God exists, and we hear those shouts. We may try to ignore them, but we hear them nonetheless.

what others say

Brendan Byrne

The revelation of God's wrath against all human suppression of the truth (v. 18). The opening statement about the "revelation of God's wrath" is thematic for the entire section down to 3:20. It evokes a key feature of the symbolic universe of apocalyptic Judaism—the sense that the entire world is being ushered to an imminent judgment where God's wrath will blaze out destructively against all human wickedness.[21]

The "wrath of God" stands in obvious contrast to the "righteousness of God." Wrath speaks of holy revulsion; God's being stands against that which in any manner contradicts his holiness—any abomination to Truth, yes any, are ultimately deeds (works) of perversity. God's wrath is man's guarantee that "heaven" will be a safe place, a godly place to live. Paul says, "The wrath of God is revealed from heaven against all ungodliness and unrighteousness of men" (Romans 1:18 NKJV). The cross was the ultimate expression of the Father's wrath. His own Son bore man's sin in his body on that tree, the innocent for the guilty!

Paul told the church at Corinth, "For He made Him who knew no sin to be sin for us, that we might become the righteousness of God in Him" (2 Corinthians 5:21 NKJV). This brings light to this matter of God's wrath. Wrath is a pure exercise of God's holy nature against all that pollutes man and who in turn pollutes God's revealed order and will. All sin carries consequences and sin's consequences often affect innocent victims as well as the guilty purveyor.

The Wrath of God

In my nearly forty-three years of ministry, preaching, and counseling, I have come to agree wholeheartedly with Karl Barth when he says, "Indeed, [judgment] is the fact most characteristic of our life."[22] Our sinfulness and all the atrocity that results from it has stirred the <u>wrath of God</u>. A holy God must of necessity reject all that is unholy. His wrath is a display of that rejection.

go to

wrath of God
2 Thessalonians
1:5–10;
Revelation 20:11–15

retribution
repayment

judgment
assessing penalties
for wrongdoing

what others say

J. Vernon McGee

This universe in which you and I live tells two things about God: His person and His power. This has been clearly seen from the time the world was created. How can invisible things be seen? Paul makes this a paradox purposely to impress upon his readers that the "dim light of nature" is a man-made falsehood. Creation is a clear light of revelation. It is the primary revelation.[23]

What Were We Thinking?

ROMANS 1:21–25 *because, although they knew God, they did not glorify Him as God, nor were thankful, but became futile in their thoughts, and their foolish hearts were darkened. Professing to be wise, they became fools, and changed the glory of the incorruptible God into an image made like corruptible man—and birds and four-footed animals and creeping things. Therefore God also gave them up to uncleanness, in the lusts of their hearts, to dishonor their bodies among themselves, who exchanged the truth of God for the lie, and worshiped and served the creature rather than the Creator, who is blessed forever. Amen. (NKJV)*

Paul points out that despite the knowledge of God people received through creation, they did not act on it. They did not give him glory, nor thank him. Their minds were clouded and their hearts were darkened. They began worshiping idols instead of God.

As mentioned before, this is true historically, but it is true psychologically as well. People who reject God become futile in their thinking and their hearts become clouded. They begin to set other things in place of God.

God turns people who reject him over to their sinful desires to reap the **retribution** of choosing to live in sin and for sinful pleasure. God judges sin in part by allowing it to run its course. Yet, it is the resulting sense of darkness that often opens our hearts to God's holy light. Therefore, we see that there is both grace and mercy in the midst of **judgment**.

vile passions
evil desires

Paul says similar things in many of his letters. For example, he tells the Ephesian church that they are not to live any longer as the Gentile world "in the futility of their mind, having their understanding darkened, being alienated from the life of God, because of the ignorance that is in them, because of the blindness of their heart" (Ephesians 4:17–18 NKJV). Note Paul's mention of the mind and the heart here, which he mentions in Romans too. He says their understanding is darkened as a result of the state of their hearts.

---

what others say

Karl Barth

The more the unbroken man marches along his road secure of himself, the more surely does he make a fool of himself, the more certainly do that mortality and that manner of life which are built upon a forgetting of the abyss, upon forgetting of men's true home, turn out to be a lie.[24]

Adolf Schlatter

The individual does not save himself from the powers that urge him to sin by a new resolution or a new idea. He is saved by him who lives and works for all . . . as the bringer of grace, takes the place of the law. The believer is saved through the message of Christ which reveals God's righteousness, rather than his wrath.[25]

Take Two

ROMANS 1:26–27 *For this reason God gave them up to* **vile passions***. For even their women exchanged the natural use for what is against nature. Likewise also the men, leaving the natural use of the woman, burned in their lust for one another, men with men committing what is shameful, and receiving in themselves the penalty of their error which was due. (NKJV)*

We come to the second "God gave them up" statement; the first was back in verse 24. This time Paul says God gave them up to immorality, sexual immorality. They exchanged the truth of God for a lie and then exchanged natural sexuality for unnatural sexuality.

Instead of using the normal Greek words for *men* and *women*, he uses the words for *males* and *females*. Ironically, humans (men and women) are the only species that engage in homosexuality. It does not exist in the animal kingdom.

It's important to understand that depraved behavior always begins with a <u>lie</u>, and Satan is the father of lies. When we choose darkness over light, we exchange God's truth for Satan's lie. While Adam and Eve were in paradise—a sinless environment—they believed Satan's lie and in so believing became liars themselves.

key point

what others say

Pelagius

Once lust is unbridled, it knows no limits. In the order of nature, those who forget God did not understand themselves either.[26]

Francis A. Schaeffer

With a realism we see throughout the Bible, Paul addresses the issue of male (and female) homosexuality. Religious people don't always like to deal with the reality of such things, but the Bible never covers up reality. It deals with humanity just the way it is.[27]

Like a Pig in Its Wallow

ROMANS 1:28–32 *And even as they did not like to retain God in their knowledge, God gave them over to a debased mind, to do those things which are not fitting; being filled with all unrighteousness, sexual immorality, **wickedness**, covetousness, maliciousness; full of envy, murder, strife, deceit, evil-mindedness; they are whisperers, backbiters, haters of God, violent, proud, boasters, inventors of evil things, disobedient to parents, undiscerning, untrustworthy, unloving, unforgiving, unmerciful; who, knowing the righteous judgment of God, that those who practice such things are deserving of death, not only do the same but also approve of those who practice them. (NKJV)*

This is a statement of judgment. God didn't just let people be depraved. God, as an act of judgment, caused them to be depraved. The fact that people become "filled with all unrighteousness, sexual immorality, wickedness, covetousness, maliciousness" (Romans 1:29 NKJV) is evidence that they have rejected God. Here, Paul is demonstrating the existence of sin and the reality that human righteousness does not exist.

Imagine a boy and a girl who are walking down a road together. Imagine their hands brush and eventually they find themselves hold-

go to

lie
Romans 1:25

wickedness
the exact opposite of righteousness

ing hands. This happens because there is an attraction between them.

Now imagine the same girl is ironing her clothes before going out with the boy and her hand touches the hot iron. She jerks it away. The fact that she jerks her hand away shows antagonism, not attraction.

Paul is saying human beings prove they are lost because they jerk away from God when they come into contact with him. Human beings are sinners and are not righteous, no matter what they pretend. People are not righteous because they have rejected God.

Chapter Wrap-Up

- Romans introduces us to Paul, the apostle. His call and commitment to the Gospel of God deeply influence both the substance and the tone of his message. (Romans 1:1–7)

- Paul holds prayer as a key to a faith that is fresh and continues to unfold as he serves Jesus Christ. Having received God's forgiveness, Paul longs to share God's love and purpose with the world. (Romans 1:8–15)

- The Gospel was Paul's deepest motivation for ministry. He knew it was God's way of reaching a world lost in darkness and evil. He knew God's power to overcome evil was centered in the Gospel message. (Romans 1:16–17)

- Paul speaks plainly about the wrath of God, a subject that many seek to ignore, but love motivates the true disciple of Christ to speak the whole counsel of God. Due to men's wickedness they began to suppress the truth. So God gave them over to wickedness to receive in themselves the due penalty of their sin. (Romans 1:18–32)

Study Questions

1. How did God confirm Paul's apostolic office?

2. On what or whom did Paul build his identity?

3. According to Paul, how was Jesus' divine nature confirmed?

4. Paul presents a worldview that is both comprehensive and built on the authority of the Bible as the Word of God. What was his key to being able to accomplish this?

5. Why was Paul not ashamed of the Gospel of Jesus Christ?

6. Paul gives the world a picture of the destruction of the human soul. Is this simply Paul's judgment, or is it God's word to man to alert us concerning his wrath?

Romans 2 Judgmentalism and Hypocrisy

Let's Get Started

Jesus taught that looking down on people, no matter who they are, is wrong. This is because Jesus knew that everyone is in the same boat. We've all sinned. We all fall short of the glory of God. We may be tempted to say, "Oh yes, but her sin is much worse than my sin," but when it comes to what we deserve, it is only by the grace of God that any of us escapes death. Looking down on anyone is wrong.

In chapter 2 Paul addresses those who may be tempted to look down on others. More specifically, he is addressing those who after reading the first chapter's description of humanity's indecency might quickly react with, "That's awful! People who do those things are terrible!"

Let's see what he says.

And That Goes for You, Too

> ROMANS 2:1–2 *Therefore you are inexcusable, O man, whoever you are who judge, for in whatever you judge another you condemn yourself; for you who judge practice the same things. But we know that the judgment of God is according to truth against those who practice such things.* (NKJV)

Judgmental people obviously have the capacity to distinguish between right and wrong, but here's the snag. If you have the ability to distinguish between right and wrong, and then you do wrong, you don't have an excuse.

Today, Paul might say something like this: "You're like a silly fool with ketchup stains all over his shirt who points out a little spot on his friend's shirt." Note the similarities between what Paul said here and what Jesus said in the Gospel of Luke: "How can you say to your brother, 'Brother, let me remove the speck that is in your eye,' when you yourself do not see the plank that is in your own eye? Hypocrite! First remove the plank from your own eye, and then you will see clearly to remove the speck that is in your brother's eye" (Luke 6:42 NKJV).

Paul then points out that judgmental people do not make judgments based on truth. If they did, they would see their own faults! God's judgments, however, are based on truth and therefore only he has the right to judge.

Some believe Jesus' plank-in-your-eye statement was meant to be taken humorously. Perhaps you'll understand why if you imagine a man with an enormous pillar sticking out of his eye reaching over to remove a little piece of dirt from another fellow's eye. It's a picture of ridiculousness.

Kindness with a Sharp Edge

ROMANS 2:3–4 *And do you think this, O man, you who judge those practicing such things, and doing the same, that you will escape the judgment of God? Or do you despise the riches of His goodness, forbearance, and longsuffering, not knowing that the goodness of God leads you to repentance?* (NKJV)

Those whose habit is to judge others have an additional habit of ignoring their own faults. Paul asks the question, "Do you think you will escape God's judgment?" Paul is implying, as Jesus did, that people should practice what they preach. Rather, ponder God's "goodness, forbearance, and longsuffering," says the apostle, and keep in mind that "the goodness of God leads you to repentance" (Romans 2:4 NKJV). That's why God does not immediately punish people for sinning; he is holding back his wrath so that people will have an opportunity to repent.

What we ought to do with our moral capacity is exercise it against ourselves. Use your ability to discern right from wrong on yourself, not on others. This will enable us to see our great need for God and for repentance. It will also create within us a deep thankfulness to God, for he has chosen to love us despite the inescapable reality that, next to his holiness, we are despicable.

what others say

Matthew Henry

What method God takes to bring sinners to repentance. He leads them, not drives them like beasts, allures them; and it is goodness that leads, bands of love. The consideration of the goodness of God, his common goodness to all, should be effectual to bring us all to repentance.[1]

Let's remember Paul had done plenty of faultfinding in his time. He was a zealous persecutor of Christians who imprisoned them and approved of their punishment, which in the case of <u>Stephen</u> was death. Surely he would have looked down on Christians. But by the time he wrote his letter to the Romans, Paul was a changed man. One possible reason for why Paul was so passionate about stomping out judgmentalism in his Roman brothers and sisters is that he had been confronted with the reality of his own judgmentalism not long before.

Stephen
Acts 7:54–60

Wake Up!

> **ROMANS 2:5–6** *But in accordance with your hardness and your **impenitent heart** you are treasuring up for yourself wrath in the day of wrath and revelation of the righteous judgment of God, who "will render to each one according to his deeds":* (*NKJV*)

impenitent
unwilling to admit guilt, to seek forgiveness, or to change

heart
seat of motivation, character

Paul uses some harsh language in an attempt to shock his listeners out of their complacency. He wants them to take this matter of looking down on others very seriously. Imagine Billy Graham walked up to you and said, "Because of the way you're living, you are filling a massive reservoir full of molten rock, sewage, and nuclear waste that will be poured out on you in the not too distant future." What would you do? Would you run in the opposite direction as fast as you could? Would you stomp on Mr. Graham's toe? Would you grab his knees and beg him to save you? You could react any number of different ways, but one thing I doubt you would do is yawn, as if he had just told you two plus two equals four. Harsh language has a way of getting people's attention, and Paul desperately wanted the attention of his readers.

Because you are judgmental, said Paul, you are, as water flowing into a dam, storing up divine wrath against yourselves. He reminds his listeners that divine wrath is nothing less than getting what they deserve.

We must realize that "there is no creature hidden from His sight" (Hebrews 4:13 NKJV). This is an awesome and freeing truth when understood properly. God is seeking to remove all pretense, all hypocrisy, and all evil from the lives of those who choose to believe in him. He is not snooping, as some suggest; rather, he is discipling

us, <u>training</u> us in righteousness. He is committed to being our heavenly Father. He disciplines us for our own good.

When on the road, we are aware of many warnings. Stop. Proceed with Caution. No Right Turn. Warnings are a form of grace to protect ourselves and others. Warnings are useless if we ignore them. But if we heed them, they can save our lives.

"Look, Ma, No Crystal Ball"

ROMANS 2:7–8 *eternal life to those who by patient continuance in doing good seek for glory, honor, and immortality; but to those who are self-seeking and do not obey the truth, but obey unrighteousness—indignation and wrath,* (NKJV)

Paul didn't need a crystal ball to tell the future. He knew from Jesus and his disciples that those who sought after and followed God would enjoy eternal peace. He also knew that those who rejected the truth and followed evil would experience eternal anguish. Paul was not exaggerating. He was delivering a sobering description of the way things really are. And guess what? If he were to sit with you over a cup of coffee today and say the same thing, his description would still be absolutely true. Those whose hope is in God will receive eternal life. Those who reject truth and follow evil will experience the wrath of God.

training
Hebrews 12:11–12

What Is Eternal Life?

partiality
showing favoritism
or respect

Christians usually think of "eternal life" in one of two ways. They either equate it with heaven, thinking heaven is a place of paradise to which Christians go after death, or they think of it as everlasting life—life that continues forever. Both of these ideas have some validity, but by themselves, they give an incomplete picture of what biblical "eternal life" is.

First, we should remember that eternal life is a gift from God and comes through Jesus Christ. It's not something we earn or will ever deserve. Second, eternal life starts from the moment a person turns to Christ. It does not start at death. If you are a Christian, you have eternal life right now. "God has given us eternal life, and this life is in His Son. He who has the Son has life; he who does not have the Son of God does not have life" (1 John 5:11–12 NKJV). Third, we should consider the question, How does "eternal life" look? It looks like obedience to God. It looks like following Jesus by loving the people around you. It looks like helping people who are less fortunate than you. It looks like bringing healing where there is pain, order where there is chaos. All of these things are a part of eternal life, which will have its fulfillment in boundless fellowship with God forever.

A Long Line Called History

> ROMANS 2:9–11 *tribulation and anguish, on every soul of man who does evil, of the Jew first and also of the Greek; but glory, honor, and peace to everyone who works what is good, to the Jew first and also to the Greek. For there is no **partiality** with God. (NKJV)*

Paul says there will be "glory, honor, and peace to everyone who works what is good" (Romans 2:10 NKJV). If we took this verse out of context, we might conclude it means that the good works of following the law will get people into heaven, but in chapter 3 we'll hear Paul say, "Therefore by the deeds of the law no flesh will be justified in [God's] sight, for by the law is the knowledge of sin" (3:20 NKJV). Is Paul contradicting himself? No, in the verse on the previous page he is saying glory, honor, and peace await those whose lives are filled with the natural outcome of turning to Jesus—good works.

law
Galatians 2:17–21

sinned
violated the standards

law
Ten Commandments and other laws that God gave to Moses

In the second verse he is making it clear that no one can be saved by the law alone.

What about this "the Jew first and also of the Greek" language (Romans 2:9 NKJV)? He said it back in chapter 1, too. Why does Paul keep saying this? To understand why, you need to think about God the same way Paul thought about him. To Paul, God was the Person who made a covenant with Israel (the Jewish nation) way back in Genesis. God said things to Israel like, "Obey My voice, and do according to all that I command you; so shall you be My people, and I will be your God" (Jeremiah 11:4 NKJV). That's an awesome statement when you consider God could have chosen whatever people he wanted to choose. The Jews did not obey God, however, so about two thousand years after God made his first covenant he sent Jesus to set things straight. God said, "Whoever calls on the name of the LORD shall be saved" (Romans 10:13 NKJV). This was the New Covenant. With Jesus the gospel floodgates swung wide open to Gentiles and prostitutes and thieves and slaves and everybody. So, when Paul says, "the Jew first and also of the Greek," he's giving a chronological description of how God laid the groundwork for saving the human race.

The Gospel shows no partiality. We are to see people as God sees them, not as we want to see them. He sees their value, their worth. In showing no partiality, God is demonstrating how to exercise grace and not judgment. We are called to serve others, not to sort them.

Partiality is both an Old and a New Covenant truth. In Leviticus 19:15 God exhorts, "You shall do no injustice in judgment. You shall not be partial to the poor, nor honor the person of the mighty. In righteousness you shall judge your neighbor" (NKJV). In this context, judge means to treat them as you would be treated. Or as Jesus put it, "Love your neighbor as yourself" (Matthew 22:39 NKJV).

Face the Facts

ROMANS 2:12–15 *For as many as have **sinned** without law will also perish without law, and as many as have sinned in the **law** will be judged by the law (for not the hearers of the law are just in the sight of God, but the doers of the law will be justified; for when Gentiles, who do not have the law, by nature do the things in the law, these, although not having the law, are a law to themselves, who show the works of the law written in their* *hearts, their **conscience** also bearing witness, and between themselves their thoughts accusing or else excusing them) (NKJV)*

Whether you've sinned does not depend on whether you know the law, said Paul. Some Jews of his day thought because they had the privilege of knowing the law, and kept it partially, they were righteous. Paul says to think again. Merely hearing the law isn't enough, you must do the law, and doing it partially won't wash either. You must do it perfectly because God is perfect. Of course, Paul knew it was impossible for the Jews to keep the law perfectly.

Though the Gentiles did not have Mosaic law, they did have conscience. Paul speaks of their consciences as "accusing or else excusing" them (Romans 2:15 NKJV). In other words, when they did something wrong, they felt guilty, but they made excuses. Both of these things, feeling guilty and defending themselves, are proof that they had violated their consciences. If the Gentiles hadn't violated their consciences, they wouldn't have felt guilty. If they hadn't violated their consciences, they wouldn't have had any need for excuses. Paul is pointing out that people are condemned apart from God's law because they know they have violated their own standards, much less God's. Every one of us is a sinner because every one of us has failed to live up to our own standards, let alone God's.

Paul is saying both Jew and Gentile, the first who knows the law and the second who doesn't, have the same problem. Both deserve condemnation because both are aware they are sinners.

Every culture in the world has some notion of right and wrong. Though the particularities of law and custom may differ from one place to another, no culture should be considered to have a totally different morality. No culture, for example, admires a man who backstabs all the people who have been kindest to him. No country praises a soldier who turns tail in the middle of battle. In some cultures, you may be allowed to have more than one wife, but no culture says you can have any woman you want any time you want her. Every culture has some idea of right and wrong.

It is not sufficient to know well, nor to promise well, but as our text says, it's important that we do well. God wants us to rely on the fact that he is just and that justice will be done. Our obedience or our disobedience, each in its own way, reveals the secrets of our hearts—secrets on which God will pronounce his righteous judgment. For the Christian, law and conscience are used by the Holy

Spirit to confront any disobedience that leads us away from God's will.

Say When

ROMANS 2:16 *in the day when God will judge the secrets of men by Jesus Christ, according to my gospel. (NKJV)*

This verse is referring back to verses 12 and 13 where Paul explained how people would be judged. Paul is letting his readers know there will come a judgment day. "It's coming," he says. "And you'd better be ready." Think of Arnold's famous line, "I'll be back," and you'll get some idea of what Paul is trying to communicate. It's not a matter of if, it's a matter of when.

Note two more things. First, for some reason Paul places special importance on "the secrets of men" (Romans 2:16 NKJV) here, as if he wanted to underscore the truth that we can run, but we can't hide from God. Second, our acts will pass through the filter of Jesus Christ on the way to judgment. If you have put your faith in Christ, God will forgive them because Jesus paid the price of punishment for you. If not, you will be punished accordingly.

We walk with a God who is really present, a God who encourages that which is righteous and confronts that which is evil or wrong.

Look at the Man in the Mirror

ROMANS 2:17–24 *Indeed, you are called a **Jew**, and rest on the **law**, and make your boast in God, and know His will, and approve the things that are excellent, being instructed out of the law, and are confident that you yourself are a guide to the blind, a light to those who are in darkness, an instructor of the foolish, a teacher of babes, having the form of knowledge and truth in the law. You, therefore, who teach another, do you not teach yourself? You who preach that a man should not steal, do you steal? You who say, "Do not commit adultery," do you commit adultery? You who abhor idols, do you rob temples? You who make your boast in the law, do you dishonor God through breaking the law? For "the name of God is blasphemed among the Gentiles because of you," as it is written. (NKJV)*

Paul turns his attention to the Jew. Jews of his day had a great deal of confidence because they knew more about moral matters than the rest of humankind. They knew more because God chose to give them the law before he gave it to anyone else. Furthermore, Jews believed that in the law they had the embodiment of all knowledge and truth. This is understandable when you consider who gave them the law. God himself inscribed the tablets with the Ten Commandments, and he did so specifically for the Jews. It's no wonder they thought they were hot stuff!

The problem was this: though the Jews had the law, they didn't keep it. Paul points out the Jews' hypocrisy by asking a series of questions. He wants the Jews to look at themselves for who they really are. The Jews were breaking the same law of which they were so proud.

Do you think Paul was being too harsh on the Jews? Consider this: in the first century the rabbis had decided that the prohibition against adultery and the sentence of stoning adulterers should be disregarded because there were so many adulteries. There was so much adultery going around, the rabbis decided they couldn't do anything about it.

In case we're tempted to think, "Oh, those nasty first-century Jews. How could they!" we would do well to remember the skeletons lurking in our own closets. Remember, Paul said God will judge the secrets of all humankind. His words are just as true for us as they were for Jews of the first century.

Counterfeit Righteousness

ROMANS 2:25–26 *For **circumcision** is indeed profitable if you keep the law; but if you are a breaker of the law, your circumcision has become uncircumcision. Therefore, if an uncircumcised man keeps the righteous requirements of the law, will not his uncircumcision be counted as circumcision? (NKJV)*

Imagine a friend presents you with a Jaguar XJR for your birthday (I know it's hard, but try). With a 370 horsepower engine, this car is reported to do 0 to 60 miles per hour in 5.4 seconds. Naturally, you want to look at the engine. You want to take in the sight and pay respect where respect is due. You slide into the leather seat and pop the hood. You walk to the front of the car, smiling, letting your

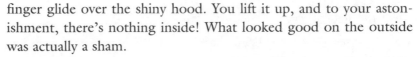

justification
legal standing as
innocent before
God

baptism
a sacred Christian
rite involving water

communion
a sacred Christian
rite involving conse-
crated bread and
wine

finger glide over the shiny hood. You lift it up, and to your astonishment, there's nothing inside! What looked good on the outside was actually a sham.

Circumcision was an outward sign of a covenant relationship with God. In the context of that covenant relationship with God, God's people were called to walk with, worship, and obey him. Just as a fancy Jaguar with no engine is a terrible disappointment, Paul told the Jews circumcision without obedience was meaningless.

Paul had to part ways with his fellow Jews on the topic of circumcision. For the Jew, circumcision was the covenant, but Paul believed what Scripture taught. Circumcision was the sign of the covenant. This difference is significant. God, through Abraham and then Moses, was creating a people from whom the Messiah would be born. Circumcision was affirmation that the covenant continued from generation to generation. It had no power to save.

Paul's view of circumcision was that it had value, but it could not bring **justification** to a sinner. It was never intended to.

Why does Paul choose to focus so much attention on the Jews? Paul's focus on the Jewish people is due to God's choice to make the Jews his vehicle of revelation. It is from the Jews that God brought forth the Messiah who is our only source of true righteousness. "Salvation is of the Jews," Jesus said (John 4:22 NKJV). Through the Jews the living God and true spirituality were revealed in the person of Jesus.

We struggle with similar issues in churches today. Many people practice the rituals of the faith (**baptism**, **communion**, recitation of formal prayers) because they know about God, but their hearts are unchanged. In this way, God's name is blasphemed throughout the world.

<u>Left Behind</u>

> **ROMANS 2:27** *And will not the physically uncircumcised, if he fulfills the law, judge you who, even with your written code and circumcision, are a transgressor of the law? (NKJV)*

Tim LaHaye and Jerry Jenkins probably weren't thinking of Romans 2:27 when they started work on their popular Left Behind series, but the title is a good description of where Paul thought the

Jews would be if Gentiles who didn't have the law obeyed it better than the Jews who did. The Jews would be left behind.

It's bad enough to get beat, but to get beat by someone you think is inferior to you is like getting a humble pie thrown in your face. It just doesn't get any more humiliating. Paul left no room for the Jews to be boastful.

Godliness Is an Internal Affair

ROMANS 2:28–29 *For he is not a Jew who is one outwardly, nor is circumcision that which is outward in the flesh; but he is a Jew who is one inwardly; and **circumcision is that of the heart**, in the Spirit, not in the letter; whose praise is not from men but from God.* (NKJV)

With these verses Paul wraps up his discussion of law and circumcision. The Jews tended to place unwarranted confidence in both. Merely knowing the law wasn't enough to be in God's favor. Circumcision by itself did not have power to save.

God was concerned with the heart. Paul wasn't forbidding circumcision—an ancient Jewish covenantal rite—but was interested in establishing its purpose in the greater light of God's **messianic mission**. Its purpose had been polluted, and as a result the God who had appointed it was being misrepresented.

There are two kinds of pride: good pride and evil pride. While good pride appreciates the beauty or meaning of something, evil pride is arrogant. People who wrestle with evil pride think they're better than others or that they have some unique advantage.

The Jews used the law in an unlawful manner. They thought that if you knew the law, you were saved, but in fact, the law is not **salvific**. The grace of the law is that it enables us to see ourselves as God sees us—needy, sinful, and in need of salvation.

what others say

Francis A. Schaeffer

External rites, whether those of Judaism or of **Christendom** are meaningless unless there is a circumcision of the heart, unless God has touched the person's heart and there is a reality to his or her faith . . . to live lives that are a scandal in the sight of nonbelievers, to profess a faith that means nothing in our inward parts, this surely places us under God's wrath.[4]

messianic mission
Isaiah 9:6–7; 57

better than others
Luke 18:9–14

circumcision of the heart
spiritual commitment to God, in contrast to mere physical descent from Abraham

messianic mission
Christ's mission to save individuals and establish God's rule

salvific
instrumental in gaining salvation

Christendom
all nations and cultures that have religious and moral roots in Christianity

Chapter Wrap-Up

- When we pass judgment on someone else we have three fingers pointing back at ourselves. Their sins are our sins, only in different expressions. (Romans 2:1–2)

- We all need to think on God's kindness. If God, who is completely holy and the source of our righteousness, is kind toward our sinful race, surely we, who share in that sin, need to follow God's example. (Romans 2:3–4)

- If man fails to repent and remains stubborn, he is storing up wrath for the day of judgment. (Romans 2:5–6)

- Paul reminds the church that God shows no favoritism. If we do evil, we store up wrath; if we seek glory and honor, God will give eternal life. (Romans 2:7–11)

- Both Jews and Gentiles are sinners. The Jews violate God's law, and the Gentiles violate their consciences. (Romans 2:12–16)

- The Jews were hypocritical in that though they had the law, they did not keep it. (Romans 2:17–24)

- Outward signs are nothing without inward realities. Truly being a part of God's family depends on obedience and devotion to God. (Romans 2:25–29)

Study Questions

1. Why is God concerned about judgmentalism?

2. How does God's kindness bring us to repentance?

3. What did Paul mean when he said judgmental people were storing up wrath for themselves?

4. What does it mean that God shows no favoritism?

5. What is meant by the phrase "the work of the law written in their hearts" (Romans 2:15 NKJV)?

Part Two
GOD'S FORGIVENESS

Romans 3 In Search of Righteousness

Chapter Highlights:
- God's Faithfulness
- Deserving Condemnation
- Silence Before God
- The Sacrifice of Christ
- No Boasting

Let's Get Started

In the everydayness of life, we tend to forget the enormity of the universe. But in our forgetfulness we also forget the One who created it, whose power and glory are awesome. The November 20, 1995, issue of *Time* magazine gave us a stunning display of activity in the Eagle Nebula through pictures that were taken from the Hubble Space Telescope. This Nebula is some seven thousand light years from earth, which is more than four hundred million times as far away as our sun.

In a similar way, the Jews in the everydayness of their religion got caught up in the activity of religion, while the wonder, grace, and beauty of a relationship with God got pushed aside. Somewhere in their distant past they chose outward ritual over a personal relationship with God. Judaism became a religion of law, void of God's grace. They thought of God as only their God, not the God of the whole world.

The Jewish Advantage

ROMANS 3:1–2 *What advantage then has the Jew, or what is the profit of circumcision? Much in every way! Chiefly because to them were committed the oracles of God. (NKJV)*

Paul, once limited by his own Jewish outlook, knew his Jewish readers would ask this question. It would have been a valid question to raise after reading what Paul had written in the first two chapters. If the Jews and Gentiles stood on a level playing field, then what advantage was it to be a Jew?

Paul's response was a positive one: "Much in every way!" (Romans 3:2 NKJV). In Paul's view, being the appointed guardians of God's Word was the chief advantage of being a Jew. They could know the will of God, and they had access to the God whose will it was!

Torah
the law and the
whole Jewish way
of life

interpretation
understanding

Eusebius of Emesa

When Paul says "to begin with," he does not go on to list a second or third item. He means rather that what he begins with is comprehensive of all good things. For what could be better than to believe the words of God?[1]

James R. Edwards

If **Torah** was the pride of the Jews, their response to it was disappointing. Torah was not a possession to be hoarded but a gift which entailed a responsibility. Calvin believed the Jews were first to be the depositories of Torah and then the dispensers of it. But in this they failed.[2]

A Heart That's True

ROMANS 3:3–4A *For what if some did not believe? Will their unbelief make the faithfulness of God without effect? Certainly not! (NKJV)*

In chapter 2 Paul pointed out that though all Jews were circumcised outwardly, only some had circumcised hearts. In other words, only some of the Jews were faithful to God. Upon hearing this, a Jew might very well ask, "So, does that mean God was unfaithful to the Jews who are not faithful?"

Paul's answer is one of the strongest expressions used in the New Testament to express disagreement: "Certainly not!" (Romans 3:4 NKJV). In the King James Version of the Bible, this phrase is always translated, "God forbid." What Paul is saying is that if a certain Jew is not faithful to God, that's not God's fault. God never stopped being faithful. Choosing not to follow God is the fault of the person who makes that choice.

A true faith is dependent on a true **interpretation** of the Word. The Jews' faithfulness (whatever degree of faithfulness they had) to the Old Covenant tended to lead them into further unbelief in Christ. This is also true in the Christian faith today. A wrong interpretation of Scripture leads people down many a blind alley. We need to handle God's Word with great care and prayer.

D. Martyn Lloyd–Jones

When the New Testament is talking about faith it is talking about something special, something new:

"By grace are ye saved through faith, and that not of yourselves; it is the gift of God." All men have not faith, says the Scriptures. This is something that is only to be found in a Christian.[3]

Damascus Road
Acts 22:6–10

Sanhedrin
a council of seventy-one members who governed the Jewish faith and lifestyle during the time of the Roman Empire

Let God Be True

ROMANS 3:4B *Indeed, let God be true but every man a liar. As it is written:*
"That You may be justified in Your words,
And may overcome when You are judged." (NKJV)

Paul says if ever there is wickedness, it does not come from God. God always proves true to his promises. To prove his point, Paul quotes a psalm in which David confesses his sin. To understand this quote, we need to look at what precedes and follows it in Scripture. Here is Psalm 51:3–5:

For I acknowledge my transgressions,
And my sin is always before me.
Against You, You only, have I sinned,
And done this evil in Your sight—
That You may be found just when You speak,
And blameless when You judge.
Behold, I was brought forth in iniquity,
And in sin my mother conceived me. (NKJV)

David came face-to-face with his own sin, and Paul hoped the Jews would come face-to-face with theirs.

Paul faced his sin on the Damascus Road (see Illustration #4). He was commissioned by the **Sanhedrin** of Jerusalem to go to Damascus and round up the Christians there. They were to be imprisoned and await sentencing in Jerusalem. Near Damascus, Jesus appeared to Paul (who was then known as Saul) and asked why Paul was persecuting him. Paul was confronted with the terrible mistakes of his past. The experience dramatically changed his life forever, for from that moment on, Paul was a missionary for Christ.

Apollinaris of Laodicea

Let it be agreed, Paul says, that God is faithful and true in every case, whereas men have been judged as unfaithful and untrue, so that God by his goodness may conquer the self-righteousness of men by bestowing his own righteousness upon them.[4]

Illustration #4
The Damascus Road—This map shows the location and route of the Damascus Road from Jerusalem to Damascus. On this road Paul heard God's voice, saw a blinding light, and was converted to Christianity.

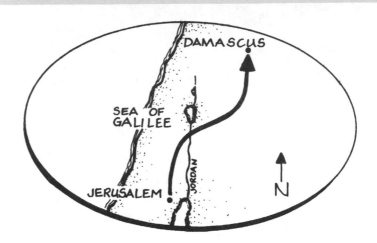

A Dumb Question

ROMANS 3:5–8 *But if our unrighteousness demonstrates the righteousness of God, what shall we say? Is God unjust who inflicts wrath? (I speak as a man.) Certainly not! For then how will God judge the world? For if the truth of God has increased through my lie to His glory, why am I also still judged as a sinner? And why not say, "Let us do evil that good may come"?—as we are slanderously reported and as some affirm that we say. Their condemnation is just. (NKJV)*

Teachers often encourage their students to learn by telling them there are no dumb questions, but Paul had to draw the line somewhere. The question Paul is addressing might be rephrased to read something like this: "If the darkness of my sin makes the brightness of God's holiness a little brighter, then shouldn't I sin all the more?" The ridiculousness of such a question is self-evident. God's holiness cannot be brightened. It would be like trying to make completeness more complete, perfection more perfect, or wholeness more whole. The Word of God becomes active when grasped by faith.

Paul answers the question by drawing from the nature and the attributes of God himself. Because God will judge the world, he cannot be unjust. It is only inadvertently that sin ever brings glory to God. God came to save sinners and he found <u>just ways</u> to accomplish this extraordinary task without changing his character in any way.

The statement "Let us do evil that good may come" (Romans 3:8 NKJV) is from hearts that are so contradictory to God, Paul says, "their condemnation is just" (3:9 NKJV). A person with such a heart has made up his or her mind to be evil.

just ways
Romans 3:21–26

Greeks
similar to the term Gentile, indicating all non-Jews

total depravity
the doctrine that anything human beings do is tainted by sin and cannot contribute to salvation

---

what others say

Sir Robert Anderson

The Gospel brings peace to the sinner, not because it makes light of sin, or lowers the inexorable claims of Divine perfection, but because it tells how Christ has made it possible for an absolutely righteous and thrice Holy God to pardon and save absolutely sinful and evil men.[5]

Who's the Better Sinner?

ROMANS 3:9 *What then? Are we better than they? Not at all. For we have previously charged both Jews and Greeks that they are all under sin. (NKJV)*

Paul addressed questions that he knew would surface from either the Jews or the **Greeks**. These are sensitive topics due to the cultural differences. Paul is trying throughout this entire epistle to neutralize any ethnic division. It is sin that keeps us from God, not race. Paul also points out that sinfulness is something we all have in common.

Sin is real. It is continuously present because of our fallen nature and Satan's activity. The law can diagnose our sinfulness and the moral illness it produces, but it has no power to cure it. Rather, it makes us more miserable, showing us what is wrong but offering no solutions. We want to escape the law and its clutches, but apart from the intervening grace of God, we lack the power to make the escape. **Total depravity** is the human lot and no one escapes the effects of sin.

In the final analysis there is no difference between the Jews and the Gentiles; we're all sinners in need of salvation. However, it was through the Jews that God sent the Messiah. Through the Jewish race he brought forth a Savior for the whole world, Jew and Gentile alike.

key point

from God
2 Timothy 3:16

Paul the Bible Thumper

ROMANS 3:10–18 *As it is written:*
"There is none righteous, no, not one;
There is none who understands;
There is none who seeks after God.
They have all turned aside;
They have together become unprofitable;
There is none who does good, no, not one."
"Their throat is an open tomb;
With their tongues they have practiced deceit";
"The poison of asps is under their lips";
"Whose mouth is full of cursing and bitterness."
"Their feet are swift to shed blood;
Destruction and misery are in their ways;
And the way of peace they have not known."
"There is no fear of God before their eyes." (NKJV)

Up to this point, Paul has demonstrated by argument that all have sinned, both Jew and Gentile. Now he proves his point by using Scripture. The Jews acknowledged that God is present in his revelation, and Scripture is God's revelation. This therefore would have been the ultimate evidence to his readers. Scripture itself says there is no one righteous.

What we learn from this is that while we can reason with the most acute logic and demonstrate with the most persuasive arguments, that which actually proves is Scripture. It is the final word on any matter. Why? Because Scripture is <u>from God</u>.

All Rise, Justice Yahweh Is Taking the Bench

ROMANS 3:19–20 *Now we know that whatever the law says, it says to those who are under the law, that every mouth may be stopped, and all the world may become guilty before God. Therefore by the deeds of the law no flesh will be justified in His sight, for by the law is the knowledge of sin. (NKJV)*

Paul sets the stage for a courtroom scene in which people stand before God as Judge. When the law is presented, detailing the right way to live, the people immediately realize they have not done so. They are silent. They have absolutely nothing to say in their defense.

Second, Paul makes sure his listeners understand that the law is not going to make anyone righteous. The law's intended purpose is not to save us but to show us our need for salvation. The law can in this way lead us to faith. This is how law and faith work with instead of oppose each other.

We might wonder why the Jews had such a hard time abandoning their trust in the law. To understand why, it may help to look at Acts 17, which is about Paul's visit to Athens, a city of **pagans** in his time. The apostle preached that it was obvious the Athenians were very religious because of all the idols around town, but he told them it was also obvious they had not heard about God, the one God, the God of the universe. When they heard this, "some mocked, while others said, 'We will hear you again on this matter'" (verse 32 NKJV).

If it was this difficult for people to give up their trust in petty idols, imagine how much more difficult it would have been for the Jews to give up their trust in a holy law that they knew came from God and on the fulfillment of which rested all their hopes for both present and eternal peace.

God gave the Ten Commandments both to reveal his righteousness and to confront sin. Take time to read the words and teachings of the Ten Commandments and see if they make you conscious of sin, your own and the sin you observe in the world. The law did not create sin; it revealed it.

Ten Commandments
Exodus 20:1–17;
Deuteronomy
5:6–22

pagans
people who worshiped the multiple gods of Greek mythology

what others say

Saint Augustine

Let us distinguish the following four states of human existence: before the law, under the law, under grace and at rest. Before the law we follow the lust of the flesh. Under the law we are dragged along by it. Under grace we neither follow it nor are dragged along by it. At rest (in glory, after the resurrection) there is no lust of the flesh.[6]

Karl Barth

If all the great outstanding figures in history, whose judgments are worthy of serious consideration, if all the prophets, Psalmists, philosophers, fathers of the Church, Reformers, poets, artists were asked their opinion, would one of them assert that men were good, or even capable of good? Is the doctrine of original sin merely one doctrine among many? Is it not rather, according to its fundamental meaning . . . the doctrine which emerges from all honest study of history? Is it

the Prophets
Old Testament
books written by
prophets

glory
perfection

not the doctrine which, in the last resort, underlies the whole teaching of history? Is it possible for us to adopt a "different point of view" from that of the Bible, Augustine, and the Reformers? What then does history teach about the things which men do or do not do?[7]

"Free Grace! Get Your Free Grace Here!"

ROMANS 3:21–24 *But now the righteousness of God apart from the law is revealed, being witnessed by the Law and* **the Prophets**, *even the righteousness of God, through faith in Jesus Christ, to all and on all who believe. For there is no difference; for all have sinned and fall short of the* **glory** *of God, being justified freely by His grace through the redemption that is in Christ Jesus,* (NKJV)

Note how Paul begins this section: "But now." What do you mean "But now," Paul? You've just demonstrated with reason and proved with Scripture that we're all a bunch of guilty sinners who deserve only God's wrath. What on earth could you say that would give us hope?

Indeed there is hope. Paul announces the good news that a righteousness we could never obtain through the law has been made available by a different means. Faith in Jesus Christ will give us the righteousness we need to be saved from our sins. Since all have sinned, it is obvious the only hope for any of us is to have righteousness credited to our account by someone who does have that righteousness. Jesus did just that, and this righteousness is available to anyone who puts his or her trust not in oneself, not in the law, but in Jesus Christ. The grace of God comes freely; nothing in us deserves such tenderness.

When Paul says "there is no difference" (Romans 3:22 NKJV), he means that when it comes to the fact of sin, both Jews and Gentiles are guilty. When it comes to who falls short of the glory of God, all of us have, regardless of who has committed greater or lesser sins. If we visited a prison, we would find people who were there for lesser crimes than others, but we would find no innocent people!

Paid in Full

ROMANS 3:25–26 *whom God set forth as a propitiation by His blood, through faith, to demonstrate His righteousness, because in His forbearance God had passed over the sins that were previously committed, to demonstrate at the present time His righteousness, that He might be just and the justifier of the one who has faith in Jesus. (NKJV)*

God had a score to settle. His justice had not yet been satisfied. He either had to condemn us for our sins or make the costliest sacrifice ever. Because he loved us (we don't know why), God made the sacrifice of Christ, which did not merely cover our sins but satisfied all the requirements of justice. It paid the penalty in full. This kind of sacrifice is known as propitiation (PRO-PI-SHEE-AY-SHUN).

Propitiation was necessary not only for our own sins of the past, present, and future, but it was also necessary for all sin from the beginning of history. When Paul says "because in His forbearance God had passed over the sins that were previously committed" (Romans 3:25 NKJV), he is pointing out that up to the death of Christ, God had let the sins of humankind go unpunished, which would have been contrary to his nature if he had not eventually presented the sacrifice of Christ. God punished everybody's sins on the crucifixion cross. He did not show favoritism to anyone. He let Christ serve as the propitiation so that people who had faith in him could be justly forgiven.

We ought to reflect on the costliness of God's sacrifice. Jesus took on the pain of sin, which was the absence of God. We have no idea what this would be like because God loved us so much he couldn't live without us. We've done nothing that he should love us. He just does.

Redemption is a costly matter. It cost the Son of God his life. The Old Covenant prefigured in its sacrificial system of worship and redemption the need for blood redemption. Jesus, called "the Lamb

something to ponder

of God," became God's ultimate sacrifice. He was made sin for us. This was God's predetermined plan of grace for the entire human race.

Matthew Henry

It is by his grace. And to make it the more emphatic, he says it is "freely by his grace." It comes freely to us, but Christ bought it, and paid dearly for it.[9]

Francis A. Schaeffer

In a way, this phrase ["so as to be just and the one who justifies those who have faith in Jesus"], and the verses that surround it constitute the center of the whole Bible, for they answer the most profound of all questions: How can God remain the absolutely just ruler of the universe, and yet justify me, an ungodly sinner?[10]

God Is the Only One with Bragger's Rights

ROMANS 3:27–31 *Where is boasting then? It is excluded. By what law? Of works? No, but by the law of faith. Therefore we conclude that a man is **justified** by faith apart from the deeds of the law. Or is He the God of the Jews only? Is He not also the God of the Gentiles? Yes, of the Gentiles also, since there is one God who will justify the circumcised by faith and the uncircumcised through faith. Do we then make void the law through faith? Certainly not! On the contrary, we establish the law. (NKJV)*

Paul is mainly talking to the Jews here because we know from verses in Romans 2:17 and 2:23 that the Jews had a tendency to boast. He says that because righteousness comes through faith, not from ourselves, boasting is eliminated.

The Jews believed that salvation came from observation of the law, so when Paul said it came through faith, Jews might very well have asked, "Well, okaaaay, but what good is the law then?" Paul anticipated this question and answered that, far from nullifying the law, Christians upheld the law because they put it in its rightful place. Law was intended to shut peoples' boastful mouths before God and to demonstrate the utter necessity of faith. The law was not a way of salvation as had been perceived within Judaism.

Chapter Wrap-Up

- There is nothing in this world system—political, religious, or academic—that will nullify God's faithfulness. Absolutely nothing! (Romans 3:1–3)

- Jew or Gentile, with the law or with conscience, we all deserve condemnation. (Romans 3:9–18)

- The law's purpose is to silence us before God. The law brings us to a knowledge of our need for salvation. (Romans 3:19–20)

- Jesus was God's propitiation. This means that God's justice is fully satisfied by the blood of Jesus Christ. Christ's death is the greatest proof of our need for righteousness. God's way is the only way for sinners to be declared righteous. (Romans 3:22–26)

- We have no room to boast because it is only by faith in Christ that we are saved. The rightful place of the law is to show us our need for salvation. It is not, nor was it ever intended to be, a way of salvation. (Romans 3:27–31)

Study Questions

1. Did the Jews have an advantage over the Gentiles?

2. Why does our unrighteousness cause God to judge the world?

3. How is it that no one is righteous?

4. How does the law make us conscious of sin?

Romans 4 Abe's Faith

Let's Get Started

We often make light of sin. We say, "Well, after all, I'm only human," or we tell others who rebuke us, "Quit being so self-righteous!"

Why do we have this lax attitude toward sin and its devastating consequences? In Jesus' conversation with a Pharisee named <u>Nicodemus</u>, who came to Jesus one night to discuss spiritual matters, Jesus reminded this educated man, "This is the condemnation, that the light has come into the world, and men loved darkness rather than light, because their deeds were evil" (John 3:19 NKJV).

In chapter 4 we move into one of the most exciting discussions of faith and its extraordinary importance in both initiating the experience of salvation and its continuing work in **sanctification**. Indeed, "without faith it is impossible to please [God]" (Hebrews 11:6 NKJV).

Nicodemus
John 3:1–16

sanctification
2 Corinthians
3:17–18;
Romans 8:11

sanctification
to become righteous in character and practice

justified
declared righteous by God

First Affidavit: Our Forefather Abraham

ROMANS 4:1–2 *What then shall we say that Abraham our father has found according to the flesh? For if Abraham was **justified** by works, he has something to boast about, but not before God. (NKJV)*

Knowing that the Jews loved to boast of Abraham as their father, Paul suggested going back to the story of Abraham to see what it said about justification.

Note that if Abraham had been justified by works—and by the way, nothing could have been further from the truth— he would have had the right to boast only before people, not before God. God is under any circumstance our Master. We are his creatures. Our rightful place, our happiest place is beneath him.

go to

through faith
Ephesians 2:8–9

Inspecting Scripture

ROMANS 4:3 *For what does the Scripture say? "Abraham believed God, and it was accounted to him for righteousness." (NKJV)*

Paul asked a loaded question and put the ball in the Jews' court: "What does the Scripture say?" (Romans 4:3 NKJV). He then took them back to Genesis 15:6. The moment Abraham took God at his word, God declared him righteous. Abraham did not do anything to earn this declaration. He simply believed. This is the doctrine of justification <u>through faith</u>.

Abraham's faith counted him as righteous long before he was circumcised and long before God had given the law to Israel. This would have been further evidence to the Jews they were placing unwarranted confidence in the wrong things because if circumcision and the law were the means to righteousness, then how was Abraham who had neither considered righteous?

> **what others say**
>
> **James D. G. Dunn**
>
> Abraham's faith was a firm confidence in God as the one who determines the future according to what he has promised.[1]

If you've ever been on a debate team, you would have been glad for a teammate like Paul. He was a master at crafting persuasive arguments. Paul's use of the scriptural account of Abraham, for example, to demonstrate that righteousness comes only by faith was nothing short of brilliant when you consider who Paul's readers were. Not only did the Jews reverence Scripture to a fault, Abraham was the founder of their race. Jews thought so much of Abraham, they kept meticulous records to prove they were his descendants. When Paul used Abraham as his example, he made his point with the Jews.

> **what others say**
>
> **Matthew Henry**
>
> Here the apostle proves that Abraham was justified not by works, but by faith. He appeals to the case of Abraham their father, and puts his own name to the relation, being a Hebrew of the Hebrews: Abraham our Father.[2]

go to

conversion
Acts 9:1–18;
16:25–31

conversion
becoming a
Christian

what others say

Saint Augustine

Since Abraham without the law obtained glory not by the works of the law (as if he would fulfill the law in his own strength), since the law had not yet been given, the glory belongs to God, not to him. For he was justified not by his own merit, as if by works, but by the grace of God through faith.[3]

Charles R. Swindoll

Justification is the sovereign act of God whereby He declares righteous the believing sinner—while he is still in a sinning state. Even though Abraham (after believing and being justified) would continue to sin from time to time, God heard Abraham when he said, "I believe . . . I believe You." And God credited divine righteousness to his account.[4]

Paul said that grace was something Abraham "found" (Romans 4:1 NKJV). **Conversion** has a characteristic of ecstasy about it. Like Abraham, we discover it is by grace and not by our works. When we believe, God credits our spiritual account with his righteousness. Abraham received what he did not deserve and was unable to earn. The object of a godly faith is God alone. Abraham believed God.

Paychecks Don't Come in Fancy Paper

ROMANS 4:4 *Now to him who works, the wages are not counted as grace but as debt.* (NKJV)

Paul is making a clear distinction between gifts and wages. Using the analogy of working for wages, Paul again is confronting potential deceptions in this matter of godly faith. If a man works for a certain wage and at the end of the day or week goes to his employer to get his paycheck, is it a gift or is it wages due? Obviously he is receiving what is due to him. A paycheck is not a gift. This is something you have rightly earned. But we cannot rightly earn our salvation.

If we attempt in any way to apply our works to our salvation, then the truth of the Gospel is defiled. There is only one work that we can count on, and that is the work of Christ on the cross! What saves is faith in him.

good works
Matthew 25:31–46;
Galatians 6:1–6

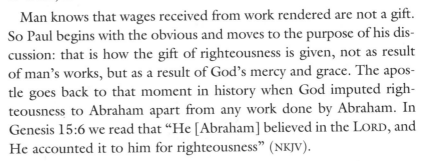

what others say

Charles R. Swindoll

But with God the economy is altogether different. There is no wage relationship with God. Spiritually speaking, you and I haven't earned anything but death. Like it or not, we are absolutely bankrupt, without eternal hope, without spiritual merit.[5]

It is true, <u>good works</u> will not get you to heaven, but that doesn't mean they aren't important. Scripture is clear that faith without works is as good as no faith at all. "Okay," you may answer, "but what kinds of works should I be doing?" That's an excellent question.

There are many different ways to serve God. Start by asking God to show you how he wants to use you. Next, be on the lookout. If you keep your eyes and ears open, God will indeed show you how to do your part in his world. He may want you to babysit. He may want you to feed the hungry or shelter the homeless. He may want you to take special action to get rid of a sin with which you've been struggling. He may want you to be with a friend who is sad. No matter how he uses you, one thing is for certain: If you ask God to put you to work, he will.

Man knows that wages received from work rendered are not a gift. So Paul begins with the obvious and moves to the purpose of his discussion: that is how the gift of righteousness is given, not as result of man's works, but as a result of God's mercy and grace. The apostle goes back to that moment in history when God imputed righteousness to Abraham apart from any work done by Abraham. In Genesis 15:6 we read that "He [Abraham] believed in the LORD, and He accounted it to him for righteousness" (NKJV).

The Covenant that God made with Abram, later known as Abraham, as spoken in Genesis 12, is now being enlarged by the Lord so that the promises given could be fulfilled. And the New Covenant commentary on Abraham gives us a divine perspective: "By faith Abraham obeyed when he was called to go out to the place which he would receive as an inheritance. And he when out, not knowing where he was going. By faith he dwelt in the land promised as in a foreign country, dwelling in tents with Isaac and Jacob, the heirs with him of the same promise, for he waited for the city which has foundations, whose builder and maker is God" (Hebrews 11:8–10 NKJV). Abraham is God's model of how he sovereignly imparts the gift of righteousness. How? "The righteousness of God, through faith in Jesus Christ, to all and on all who believe" (Romans 3:23 NKJV). This is Paul's consistent refrain in all his letters.

It is true, good works are not a man's ticket to heaven, but once a person becomes a disciple of Jesus there will be a heart's desire to serve one's Lord.

Much service in God's Kingdom is related to how we are gifted. Every believer is given spiritual gifts that enable the Holy Spirit to guide our works-activity. Paul in Romans 12 tells the church, "Having then gifts differing according to the grace that is given to us, let us use them" (12:6 NKJV). There are also natural talents if used humbly that can be exercised for the glory of God, but we need to seek God's will in these matters. The gift of leadership has been given "for the equipping of the saints for the work of ministry, for the edifying of the body of Christ" (Ephesians 4:12 NKJV).

What Paul wants his readers to clearly understand is this: works follow salvation and are not the meritorious cause of salvation. It must be very clear. Works add no merit to the perfect and all-sufficient merit of Jesus Christ.

Second Affidavit: Our Forefather David

> ROMANS 4:5–8 *But to him who does not work but believes on Him who justifies the ungodly, his faith is accounted for righteousness, just as David also describes the blessedness of the man to whom God imputes righteousness apart from works:*
> *"Blessed are those whose lawless deeds are forgiven,*
> *And whose sins are covered;*
> *Blessed is the man to whom the LORD shall not impute sin."*
> *(NKJV)*

Now Paul brings his second powerful witness: **David**. He reminds the people in Rome that David speaks of this same truth. Faith saves apart from the law. Those who oppose this great truth say we must satisfy the justice of God by our works. Here again we find God crediting righteousness to a Jewish forefather apart from his spiritual accomplishments.

David was profoundly blessed with the knowledge of his forgive-

go to

justification
Psalm 32:1–2;
Psalm 103:12

Reformation
a movement in the
sixteenth century led
by Martin Luther
that resulted in the
establishment of the
Protestant Church

ness. That is what <u>justification</u> does; it assures us we are forgiven. David repeatedly put the concept and his feelings about it into songs and prayers.

Justification was a great part of the battle for truth that the men and women of the **Reformation** had to confront. Luther, Calvin, Melanchthon, Zwingli, and many other faithful servants of the Lord changed the course of history in their battle for this truth. Paul was their primary mentor in this struggle for reform.

what others say

Francis A. Schaeffer

The basis of salvation by grace is the finished work of Jesus Christ. The instrument is our faith. Nothing else is allowed.[6]

The Divine Verdict

Picture yourself standing before God in heaven's great courtroom. God looks around and says there is "none righteous, no, not one" (Romans 3:10 NKJV). What do you say in your defense? Nothing, you're speechless. You know the Judge has spoken true.

Your heart begins racing, but wait. A chair creaks. Who's that? A lawyer takes his place between you and the Judge. He looks at you with burning love in his eyes. He faces the Judge.

"May it please the court, Father. The defendant has put his faith not in himself, not in the law, not in riches," he says confidently. "The defendant, whom I love, has put his faith in me."

"Very well," the Judge says to you. "On the basis of your faith in my Son, Jesus Christ, I hereby pronounce you NOT GUILTY."

Augustine reminds us that "God gave by grace, because he gave to sinners so that by faith they might live justly, that is, do good works."[7] Paul saw the underpinning of God's justification as grace—undiluted, unadulterated grace.

what others say

Larry Richards

To "justify" is to declare righteous as a judicial act. But God does more than this for us. He acts in our lives to actually make us righteous.[8]

what others say

Martin Luther

It is foolish and absurd to say: God has obligated us to possess grace and thus to do the impossible. I excuse our most faithful God. He is innocent of this imposture. He has not done this. He has not obligated us to possess grace, but he has obligated us to fulfill the Law, in order that he might give this grace to those of us who have been humbled and who implore his grace.[9]

A Righteous Brother

ROMANS 4:9–11A *Does this blessedness then come upon the circumcised only, or upon the uncircumcised also? For we say that faith was accounted to Abraham for righteousness. How then was it accounted? While he was circumcised, or uncircumcised? Not while circumcised, but while uncircumcised. And he received the sign of circumcision, a seal of the righteousness of the faith which he had while still uncircumcised,* (NKJV)

The Jews put their trust in the outward sign of circumcision, ignoring that Abraham's faith was credited to him as righteousness fourteen or fifteen years before he was circumcised. Circumcision was merely a sign, to Abraham and to the world, that Abraham had been set apart for God.

Today baptism serves a similar function to that which circumcision served in Abraham's day. Baptism is a sign that those baptized belong to Christ, not the world. As with first-century Jews and circumcision, people sometimes place too much trust in baptism. Some people think baptism will get them into heaven, but this is not true. Faith is the only thing that can do that. Baptism is only a sign and apart from faith it means nothing.

God of All

ROMANS 4:11B–12 *that he might be the **father** of all those who believe, though they are uncircumcised, that righteousness might be imputed to them also, and the father of circumcision to those who not only are of the circumcision, but who also walk in the steps of the faith which our father Abraham had while still uncircumcised.* (NKJV)

barrier
reason to exclude

extant
in existence

Paul argues that Abraham is the father of all who believe, regardless of ethnicity. This supports the words of our Lord at his ascension. He told the eleven disciples, "Go therefore and make disciples of all the nations, baptizing them in the name of the Father and of the Son and of the Holy Spirit, teaching them to observe all things that I have commanded you" (Matthew 28:19–20 NKJV).

As baptism follows conversion as a sign of union with and commitment to Jesus Christ, so with Abraham circumcision followed as an outward sign of the righteousness that had been credited to his account. Abraham was uncircumcised at the time he was justified, so uncircumcision was not a **barrier** to the Gentiles, as some of them feared.

what others say

John Piper

The faith of Abraham was a faith in the promise of God to make him the father of many nations. This faith glorified God because it called attention to all the resources of God that would be required to fulfill it. Abraham was too old to have children, and Sarah was barren. Not only that: how do you turn a son or two into "many nations" which God said Abraham would be the Father of? It all seemed totally impossible. Therefore Abraham's faith glorified God by being fully assured that he could and would do the impossible.[10]

Matthew Henry

In [Abraham] commenced a much clearer and fuller dispensation of the covenant of grace than any that had been before **extant**; and therefore he is called the father of all that believe.[11]

James R. Edwards

Since Abraham was justified before he was circumcised, his circumcision was a "sign" of righteousness, not a cause of it. Whereas Judaism came to regard circumcision as a good work, as something achieved, Paul refers to it as something received [Romans 4:11]. Judaism emphasized the doer of the act; Paul emphasizes the Giver of the sign.[12]

Heir of the World

ROMANS 4:13–15 *For the promise that he would be the heir of the world was not to Abraham or to his seed through the law, but through the righteousness of faith. For if those who are of the law are heirs, faith is made void and the promise made of no effect, because the law brings about wrath; for where there is no law there is no transgression. (NKJV)*

One night the word of the Lord came to Abraham. God took him outside and said, "Look now toward heaven, and count the stars . . . So shall your descendants be" (Genesis 15:5 NKJV). God promised Abraham that he would be "heir of the world." In other words, Abraham would be the father of all believers. Paul points out that this would not happen through Abraham's observance of the law. In fact, Abraham <u>disobeyed God</u> several times. It would happen through Abraham's faith.

He further points out that because no one can keep the law, the law brings wrath. Many of the Jews treasured their law highly. The idea that the law brought wrath was probably completely foreign to them.

disobeyed God
Genesis 12:1–4, 10–20; 20

promise
Deuteronomy 9:28; 10:9; 1 Kings 9:5; Hebrews 10:23

of the law
Jews

The Purpose of Promise

ROMANS 4:16–17 *Therefore it is of faith that it might be according to grace, so that the promise might be sure to all the seed, not only to those who are **of the law**, but also to those who are of the faith of Abraham, who is the father of us all (as it is written, "I have made you a father of many nations") in the presence of Him whom he believed—God, who gives life to the dead and calls those things which do not exist as though they did; (NKJV)*

<u>Promise</u> is one of the great spiritual terms used throughout Scripture. The promises of God open the path of faith to fallen and finite people, which in turn opens the door to the grace of God. Promise, by nature, requires faith on behalf of the one to whom the promise is given, while at the same time it exalts the sovereign nature of the One who makes the promise. God chose this as a way to give us sinners a sure way to enter his kingdom.

Because Abraham was made to be the "father of many nations" (Genesis 17:5 NKJV), and this according to promise, he has become "the father of us all" (Romans 4:16 NKJV). This makes both Jews and Gentiles heirs of promise. This great truth had escaped Paul when he was still Saul the Pharisee. Without a doubt, this is why he was so capable of tracing all the implications of this most essential doctrine.

John Piper

He says, "If those who are of the Law are heirs, faith is made void and the promise is nullified" [Romans 4:14]. In other words, the "promise" of God's grace was meant to be received by "faith," not earned by what he calls, "Being of the Law"—a phrase that probably implies relying on our religious culture or morality rather than on God's grace.[13]

The Very First Promise Keeper

ROMANS 4:18–22 *who, contrary to hope, in hope believed, so that he became the father of many nations, according to what was spoken, "So shall your descendants be." And not being weak in faith, he did not consider his own body, already dead (since he was about a hundred years old), and the* **deadness** *of Sarah's womb. He did not waver at the promise of God through unbelief, but was strengthened in faith, giving glory to God, and being fully convinced that what He had promised He was also able to perform. And therefore "it was accounted to him for righteousness." (NKJV)*

From a human perspective, God's promise that he would have a son and inherit the world looked impossible. Abraham was a hundred years old ("his own body, already dead" [Romans 4:19 NKJV]) and Sarah, his wife, was beyond childbearing years, yet Abraham did not allow unbelief to rob him of the promise God had made to him. Rather, he chose to believe that God, who came to him unsolicited, would keep his word.

When God makes a promise, we ought to focus on the truth that God never lies and that he is capable of doing whatever he wants to do. Though we may be limited by our circumstances and the natural world, God is not.

For Me? Thank You!

ROMANS 4:23–25 *Now it was not written for his sake alone that it was imputed to him, but also for us. It shall be imputed to us who believe in Him who raised up Jesus our Lord from the dead, who was delivered up because of our offenses, and was raised because of our justification. (NKJV)*

Did you know Genesis was written for you? "It was!" said Paul. The assurance that Abraham's faith equaled righteousness is as much for us as it was for Abraham. Just as God credited Abraham's faith to him as righteousness, he will credit our faith to us as righteousness.

new creations
Galatians 6:15

Jesus suffered the unspeakable for our sins. He endured being forsaken by his Father. If he had not done this, God would have forsaken us forever. Not only are we saved from the penalty of our sin, but also Christ's resurrection gives us an entirely new position before God. If we are in Christ, we are <u>new creations</u>.

Abraham's faith transcends time, reminding us that the words "it was accounted to him for righteousness" were "not written for his sake alone that it was imputed to him, but also for us" (Romans 4:22–24 NKJV).

What does this reveal to every believer today? That the faith we embrace is not just for us, but for the world we are called to love and serve in Christ's name. God dropped a pebble of truth into the pool of Abraham's heart and the ringlets reach out to us and farther and farther and farther.

In Galatians Paul gives more details for us to ponder. He writes, "Now we, brethren, as Isaac was, are children of promise. But, as he who was born according to the flesh [Ishmael] then persecuted him who was born according to the Spirit [Isaac], even so it is now" (Galatians 4:28–29 NKJV). The message here is that just as Christians are like Isaac, who had a supernatural birth, instead of like Ishmael, Christians can expect their experiences to be like that of Isaac. Specifically, just as Isaac was persecuted by his half brother Ishmael, Christians can expect to be persecuted by their half brothers—unbelieving religious people like the Pharisees and religious leaders of Jesus' day, the fanatically religious Judaizers of Paul's day, and the unbelieving members and leaders of churches in our own day.

something to ponder

what others say

John Calvin

It becomes more clear now why and how his faith brought righteousness to Abraham: it was because he depended on the Word of God, and did not reject the grace that God promised. This relationship between faith and the Word is to be continually maintained and committed to memory.[14]

Theodoret of Cyr

Abraham believed against the hope of nature but in the hope of the promise of God.[15]

John Chrysostom

Abraham trusted God even though God gave him no proof, nor even a sign. Rather, there were only mere words promising things which by nature were impossible.[16]

Chapter Wrap-Up

- Paul pointed out to the Roman Christians that it was Abraham's faith that was credited to him as righteous, not his observance of the law. (Romans 4:1–3)

- Wages are not a gift, but what a person deserves for his or her labor. Grace is a gift that we can do nothing to earn. David wrote poems and songs about the blessing of being forgiven. (Romans 4:4–8)

- Faith and grace, forgiveness and justification are couplets that help explain the vastness of God's love and his matchless plan. (Romans 4:9–25)

Study Questions

1. What one word summarizes Abraham's life and why?

2. Did circumcision precede or follow the promise given to Abraham? Why is this order significant?

3. Why did Abraham believe he would have a son when he and his wife were beyond the age of having children?

4. Why is righteousness such an important matter for us? For God?

Romans 5 The Benefits of Belonging to Christ

Chapter Highlights:
- God's Path to Peace
- Proof of God's Love
- God's Love Keeps Going
- Grace Bigger Than Sin

Let's Get Started

As we begin this chapter, it is good to keep in mind Paul is not writing a theological textbook, even though at times it surely seems that way. There is definite order to the letter. There is a progression of thought and serious theological content throughout. Paul's purpose for writing is apparent, chapter by chapter: He wants to proclaim the grace of God in Jesus Christ.

As a missionary and teacher, this proclamation is in agreement with the materials he taught in Galatia, Pontius, Phrygia, Cilicia, and Asia (all provinces in Asia Minor). Paul spent years studying the **Old Covenant** while he was discovering what life is like under the **New Covenant**. Paul's faith and the truth he presents are grounded in Scripture and in spiritual reality.

Paul lived, as we do, amidst the tension between how life is and how it ought to be. Thus, his teaching is very practical. He uses spiritual insight, doctrines, history, and examples, all with the desire to encourage his readers and help make their lives more fruitful in the work of the kingdom of God.

As he leaves the discussion of sin and justification in chapters 1–4, he moves to topics that deal more with spiritual growth now that the believer has an understanding of sin and the need for righteousness.

Paul doesn't present a glorified view of the Christian way of life, quite the opposite. He was in touch with the influences of **the world**, **the flesh**, and **the demonic**, and he faced each one in Christ's grace and power.

Old Covenant
Moses' law

New Covenant
the Gospel

the world
aspects of culture and society that oppose Christianity

the flesh
one's own tendencies toward evil

the demonic
supernatural evil

Therefore—What's It There For?

ROMANS 5:1–2 *Therefore, having been justified by faith, we have peace with God through our Lord Jesus Christ, through whom also we have access by faith into this grace in which we stand, and rejoice in hope of the glory of God.* (NKJV)

go to

Abraham
Isaiah 41:8

worship
John 4:23–24

My seminary professor, Dr. Howard Hendricks, always instructed us, "When you see a 'therefore,' be sure to answer the question, 'What's it there for?'" That has been good counsel to follow. Here, in Romans 5, Paul begins with "therefore." Paul's therefore serves to remind us of the journey we have just made through chapters 1–4 where Paul mapped out God's road to freedom from sin and the gift of righteousness through faith for the sinner. He now proceeds on the assumption that his readers have an understanding of justification by faith and indeed that this justification is a reality in his life as well as in the lives of his readers.

Because we are justified by faith, we are at peace with God. Washed continually in grace, no longer are we God's enemies. We are God's friends, just like <u>Abraham</u> was. No longer should we fear the wrath of God. We should look for the blessings of God. Jesus has introduced us to his Father, and the Father loves us. Futhermore, because we are completely justified by faith in Jesus, we can look forward to a time when we will enjoy the full presence of Almighty God. We have hope. No matter what happens here on earth, we know that everything will turn out all right in the end.

Justification, peace, and access ought to motivate us to <u>worship</u> and praise. We "rejoice in hope of the glory of God" (Romans 5:2 NKJV). God knows how to repair a broken vessel and make it useful once again. Why do we rejoice? We believe that now our worship will truly bring glory to God. Our faith has been renewed. Our hope has been restored. Let's praise him! The king has given us access to the grace of God. Let us stand in awe!

In chapter 5 Paul gives several benefits of justification.

key point

- We have access to God and his grace (Romans 5:2).
- We have (present tense) absolute salvation (Romans 5:10).
- We have reconciliation (Romans 5:11).
- We have the capacity to live a righteous life (Romans 5:17).
- We have life itself (Romans 5:18).
- We have eternal life (Romans 5:21).
- We don't have to try to create peace because God has granted us peace through Christ. (Romans 10:11)

sufferings
Psalm 116:8–11;
Romans 8:17–27;
2 Corinthians
4:7–12;
James 1:2–4

what others say

John Calvin

Peace, therefore, means serenity of conscience, which originates from the awareness of having God reconciled to oneself. This serenity is possessed neither by the Pharisee, who is inflated by a false confidence in his work, nor by the senseless sinner, who, since he is intoxicated with the pleasure of his vices, feels no lack of peace . . . a dull conscience implies a departure from God.[1]

But Wait, There's More

ROMANS 5:3–5 *And not only that, but we also glory in tribulations, knowing that tribulation produces perseverance; and perseverance, character; and character, hope. Now hope does not disappoint, because the love of God has been poured out in our hearts by the Holy Spirit who was given to us.* (NKJV)

After talking about the good things that come from being justified by faith, Paul goes on to add another benefit that may seem strange when we first hear of it. He says we now rejoice in our sufferings. Notice that he does not say we rejoice at our sufferings. We don't like to suffer, and we shouldn't. What Paul is saying, however, is that now our sufferings have meaning and purpose. Our sufferings are leading us somewhere.

Paul says that suffering produces perseverance. Perseverance is the ability to continue onward in the face of hard times. If we are persevering people, we don't give up. We push forward. Paul then says perseverance produces character. By facing trials and working through them, God is molding us into better people. We give up bad habits, for example, and replace them with good ones. Lastly, Paul says character produces hope. When we look back on the process through which God has brought us and realize that we are still in this process, we have a firm basis for hope. We know that just as he has brought us through trials of the past, he will bring us through trials of the future, and this will continue, because he loves us, until the very end when we will enjoy his presence forever.

something to ponder

Joni Eareckson Tada was seventeen, full of life and hope, when she dived into the Chesapeake Bay, struck a submerged rock, and instantly became a quadriplegic. Twenty-eight years following the accident, an interview in *Leadership* magazine records these words spoken by Tada: "Pain and suffering have purpose. . . . I get impatient with people who want to get all their needs met. . . . With my disability, some days are easier than others. But for me, life is always difficult. These are issues I must face every single morning. Every morning somebody has to give me a bath in bed, dress me, lift me into a wheel chair, comb my hair, brush my teeth, fix my breakfast, cut up my food, feed me. . . . I have to turn them, by the grace of God, into something that has meaning and purpose."[2]

When we are in the throes of suffering, we are so busy hurting, sometimes it can be difficult to see any purpose in it. Often it is not until afterwards that we can look back and see that God had a reason for the suffering. He was pushing us to a higher level. He was sculpting us to look more like Jesus. We will not reach perfection before we die, but God means to bring us as far as he can. We will reduce the pain we experience if while we suffer we can somehow remember that suffering has purpose.

Some Christian martyrs actually sang praises to God while burning in the flames of their persecutors. How did they do this? They had a remarkably clear understanding of the truth that suffering has purpose.

Paul was not unaccustomed to suffering himself. In 2 Corinthians 11:23–29 (NKJV) he recounts:

- "From the Jews five times I received forty stripes minus one" (verse 24).
- "Three times I was beaten with rods" (verse 25).
- "Once I was stoned" (verse 25).
- "Three times I was shipwrecked" (verse 25).
- "A night and a day I have been in the deep" (verse 25).
- "In journeys often" (verse 26).
- "In perils of waters, in perils of robbers, in perils of my own countrymen, in perils of the Gentiles" (verse 26).
- "In perils in the city, in perils in the wilderness, in perils in the sea" (verse 26).
- "In perils among false brethren" (verse 26).
- "In weariness and toil, in sleeplessness often, in hunger and thirst, in fastings often" (verse 27).
- "In cold and nakedness" (verse 27).

Charles R. Swindoll

Paul viewed his circumstances as having cleared the way "for the greater progress of the gospel" of Christ to be released.[3]

Francis A. Schaeffer

This ["hope does not disappoint us"] takes us all the way back to our theme verses, where Paul says that he is "not ashamed of the gospel of Christ" (Romans 1:16) . . . he is proud of the Gospel because of the great hope it has given him; it is a hope that has not disappointed him, and therefore a hope of which he need never be ashamed.[4]

Dietrich Bonhoeffer

So the Christian, too, belongs not in the seclusion of a cloistered life but in the thick of foes.[5]

Loving the Ugly Duckling

ROMANS 5:6–8 *For when we were still without strength, in due time Christ died for the ungodly. For scarcely for a righteous man will one die; yet perhaps for a good man someone would even dare to die. But God demonstrates His own love toward us, in that while we were still sinners, Christ died for us. (NKJV)*

We were completely powerless to do what was right when Jesus died for us. Few, if any, will die for a good man, though someone might. God's love, however, is so gracious that he died for us when we were still sinners. He did not wait for us to clean up our acts. He died for the ungodly.

Our experience of God's love is subjective, but there is an objectiveness to God's love as well. That Jesus died for us when we were sinners is unmistakable proof that God loves us. You can stake your life on it. Where you find love, you find God; when you find love, you find God.

Philip Yancey

Jesus said God is like a shepherd who leaves ninety-nine sheep inside the fence to hunt frantically for one stray; like a father who can't stop thinking about his rebellious ingrate of a son though he has another who is respectful and obedient; like a rich host who opens the doors of the banquet hall to a

blood
a symbol of Jesus'
death

reconciled
brought into har-
mony with God

menagerie of bag-ladies and bums. God loves people not as a race or species, but rather just as you and I love them: one at a time.[6]

Frederick Buechner

Love: the first stage is to believe that there is only one kind of love. The middle stage is to believe that there are many kinds of love and that the Greeks had a different word for each of them. The last stage is to believe that there is only one kind of love . . . of all powers, love is the most powerful and the most powerless. It is the most powerful because it alone can conquer that final and most impregnable stronghold which is the human heart. It is the most powerless because it can do nothing except by consent. To say that love is God is romantic idealism. To say that God is love is either the last straw or the ultimate truth.[7]

Celebrate Good Times, Come On!

ROMANS 5:9–11 *Much more then, having now been justified by His* **blood**, *we shall be saved from wrath through Him. For if when we were enemies we were* **reconciled** *to God through the death of His Son, much more, having been reconciled, we shall be saved by His life. And not only that, but we also rejoice in God through our Lord Jesus Christ, through whom we have now received the reconciliation.* (NKJV)

We were busy hating God—spitting on him, throwing dirt in his face, kicking him—while he was busy taking our sin upon his own back and dying for us, so Paul asks a simple question. If that's how God treated us when we were his enemies, don't you think he'll be good to us now that we are his own? God has done that which is difficult (loving one's enemies); of course he will do that which is easy (loving one's friends).

Christ's death reconciled us to God, Christ's resurrection ensures that we will live new lives in him. We are new creations! Lastly, Paul writes that we will praise God. What a change from three chapters ago! In chapter 2, we were standing guilty and silent before a holy Judge. Now through our Lord Jesus Christ, we are praising God who used to be our Judge! We need not, indeed we cannot, do anything to earn this reconciliation. The reconciliation is done. All we have to do is receive it.

death
both biological and
spiritual

Our reconciliation is established on the foundation of Christ's finished work and now, right now, we are being saved by our risen Savior. His fellowship, his counsel, and his gift of presence flow from the promise of the Word. With the exercise of our gifts and the recognition of our call, God receives glory from our lives.

Wanted: A New Covenant

ROMANS 5:12–14 *Therefore, just as through one man sin entered the world, and **death** through sin, and thus death spread to all men, because all sinned—(For until the law sin was in the world, but sin is not imputed when there is no law. Nevertheless death reigned from Adam to Moses, even over those who had not sinned according to the likeness of the transgression of Adam, who is a type of Him who was to come. (NKJV)*

There was no sin in the Garden of Eden. It was a perfect environment, and Adam and Eve were free to live in perfect happiness, having fellowship with God and with each other. They were capable of perfect obedience. How long they enjoyed this state of grace is unknown.

go to

the Fall
Genesis 3

Genesis account
Luke 3:38;
Romans 5:14;
1 Corinthians 15:22, 45;
1 Timothy 2:13–14

depraved
morally corrupt

Paul explains the sequence of events at the point where sin entered their experience as the consequence of their action. This is what we refer to as <u>the Fall</u>, the historical event when Adam and Eve sinned and death, both spiritual and physical, became a part of human experience. This is also referred to as original sin—original because it was the very first. Paul says "death spread to all men, because all sinned." This means that we are **depraved** from birth. The entrance of sin into life on this planet created an immediate need for a new approach to God, who knew no sin. Here God began to make a way for sinners to be received into his holy kingdom through a covenant of grace.

God's Plan: The "Reign of Grace" Through Christ

The Two Men	Adam (verse 14)	Christ (verse 14)
The Two Acts	Adam—one trespass: verses 12, 15, 17–19	Christ—one righteous act (on the cross): verse 18
The Two Results	By Adam—condemnation, guilt, death: verses 15–16, 18–19	By Christ—justification, life, kingship: verses 17–19
The Two Differences	*In degree*—the grace of God by Christ abounds beyond the sin of the creature, Adam: verse 15	In type—one sin, by Adam—condemnation and reign of death: verse 16 Many sins on Christ—justification and "reigning in life" for those accepting God's grace by him.
The Two Kings	Sin—reigning through death: verse 17	Grace—reigning through righteousness: verse 21
The Two Contrasted States	Condemned people, slaves of death, by Adam	Justified people, reigning in life, by Christ

Source: William R. Newell, *Romans Verse by Verse* (Chicago: Moody Press, 1938), 176.

It is good to take note that Paul believed the Genesis account. He makes a number of references to it in this and other epistles. He didn't consider the Genesis account to be a myth containing some amount of truth. Rather, Paul, like Jesus in the Gospel accounts, treated the account of the Fall as fact.

The generations between Adam and Moses had no written law, but there was still death during this time because people willfully violated their God-given consciences. The Old Testament does give us several accounts of people who lived godly lives beyond the Fall. These are examples of the grace of God at work in the midst of human evil.

one man's
Adam's

what others say

Origen

The death which entered through sin is without doubt that death which the prophet speaks when he says: "The soul which sins shall surely die" [Ezekiel 18:4].[10]

Mark Driscoll

To be under law means to operate under a covenant of works. The law demands of us how we should live, but does not give us the power to achieve its demands. . . . To be under grace means to operate under a covenant of blessing. Grace empowers us to live a life free of sin and free to God. Therefore, to be under grace means that we would not continue in habitual sin because we have been freed from the impossible task of living up to the law by our own efforts.[11]

Grace Is on the House

ROMANS 5:15–17 *But the free gift is not like the offense. For if by the* **one man's** *offense many died, much more the grace of God and the gift by the grace of the one Man, Jesus Christ, abounded to many. And the gift is not like that which came through the one who sinned. For the judgment which came from one offense resulted in condemnation, but the free gift which came from many offenses resulted in justification. For if by the one man's offense death reigned through the one, much more those who receive abundance of grace and of the gift of righteousness will reign in life through the One, Jesus Christ.)* (NKJV)

"The free gift is not like the offense" (Romans 5:15 NKJV) in that while sin made us all black with sin, God's grace is more than enough to wash the blackness away until we gleam with the bright holiness of God. To put it simply, God's grace is bigger than sin, and the final results of grace will be far beyond the results of sin.

Paul is seeking to show that the sin of the one man, Adam, brought all people into condemnation. But God's grace is sufficient to overcome that condemnation. While sin destroys lives, grace helps us to live full lives—lives of abundant blessing. God's gift of life through Jesus Christ eradicates the consequences of sin.

Eight times in Romans 5:15–17 (NKJV), Paul speaks of grace and the gift:

1. the free gift is not like the offense (verse 15)

2. the grace of God (verse 15)

3. the gift (verse 15)

4. the grace of the one Man (verse 15)

5. the gift (verse 16)

6. the free gift which came from many offenses (verse 16)

7. abundance of (verse 17)

8. the gift of righteousness (verse 17)

Paul was stumbling over himself to make certain his readers understood they didn't have to do anything to have their sins forgiven except receive through faith in Jesus Christ the reconciliation that had already been made.

what others say

Francis A. Schaeffer

Just as in the Old Testament a brother raised up seed to his brother who had died childless (Deuteronomy 25:5–6) so, with humanity having died in the sin of Adam, Christ came to raise up a real, living humanity. The man who raised up seed for his dead brother under Old Testament law was called a kinsman redeemer. Christ is the true kinsman redeemer. He raised up a seed to God.[12]

John Chrysostom

If a Jew should ask you: How was the world saved by the power of the one Christ? you can answer him and say: How was the world damned by the one disobedient Adam? Nevertheless, grace and sin are not equal, and neither are death and life nor God and the devil.[13]

Martin Luther

For God has arranged to remove through Christ whatever the devil brought in through Adam. And it was the devil who brought in sin and death. Therefore God brought about the death of death and the sin of sin, the poison of poison, the captivity of captivity. As he says through Hosea: "O Death, I will be your death; O Hell, I will be your bite" [Hosea 13:14].[14]

grace abounds
Matthew 6:33

One Part Sin, Five Bezillion Parts Grace

ROMANS 5:18–21 *Therefore, as through one man's offense judgment came to all men, resulting in condemnation, even so through one Man's righteous act the free gift came to all men, resulting in justification of life. For as by one man's disobedience many were made sinners, so also by one Man's obedience many will be made righteous. Moreover the law entered that the offense might abound. But where sin abounded, grace abounded much more, so that as sin reigned in death, even so grace might reign through righteousness to eternal life through Jesus Christ our Lord. (NKJV)*

Here Paul offers concluding statements on the nature of the Fall and the condemnation it brought upon humanity. What one man's sin brought upon the entire human race is mind-boggling.

Paul reviews the consequences of Adam's sin and Jesus' gift of life for all who believe. He addresses the following: offense, condemnation, righteousness, justification, life, sin, grace, death, obedience, and law. Paul explains how all of these work together to point us once again to Jesus Christ.

When Paul says, "The law entered that the offense might abound" (Romans 5:20 NKJV), he's saying the more clearly we see what's right, the more things we discover are wrong. Furthermore, the more people realize they are sinners and are dead, the more aware they become of the penalty from which God saved them.

Paul's emphasis is on life, not death. Those in Jesus Christ past, present, and future are not dead, but alive! Grace abounds for those whose hearts are anchored in Christ Jesus as Lord and Savior. At great cost, Jesus paid our debt of sin. His grace abounds to all who believe.

Chapter Wrap-Up

- Being justified by faith brings peace, access to God, hope for heaven, and purpose for our suffering. (Romans 5:1–5)
- Christ died for us when we were sinners, which is unmistakable proof of God's love. (Romans 5:6–8)
- If Christ loved us when we were sinners, he will of course continue to love us after we have become his own. (Romans 5:9–11)
- God knew that sin would enter the world, but he had a plan to put the world right. In Christ Jesus, God's grace abounds. (Romans 5:15–19)
- The law showed us more clearly what righteousness is so that we might also see more clearly what the breadth of sin is. God's grace is bigger than sin. (Romans 5:20–21)

Study Questions

1. Peace is a wonderful grace of God. How do we find peace?
2. Why would we rejoice in suffering?
3. What is unmistakable proof that God loves us?
4. What does Paul mean when he says, "The free gift is not like the offense" (Romans 5:15 NKJV)?
5. Why was the law added?

Part Three
EXPERIENCING GRACE

Romans 6 A Life-or-Death Situation

Chapter Highlights:
* A Brand-New Life
* Sin Is No Longer Our Master
* Three Verbs
* Two Outcomes

Let's Get Started

If you've flown on airplanes much at all, you've probably had the experience of circling the airport, either because the field is too busy for the plane to land or because there's a problem in the tower that necessitates a temporary delay. As we come to Paul's discourse in Romans 6, we get the feeling that he's been circling the runway for some time and is about to prepare for landing.

At this point in the apostle's discussion, he makes a major transition. In Romans 1:18–3:20 Paul establishes a need for righteousness. In Romans 3:21–4:25 he explains how God justifies sinners. He uses Abraham as an example of what it means to be **justified by faith**.

justified by faith
declared innocent by God through trust in Jesus

Then in Romans 5 Paul describes some of the results of justification: we have peace with God, through faith we have access to Jesus, and we are able to rejoice in the truth that our suffering has purpose. He concludes this chapter by reflecting on the entrance of sin into human experience and on the consequences of that tragic moment in history. Grace steps in and reveals both the love and the power of God. This is the good news.

Finally, Paul explains how Jesus, God's second Adam, became salvation for us. Here we see the wonderful coming together of faith and grace, righteousness and justification, bringing "eternal life through Jesus Christ our Lord" (Romans 5:21 NKJV).

In Romans 6 Paul makes the point that righteousness is not only a matter of how God sees us through faith in Jesus Christ.

Righteousness is also something we should experience. Let's see how his discussion unfolds.

There's No Winning in Sinning

ROMANS 6:1–2 *What shall we say then? Shall we continue in sin that grace may abound? Certainly not! How shall we who died to sin live any longer in it? (NKJV)*

We have learned God's grace is enough to justify us. That's the good news of the Gospel, but the question remains: "Shall we continue in sin that grace may abound?" (Romans 6:1 NKJV). This might at first appear like a foolish question, but Paul's been around the block a few times. He had preached this message on several occasions, and he knew how difficult it was to walk a sinless path, despite God's grace and mercy.

Some misinformed people were tempted to give up all self-control. They reasoned that since God forgave all their sins, the more they sinned, the more grace God would give them. If one measure of grace was good, they figured they could get a double measure by being even more sinful.

Paul's reply to his question is, "Certainly not!" (Romans 6:2 NKJV; or "God forbid" in the KJV). It is an exclamation of the highest degree in Jewish thought—not shock, but disgust. The phrase is used when truth is being trashed. When Paul speaks of being dead to sin, he is expressing how powerful God's righteousness can be for those who believe and walk in it. The righteousness God grants believers is so powerful, it can keep Christians from wanting to sin.

A Second Definition for Baptism

> ROMANS 6:3–4 *Or do you not know that as many of us as were baptized into Christ Jesus were baptized into His death? Therefore we were buried with Him through baptism into death, that just as Christ was raised from the dead by the glory of the Father, even so we also should walk in newness of life. (NKJV)*

Paul uses some difficult language here. What does it mean to be "baptized into Christ Jesus" (Romans 6:3 NKJV)? When we hear the word *baptism*, we normally think of water baptism, but here, Paul is using the word in a different way. He's using baptism as a metaphor for when one person is united with another person or other people. Remember when God used Moses to part the Red Sea, and all the Israelites were saved? In 1 Corinthians 10:2 (NKJV), Paul refers to this event by saying the Israelites were "baptized into Moses," which is to say they were united to Moses like never before. They recognized his leadership and their dependence on him. In the same way, we are "baptized into Christ Jesus." We are united to Jesus. The identity of Jesus is inseparably linked with our own identities.

That's why Paul says we are "baptized into His death" (Romans 6:3 NKJV). What he means is that we are so perfectly united to Christ that his death becomes our death, not in the physical sense but in the spiritual sense. In other words, Christ's death was the death of our sin. It was the death of our old relationship with Adam, the essence of which was sin.

It is interesting to note that although Jesus emphasized the importance of following him throughout his ministry, he never talked about <u>union</u> with himself until his crucifixion was near.

go to

union
John 14–16

Two Types of Baptism

References to Water Baptism	References to Spiritual Baptism
Mark 16:16	Matthew 3:11
John 4:2	Mark 1:8
Acts 2:38–41	Luke 3:16
Acts 8:12–16	John 1:26, 33
Acts 9:18	Acts 2:38–39
Acts 10:47–48	Acts 8:16
Acts 16:15, 33	Acts 11:16
Acts 18:8	Romans 6:3–4
Acts 19:5	1 Corinthians 10:2
Acts 22:16	1 Corinthians 12:13
1 Corinthians 1.13–17	Galatians 3:27
Hebrews 6:2	Ephesians 4:5
1 Peter 3:21	Colossians 2:12
	1 Peter 3:21

United with Christ

ROMANS 6:5 *For if we have been united together in the likeness of His death, certainly we also shall be in the likeness of His resurrection,* (NKJV)

The strength of Paul's argument is in the word *united* (*sumfutos*), a beautiful Greek word. To be united with Christ Jesus means "to be planted together" with Christ. Paul is suggesting that through the death and the resurrection of Jesus, we have become one and the same plant with Him. As taught in verse 4, we were buried by bap-

Gospel
John 1:12–13

work of righteousness
something we do that makes us better or gains merit with God

tism only with the intention of rising again. So the formulation goes like this: The man who participates in the death of Christ cannot but participate in the resurrection, i.e., the very life of Christ!

Paul illustrates the power of what he has written, in chapter 11, when he wrote that "some of the branches were broken off, and you, being a wild olive tree, were grafted in among them, and with them become a partaker of the root and the fatness of the olive tree" (Romans 11:17 NKJV).

Paul says that we are not only united with Christ in his death, we are united with Christ in his resurrection. We too have new life. A new relationship has been born between us and Christ, the essence of which is life. We may not be completely at peace all the time, but we do know that God is always with us, that trials have a purpose, and that one day we'll enjoy the paradise of the full presence of God.

> **what others say**
>
> **James R. Edwards**
>
> God's grace is indeed freedom, but freedom from sin, not freedom for it—whoever sees in grace a pretext to get away with as much as possible is simply showing contempt for Christ who died for sin. The freedom created by grace leads not to license but to obedience. Obedience honors God's boundless love and responds to that love in the freedom which love creates.[1]

It is the Holy Spirit, not water, who joins a person to Christ. This is the dynamic work of the Gospel. Water is an outward sign, practiced as an ordinance or sacrament, of one's profession of faith. This has been a doctrine in the church since its inception.

When adult Christians decide to be baptized, it is not a **work of righteousness**. Rather, it is, or should be, their response to a God who loved them and was willing to take on their sin. Baptism is also an act of Christian obedience. It is our affirmation that we have believed and want to follow in Christ's footsteps.

No longer are we slaves to sin. We are now servants of Christ. We have become part of a new priestly order. Spiritually speaking, we are in paradise. If we were to act as if we were in spiritual paradise, how would our lives be different? Would we worry as much as we do? Would we get angry as often as we do? Would we look to the needs

apply it

of others more often? Would we be more deliberate in how we live our lives?

Paul takes up this same discussion in his letter to the Galatians. He writes to the people in the churches of Galatia, a Roman province where Paul went on his first missionary journey (see Illustration #5), reminding them of this very essential matter: "You are all sons of God through faith in Christ Jesus. For as many of you as were baptized into Christ have put on Christ" (Galatians 3:26–27 NKJV). Paul's message is consistent. We are united with Christ.

old man
our sinful nature

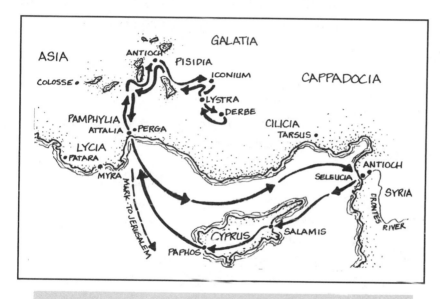

Illustration #5
Paul's First Missionary Journey—This map shows the route Paul took through Galatia on his first missionary journey.

what others say

John Chrysostom

Being dead to sin means not obeying it anymore. Baptism has made us dead to sin once and for all, but we must strive to maintain this state of affairs, so that however many commands sin may give us, we no longer obey it but remain unmoved by it, as a corpse does.[2]

Follow the New Captain

ROMANS 6:6–7 *knowing this, that our **old man** was crucified with Him, that the body of sin might be done away with, that we should no longer be slaves of sin. For he who has died has been freed from sin.* (NKJV)

What Paul is saying in these verses may be best illustrated with a story.

Once there was a crew of sailors whose captain was insane. For a long time the crew obeyed the man because, insane or not, he was their captain. There was only one problem. The insane captain's leadership often brought disaster.

One night the crew came very close to death because the captain led the crew into a frightening storm. On the following morning the first mate went around to each of the men and explained they no longer needed to pay attention to the insane captain. He was now so crazy that he wouldn't know the difference. The first mate became their new captain, and the crew eventually learned to ignore the old captain when he shouted orders. They did only what their new captain commanded. The wise leadership of the new captain brought joy and wealth to all the crew.

This story illustrates what our union with Christ is like. The old captain is our "old man" (Romans 6:6 NKJV), from whom we used to take all our orders and to whom we need no longer pay attention. The new captain is Christ, whose leadership will bring us abundant life.

Paul wants the believer to see that the "body of sin" (6:6 NKJV) has truly been done away with. As Jesus' death and resurrection were historical facts, so the believer's death and resurrection in Christ are rooted in objective truth.

apply it

Sometimes it takes a lot to convince ourselves that we are "freed from sin" (Romans 6:7 NKJV). After all, sin is still evident both in us and around us. This is one reason why faith is so important. Paul tells us that faith (in our freedom from sin) must come first; then we will see the results. It doesn't work the other way around. We can't wait to be convinced that we are free and then have faith that we are. That's not the way God set things up. He says to have faith, and the rest will come.

how to behave." It is a multi-textured vision, woven together to meet various specific needs, and promoted with all the energy that, Paul declared, his God had inspired within him."[3]

Knowing Is Half the Battle

ROMANS 6:8–10 *Now if we died with Christ, we believe that we shall also live with Him, knowing that Christ, having been raised from the dead, dies no more. Death no longer has dominion over Him. For the death that He died, He died to sin once for all; but the life that He lives, He lives to God.* (NKJV)

Here Paul begins using a series of three active verbs that we can think of as three steps to overcoming sin. The first verb is "to know." Paul says that knowing Jesus rose from the dead, he cannot die again, and therefore death has no mastery over him. This is the first step in overcoming sin—knowing that Christ died to sin and lives for God.

Oswald Chambers

To become one with Jesus Christ, a person must be willing not only to give up sin, but also to surrender his whole way of looking at things. . . . No one experiences complete sanctification without going through a "white funeral"—the burial of the old life. . . . You cannot die or go to your funeral in a mood of excitement. Death means you stop being.[4]

Take It As True

ROMANS 6:11–14 *Likewise you also, reckon yourselves to be dead indeed to sin, but alive to God in Christ Jesus our Lord. Therefore do not let sin reign in your mortal body, that you should obey it in its lusts. And do not present your members as instruments of unrighteousness to sin, but present yourselves to God as being alive from the dead, and your members as instruments of righteousness to God. For sin shall not have dominion over you, for you are not under law but under grace.* (NKJV)

Here are the second and third steps to overcoming sin. In the same way we know death has no mastery over Christ, we ought to take it as true that we are no longer in slavery to sin because we are joined with Christ in his death through the power of the Holy Spirit.

The New King James Version uses the verb *reckon*. We ought to reckon ourselves dead to sin. Paul is saying, "Make up your minds that sin does not have power over you."

The third and final step in overcoming sin is to yield to God. We should not offer our bodies to sin. We should offer them to God. It is not a matter of doing nothing. It is a matter of doing the right thing.

Jesus is both our example of a life that is fully surrendered to the will of God and the one who enables us to walk in that same surrender. It is our faith that makes the connection. Faith overrules our own will and allows us to abide in God's will. Ultimately, there is only one will that is holy: God's.

Paul reminded the Galatians, "Do not be deceived, God is not mocked; for whatever a man sows, that he will also reap. For he who sows to his flesh will of the flesh reap corruption, but he who sows to the Spirit will of the Spirit reap everlasting life" (Galatians 6:7–8 NKJV). People may breathe a sigh of relief after doing something wrong, thinking, "Great! I didn't get caught," but the reality is there is no such thing as not getting caught. There is no avoiding the destructive consequences of sin. Sometimes they come immediately, sometimes they come later, but they do come.

We have to live in these bodies the rest of our lives on earth. Just as Jesus carries scars on his hands and feet, sin, even when confessed and forgiven and cleansed by his blood, often leaves an indelible mark. One day we will look upon Christ's scars and realize we participated in putting them there.

Paul entreats, "Do not present your members as instruments of unrighteousness to sin, but present yourselves to God as being alive from the dead" (Romans 6:13 NKJV). This is a faith offer. Your body will fight against a righteous walk with God until it is brought into submission to God's will. This means we have to choose, carefully, what we look upon, what (and how) we touch, what we listen to, and, if we are overcome with the sin of gluttony, we need to watch what we taste and smell.

what others say

Francis A. Schaeffer

As Christians we have the possibility of living by faith, on the basis of the blood and in the power of the Spirit. Therefore, it isn't necessary that sin should have dominion over us. As Paul will say later, ". . . that the righteousness of the law might be fulfilled in us, who walk not after the flesh, but after the Spirit" [Romans 8:4] . . . we are under grace. The finished work of Christ and the indwelling of the Spirit are ours. It is possible for us to yield to the power of Christ.[5]

Martin Luther

Nothing lives to God, however, except that which lives eternally and spiritually, because God is eternal and a spirit, before whom nothing counts except what is spiritual and eternal; but the flesh and temporal things are nothing to Him.[6]

Dietrich Bonhoeffer

Baptismal death means justification from sin. The sinner must die that he may be delivered from his sin (Romans 6; Colossians 2). Sin has no further claim on him, for death's demand has been met, and its account settled. Justification from sin can only happen through death. Forgiveness of sin does not mean that sin is overlooked and forgotten, it means a real death on the part of the sinner and his separation from sin.[7]

righteous demands
Matthew 5:17

Whose Slave Are You?

ROMANS 6:15–18 *What then? Shall we sin because we are not under law but under grace? Certainly not! Do you not know that to whom you present yourselves slaves to obey, you are that one's slaves whom you obey, whether of sin leading to death, or of obedience leading to righteousness? But God be thanked that though you were slaves of sin, yet you obeyed from the heart that form of doctrine to which you were delivered. And having been set free from sin, you became slaves of righteousness.* (NKJV)

Paul wants it to be understood that being under grace in no way lessens the <u>righteous demands</u> of the law. If anything, grace becomes more demanding.

In the Roman Empire people became slaves a number of different ways. One way was to be born into a slave family, another was to be captured in battle, and still another was to be forced into slavery if one's nation was taken over. One final way was if an otherwise free person went into another's household and acted as a slave. Under Roman rule, if a person did this, he or she was a slave. The idea was, "A man is as he does."

Paul says if you act as a slave to sin by doing sinful things, you are a slave to sin. If you act as a slave to God by doing good things, you are a slave to God.

Note there are only two options. Slavery to sin or slavery to God. There is no such thing as not having a master. We all have a master. The question is, Which one? The way we act is a demonstration of our choice.

Paul keeps bringing grace into his discussion with the church in Rome. He knows that while the law reveals sin, grace brings healing to the sinner. While the law points out our sins and weaknesses, grace points up to our Savior and his strength. We are "under grace." It's our umbrella to protect us from the spiritual turmoil that surrounds us. If we fail to grasp the significance of the grace of God in Christ Jesus, we will always be in bondage to sin.

Our struggle is not with the law, nor with grace; our struggle is with sin. The law drags us out into the light, exposing our sin, and grace leads us to the Cross where our sin is paid for and done away with.

As believers we have changed masters; once we were slaves to sin, finding no way out, but now we are servants of righteousness. Paul states it more definitively: "you became slaves of righteousness" (Romans 6:18 NKJV).

something to ponder

what others say

Martin Luther

But temptation becomes a servant when we resist it, because it then produces a hatred of iniquity and a love of righteousness.[8]

John Calvin

"And being set free from sin." The meaning is that it is absurd for anyone to continue in bondage after he has gained his freedom. He ought to maintain the state of freedom which he has received. It is not fitting, therefore, for believers to be brought again under the dominion of sin, from which they have been set at liberty by Christ.[9]

Speaking Your Language

ROMANS 6:19 *I speak in human terms because of the weakness of your flesh. For just as you presented your members as slaves of uncleanness, and of lawlessness leading to more lawlessness, so now present your members as slaves of righteousness for holiness.* (NKJV)

When Paul says, "I speak in human terms" (Romans 6:19 NKJV), what he's saying is this: "I'm using this slavery analogy because slavery is something you're familiar with." Slavery would have been an effective reference point because slaves were a major economic asset in first-century Rome. A large percentage of the professionals, including teachers and doctors, were slaves. The Roman church would have known all about slavery—its advantages and disadvantages, its binding nature, and how to avoid or enter into it.

What's in It for Me?

ROMANS 6:20–23 *For when you were slaves of sin, you were free in regard to righteousness. What fruit did you have then in the things of which you are now ashamed? For the end of those things is death. But now having been set **free from sin**, having become slaves of God, you have your fruit to holiness, and the end, everlasting life. For the wages of sin is death, but the gift of God is eternal life in Christ Jesus our Lord.* (NKJV)

Paul goes on to discuss what results from servitude to either master. Here is what sin offers:

- Slavery to uncleanness (6:19)
- Ever-increasing lawlessness (6:19)
- Slavery to sin (6:20)
- Shame (6:21)
- Death (6:21, 23)

Paul reminds believers that God's righteousness leads to **holiness**. To understand real holiness, we need to look at Jesus in the Gospels. His is a holiness that fits the plan and purposes of God. He wasn't self-righteous. Rather, his piety led to charity, kindness, compassion, service, mercy, tenderness, and forgiveness. His purity led to devotion to his Father. His compassion enabled him to reach out to the

written
Leviticus 19:2

poor, the needy, and the religious. His tenderness led him to stop and talk with the children, to make them a real part of the kingdom of God.

Holiness is not an escape from the world, it's the godly way to enter the world—to glorify God and to be a blessing to others. The apostle Peter understood holiness after years of missing the mark. He wrote in his first epistle, "As He who called you is holy, you also be holy in all your conduct, because it is <u>written</u>, 'Be holy, for I am holy'" (1 Peter 1:15–16 NKJV). Holiness means separation from all that is sinful and consecration to all that is holy. It requires our total person to be set apart for God.

> ### what others say
>
> #### Charles Hodge
>
> The leading doctrine of this section, and of the whole gospel, in reference to sanctification, is, that grace, instead of leading to the indulgence of sin, is essential to the exercise of holiness. So long as we are under the influence of a self-righteous or legal spirit, the motive and the aim of all good works are wrong or defective.[10]

Chapter Wrap-Up

- Paul speaks about death and life. Because we have been baptized in Christ, we now share his identity and rejoice in hope. (Romans 6:1–4)

- We have been identified and united with Christ in his death, burial, and resurrection. Through the exercise of faith we receive the benefits that accompany this great work of grace on behalf of humanity. (Romans 6:5–7)

- Because of the resurrection, sin is no longer our master. By faith, we can count ourselves "dead indeed to sin, but alive to God in Christ Jesus" (verse 11 NKJV). (Romans 6:8–11)

- In addition to knowing that we are joined with Christ in his death and resurrection, we need to take this as true and choose to obey God. In this way, we will demonstrate who our master is. A man is as he does. (Romans 6:12–14)

- We must choose between two masters, sin or God. The result of sin is death, and the reward of God is righteousness and eternal life. (Romans 6:15–23)

Study Questions

1. Does sin cause grace to abound?

2. What does it mean to be baptized into Christ's death?

3. What does it mean to be "united together [with Christ] in the likeness of His resurrection" (Romans 6:5 NKJV)?

4. We have been united with Christ in his resurrection. How does that free us from sin?

5. Since we have been set free from sin, how is it that so many Christians live in sin?

Romans 7 The Tension of Two Natures

Chapter Highlights:
- Freedom by Death
- Two Natures
- Goodness of the Law
- Badness of Sin
- Deliverance and Thanksgiving

Let's Get Started

Paul's writings are the key that enables the church to unlock the gospel message. We have seen from the first six chapters how precious the Gospel is to Paul. It is easy for us to forget how good God is and to put conditions on his grace—especially conditions that we apply to others.

As a committed Pharisee, Paul was well schooled in the law, which included the Ten Commandments as well as other God-given laws. There were laws that guided temple worship, laws about what to eat and what not to eat, laws surrounding childbirth, laws related to various infections and diseases, and laws that set moral standards.

While the law was never intended to bring about salvation, the law was holy in that it was an expression of God's character. The law helped people recognize their need for salvation.

Death Unlocks the Shackles

> ROMANS 7:1–3 *Or do you not know, brethren (for I speak to those who know the law), that the law has dominion over a man as long as he lives? For the woman who has a husband is bound by the law to her husband as long as he lives. But if the husband dies, she is released from the law of her husband. So then if, while her husband lives, she marries another man, she will be called an adulteress; but if her husband dies, she is free from that law, so that she is no adulteress, though she has married another man.* (NKJV)

As chapter 7 opens, Paul is answering a question that his Jewish readers would have been sure to ask: How can we be legally freed from the law? Paul answers this question by using marriage as an illustration. The law binds a wife to her husband for as long as the man lives and no longer.

Paul uses the marriage covenant as a lens to sharpen our vision. It is an apt analogy. Here's Paul's rationale:

reign
control, authority

- The law has authority over people for as long as they live.

- Only death can break or end that authority (as death ends marriage).

- All attempts to circumvent the law's authority lead to a violation.

- Death frees one from the law.

- Jesus died to the law in order that the law would be dead to us, and we to the law.

It takes discernment to know when we are under the law or just being obedient on the basis of our faith. If we are still under the rule of law, trying to obey the law instead of being submissive to the law of Christ, we are still under the **reign** of sin. Remember that the power of sin resides in the power of the law. It is Jesus Christ who fulfilled the just requirements of the law and, in so doing, broke the power of sin. Dying to the law does not mean practicing lawlessness. It means discovering the joy and freedom of following the Lawgiver, for the Lawgiver revealed himself in the person of Jesus.

God did for us, in the death of his Son, what we could not do for ourselves. We would still be under law—every precept, every command, every ordinance—if we had not "become dead to the law through the body of Christ, that [we] may be married to another" (Romans 7:4 NKJV). By the grace of God, we belong to Jesus, our Savior, Mediator, High Priest, and Lord.

what others say

William Barclay

When a man rules his life by union with Christ he rules it not by obedience to a written code of law which may actually awaken the desires of sin, but by an allegiance to Jesus Christ within his spirit and his heart. Not law, but love, is the motive of his life: and the inspiration of love can make him able to do what the restraint of law was powerless to help him do.[1]

Rotten Fruit

ROMANS 7:4–6 *Therefore, my brethren, you also have become dead to the law through the body of Christ, that you may be married to another—to Him who was raised from the dead, that we should bear fruit to God. For when we were in the flesh, the sinful passions which were aroused by the law were at work in our members to bear fruit to death. But now we have been delivered from the law, having died to what we were held by, so that we should serve in the newness of the Spirit and not in the oldness of the letter. (NKJV)*

When we relate to God through the law by trying our hardest to do what's right, all that happens is the old nature is stimulated by the law to produce fruit that is contrary to God, "fruit to death," Paul calls it (Romans 7:5 NKJV).

Here's an example. Let's say a man makes up his mind to stop taking the Lord's name in vain. Let's say he succeeds, but now he looks down on everyone around him who does take the Lord's name in vain, and he also becomes very proud of his own accomplishment. The man succeeds in not taking the Lord's name in vain, but he becomes judgmental and prideful in the process. This is the way of the old nature. One step forward, two steps back.

The way of the new nature is different. The new nature looks to God for guidance, not the law. You might say, "Well, okay, but didn't the law come from God?" The answer is yes, but the law is not meant to be a guide for our lives. If you're an apprentice in carpentry and the master carpenter gives you a box of tools, will you use the hammer to tighten screws? Of course not! Every tool has its purpose.

The law's purpose is to show us how much we need the Holy Spirit to guide us. To use the carpentry analogy again, when we compare our work to the work of the master carpenter, we see how far we have to go. We are therefore motivated to listen and learn from the master. In the same way, the law shows us how much we need to listen to God.

Two Natures and Their Outcomes

Nature	Stimulated by . . .	To Produce . . .
Old Nature	The law	Fruit for death
New Nature	The Holy Spirit	Fruit for God

It was the apostle James who wrote, "As the body without the spirit is dead, so faith without works is dead also" (James 2:26 NKJV). This is what Paul means when he speaks of being controlled by the old nature, bearing "fruit to death" (Romans 7:5 NKJV). When the Holy Spirit indwells our body, in accordance with the teaching

glory
John 5:40; 8:50; 17:5;
Colossians 1:27;
2 Peter 1:3

of the New Covenant, we will "bear fruit to God" (7:4 NKJV). Fruit is produced in both the old and the new natures. Whoever we are in union with will determine the kind of fruit we bear.

what others say

Matthew Henry

Good works are the children of the new nature . . . there is no fruit brought forth to God till we are married to Christ. This distinguishes the good works of believers from the good works of hypocrites and self-justifiers, that they are done in union with Christ.[2]

Christ's purpose is unswerving: He came to fulfill the divine will and to make known the glory of God. This is a guide for believers in our service for the kingdom of God. Paul spells it out plainly to the Corinthians: "Whether you eat or drink, or whatever you do, do all to the glory of God . . . Just as I also please all men in all things, not seeking my own profit, but the profit of many" (1 Corinthians 10:31, 33 NKJV). To glorify God is to reveal, by word and by life, what God is like. We are called upon by the Spirit of God to reflect the Person whose life we possess. We are to "do all to the glory of God." God's expectations are of the highest order because he has given us his greatest good: the very life of his Son.

what others say

Adolf Schlatter

As long as [Jesus Christ] had a body, he was under the law (Galatians 4:4), and there would have been no liberation from the law, if the judgment of death had not been carried out in his body. All those who belong to him are included in what Jesus did. His divine, powerful love renders his association complete and effective for all.[3]

William S. Plumer

The legal spirit is a great enemy of the gospel. Legal repentance is wholly diverse from evangelical sorrow for sin. Mount Sinai is far from Mount Calvary. It was Joshua, not Moses, that let Israel into Canaan . . . great is the mystery of godliness.[4]

Magnifying Our Sin

ROMANS 7:7–8 *What shall we say then? Is the law sin? Certainly not! On the contrary, I would not have known sin except through the law. For I would not have known covetousness unless the law had said, "You shall not covet." But sin, taking opportunity by the commandment, produced in me all manner of evil desire. For apart from the law sin was dead. (NKJV)*

covetousness
a desire for the possessions of others

Sin is used several times in verses 7–12. In these verses it is referring not to an act of sin, but to the sin principle, the powerful force within us that stays relatively quiet until we are told we should not do certain things (the law). "You shall not covet" (Romans 7:7 NKJV) is one example. Then sin wells up within us. The surest way to lose flowers from your garden bed is to post a sign that reads, "Don't Pick the Flowers." If sin is allowed to run its full course, it eventually destroys us.

The apostle knew his discussion of the law would raise a number of questions in his readers' minds. For example, because our "sinful passions" are "aroused by the law" (Romans 7:5 NKJV), is the law not wicked?

Paul responds, "Certainly not!" (7:7 NKJV). The issue at hand is our awareness of sin, which is created by the law. The law does not cause sin, it identifies sin. The law acts like a magnifying glass; it helps us see our sin in large, bold type. God's commandments make it clear to us that we prefer to follow our own will instead of his. Adolf Schlatter, a professor in theology at Tubingen University in the late nineteenth and early twentieth centuries, brings clarity to what the apostle communicated. He writes, "The law gives rise, not to sin, but to the knowledge of sin, which is non-existent without the law."[5]

It is because of this law-provoked inclination toward sin that Paul tells the believers in Rome to look carefully at "the newness of the Spirit and not . . . the oldness of the letter" (Romans 7:6 NKJV). Paul had learned that we must be dead to the law before we can truly lay hold of Christ.

something to ponder

Covetousness is a sin that shows up early in childhood. It's a sign for parents to begin praying for the salvation of their child. The flame of covetousness cannot be beaten away with a rod, but it can be enveloped and consumed in the fire of God's blessing. The way to stop coveting is to realize how much we have in Christ. We torture ourselves thinking, "If only," while the infinite joy of God sits neglected under our noses.

Paul's Different Uses for "Law"

context
the textual setting of
a word that can
shed light on its
meaning

Paul used the word *law* in three different ways, as follows:

1. The Old Testament and its commandments

2. The principle of the sin nature (we act against that which God says is right)

3. The principle of the new nature (we follow God)

The way to discern which definition Paul is using is by looking at the **context** of the word. For example, when Paul says in Romans 7:21, "I find then a law, that evil is present with me, the one who wills to do good" (NKJV), we know from the context that Paul is not talking about the Old Testament and its commandments or the principle of the new nature. He's talking about the principle of the sin nature.

Paul is challenging the confusion that men make when they "turn the Gospel into a law" (Luther). The Mosaic law has a divine function that continues to this very hour. It gives mankind God's perspective on sin and his sin nature, the result of the Fall. The commandments, literally, according to Paul, open the floodgates to sin, which in turn "produced in me all *manner* of evil desire." Now "desire" in itself is not sin, according to James (1:12–15), but it is a step in that direction, and that step is our opportunity to say no to the enticement of sin and yes to the will of God.

When you contrast the whole of Mosaic law with the one law in the Garden of Eden: "Of the tree of the knowledge of good and evil you shall not eat, for in that day that you eat of it you shall surely die" (Genesis 2:17 NKJV): it is easy to see how the commandments gave sin an open field to play in! Paul had learned and is teaching every generation since, "For apart from the law sin was dead."

Yes, sin lay dead, but so was man! You were "dead in trespasses and sin, in which you once walked according to the course of this world" (Ephesians 2:1–2 NKJV). But when the commandments entered man's consciousness, the power of God came home with power and authority. Sin was aroused, became active, like the sudden eruption of a volcano. The urge to sin, to violate the commandments is a powerful urge.

what others say

John Murray

It must not be assumed, however, that what the apostle is dealing with here is the principle stated elsewhere that "where no law is, there is no transgression" (4:15; cf 5:13; 1 Corinthians 15:56). Paul here in verse 8 is not speaking about the nonexistence of sin but of sin as existing, yet as dead. And what he is referring to is the inertness, inactivity, in that sense of deadness, of sin, in contrast with the life of sin to which he will presently refer. [6]

Douglas J. Moo

God's work in Christ, mediated by the Spirit, is what overcomes the inability of the law, weakened by the flesh, and liberates the believer from the "law of sin and death."[7]

Commandment and Conviction

ROMANS 7:9–11 *I was alive once without the law, but when the commandment came, sin revived and I died. And the commandment, which was to bring life, I found to bring death. For sin, taking occasion by the commandment, deceived me, and by it killed me. (NKJV)*

When Paul says he was "alive once without the law" (Romans 7:9 NKJV), he is referring to a time in his life when he assumed that he was fulfilling God's commandments. Before his conversion Paul was, like other Pharisees, proud of his commitment to keep God's rules and observe his rituals. But the Pharisees focused on outward things. As long as they seemed to keep the commandments and remained ceremonially clean, they believed they were right with God. During this time in his life Paul was unaware of the sin within him.

Sometime after his conversion, however, Paul realized he was sinful ("the commandment came" [7:9 NKJV]). He was so intensely convicted that he likened the experience to death.

Paul did not see the condemnation of the law until he came face-to-face with Jesus. It was in the light of his grace and kindness that this hostile, angry man was brought to his knees. Until that point, Paul considered himself "alive . . . without the law" (Romans 7:9 NKJV). Once Paul was in the presence of true righteousness, he was <u>convicted</u> like never before.

How are the commandments intended to "bring life" (Romans

7:10 NKJV)? They confront people with their need for righteousness. People are then called to turn to the Lawgiver, and to seek mercy and forgiveness. Upon receiving God's grace, life expands in the heart of the believer to the point of breaking open and doing away with the shell of the old self.

Don't Fault the Law

ROMANS 7:12 *Therefore the law is holy, and the commandment holy and just and good. (NKJV)*

After arguing for the goodness of the law at length, Paul concludes his thesis by making it absolutely clear that the law is holy, righteous, and good. Paul wanted to dispel any remaining false notions concerning the law. He therefore gives it his highest commendation.

what others say

Saint Augustine

Man needed to be shown the foulness of his malady. Against his wickedness not even a holy and good commandment could avail; by it the wickedness was increased rather than diminished.[8]

William S. Plumer

The moral law is unto life among unsinning angels. It was unto life to our first parents till they ate the forbidden fruit . . . but every man, who has had conviction of sin, has, like Paul, found the law to be unto death, that is to condemnation, to the death of legal hope, and to the arousing of wicked principles in the soul into lively action. The law, rightly used, conduces to holiness and happiness; broken or misused, it **conduces** only sin and misery.[9]

Law vs. Sin

ROMANS 7:13 *Has then what is good become death to me? Certainly not! But sin, that it might appear sin, was producing death in me through what is good, so that sin through the commandment might become exceedingly sinful. (NKJV)*

Paul finds himself in front of a question that he had not fully pondered: "Has then what is good become death to me?" (Romans 7:13 NKJV). Is that possible? What was the relationship between the law and **death**? Having concluded the commandment not to covet, which Paul used to represent the whole law, was "holy and just and good" (7:12 NKJV), was it possible the law produced death in him?

Paul concludes, "Certainly not!" (7:13 NKJV). It's not the law that produces death in individuals; it's sin. He concludes that sin uses that which is "good" (the law) as an instrument to produce death in a person. This happens because we cannot keep the standard of God's righteousness.

Paul concludes that because sin uses the law to bring death, sin reveals itself as truly despicable. The law triumphs: it fully exposes sin for the evil thing it is.

Spirit
John 4:24

Bewitched, Bothered, and Bewildered

ROMANS 7:14–16 For we know that the law is spiritual, but I am carnal, sold under sin. For what I am doing, I do not understand. For what I will to do, that I do not practice; but what I hate, that I do. If, then, I do what I will not to do, I agree with the law that it is good. (NKJV)

Paul switches to the present tense here, whereas before he was using the past tense. He is obviously referring to his present struggles with sin, which daily try to gain control of his life.

Paul wonders why he can't control the advance of sin within him. He has the right attitude—he wants to do what is right and good. Yet, he still wallows in the mud that consumes his heart and soul. He believes in God, but wonders where God is.

Herein we see the conflict, the step that most, if not all, resist in some manner. Paul discovers that there is a difference between what he wants to do and what he actually does. He is "sold under sin" (Romans 7:14 NKJV). He has no capital, no assets to buy himself out of the slave market.

He can readily agree that the law is good, but the law is powerless to change him on the inside. It's unable to give him the resources he needs to fulfill the demands of the law, the very same law that is considered good.

When Paul says the law is spiritual, he's referring to the source of the law, which is God, who is <u>Spirit</u>. When he says he is unspiritual, he is contrasting himself with the nature of the law. The law was pure, but he was full of sin.

go to

sanctification
2 Corinthians
3:17–18;
Romans 8:11

sanctification
to become righteous in character and practice

imperfect and aorist
two Greek tenses which when used together place an action in the past

The <u>sanctification</u> process is fraught with conflict. Sin and death have been an integral part of Paul's discussion since the middle of chapter 5.

Paul does not retreat from life's conflicts. Rather, he puts himself squarely in life's path. We will never find answers by hiding from the difficulties of life. Paul searched diligently for the will of God as well as the ways of God. He wanted his life, and the lives of those he was responsible to teach, to express what it means to live for the glory of God. We are called to do likewise.

> **what others say**
>
> **Joseph Shulam**
>
> Paul now feels confident to claim that everyone "knows" that the truth is that God's law is holy, righteous, and good, and that man's human inclination is evil. Just as God's faithfulness is not impugned by Israel's unfaithfulness (cf. 3:3ff), the Torah is not contaminated because man does not fulfil its commandments. Although God intended the Torah to give life, because its commandments also hold the "power of sin" it is also a means of death, for the "sons of darkness," or those who use it unlawfully (cf. 1 Timothy 1:8f).[10]
>
> **John F. Walvoord and Roy B. Zuck**
>
> Understanding the conflict in personal sanctification involves seeing the relationship between a believer and his indwelling sin . . . in relating his personal experience in 7:14–25 Paul consistently used the present tense whereas he had used the **imperfect and aorist** tenses. Obviously he was describing his present conflict as a Christian with indwelling sin and its continuing efforts to control his daily life.[11]

A Noble Struggle

ROMANS 7:17–20 *But now, it is no longer I who do it, but sin that dwells in me. For I know that in me (that is, in my flesh) nothing good dwells; for to will is present with me, but how to perform what is good I do not find. For the good that I will to do, I do not do; but the evil I will not to do, that I practice. Now if I do what I will not to do, it is no longer I who do it, but sin that dwells in me.* (NKJV)

After debunking the idea that the law is sin or that the law brings death, Paul addresses the question, Does the believer struggle with the law too? He answers by sharing from his own experience as a believer trying to keep the law.

Larry Richards writes a paraphrase that highlights the key points of Paul's argument. The paraphrase starts at verse 15: "I don't understand my own actions. I don't do what I want—I do the very thing I hate. Because I don't want to do the things I do, it's clear that I agree that what the law says is good and right. I'm that much in harmony with God. But somehow I'm not in control of my own actions! Some sinful force within takes over and acts through my body."[12] A change was underway, but Paul was still struggling.

Just because we struggle with sin doesn't mean we are not Christians. It takes self-control and diligence to overcome the temptations that the world around us presents. Christ fought and won the final battle over sin, but we need to apply that victory to daily life. Satan loves to whisper to us, saying we deserve this or that and making evil look like a reward. Often we find a set of rigid rules easier to follow than examining and changing our wrong attitudes and motives. In chapter 8 Paul will give us some very valuable information about how to overcome sin.

Earlier Paul said his sinful nature could not save him and neither could the law, though in itself the law is holy and righteous and good. Paul then explains that even with a new nature, **his will** could not save him. Here Paul says the sin "dwells in [him]" (Romans 7:17 NKJV) and is responsible for his doing evil. In this way, Paul avoids Satan's false promise of **sinless perfection**.

key point

his will
his determined intention to do good

sinless perfection
what the serpent promised Adam and Eve in the Garden of Eden

what others say

Martin Luther

Therefore sin remains in the spiritual man for the exercise of grace, for the humbling of pride, for the repression of presumptuousness.[13]

William S. Plumer

Here then it is conceded that the language of Romans 7:14–25 is appropriate to the case of Christians; that all Christians have a contest like that here described; and that the matter is of a very weighty character—a matter of universal Christian experience, than which nothing is to us more important to be rightly understood.[14]

"I Can't Do It"

> **ROMANS 7:21–25a** *I find then a law, that evil is present with me, the one who wills to do good. For I delight in the law of God according to the inward man. But I see another law in my members, warring against the law of my mind, and bringing me into captivity to the law of sin which is in my members. O wretched man that I am! Who will deliver me from this body of death? I thank God—through Jesus Christ our Lord!* (NKJV)

Paul continues to chronicle his experience. He carefully thought out what he was observing and feeling so others could benefit from his grueling experience.

The apostle is recounting a profound conflict that every Christian finds inherent in his life in Christ Jesus. It seems to be a dilemma beyond total understanding, and yet very real. We know from Scripture that Christ dwells in Paul (Galatians 2:20; Colossians 3:3–4), yes, and in all who believe in Jesus as Savior and Lord, yet sin also dwells in Paul (verses 17, 20).

1. *Dilemma Number One (7:15–16):* "For what I am doing, I do not understand . . . but what I hate, that I do." Out of this dilemma Paul discovers: since he cannot do what he wills to do, it confirms that the law is good. He sees that sin has the power to overrule his ability to will what is right! Somehow there is a complete split between the "I" that wills, that decides, and the "I" that finally expresses the will of God.

2. *Dilemma Number Two (7:20):* He comes to an important insight: "Now if I do what I will not to do, it is no longer I who do it, but sin that dwells in me." He has come to the conclusion "nothing good dwells" in him, that is, in his "flesh." So he has nothing to offer God! This is confirmed in the first eight chapters of Romans.

3. *Dilemma Number Three (7:21–23):* Here Paul personifies evil. The expression, "evil is present with me," presents an existential moment in Paul's theological processing. He is acknowledging that everyone is presented with the choice between obeying his evil proclivity and determining the will of God: who is master? I believe that the text strongly suggests that Paul is referencing the Evil One, the world of Belial or Satan, as the source of conflict.

Yet in spite of the dilemma Paul is experiencing, he still "delights" in the law (*nomos*) of God. The conflict was driving him to the only answer God would give, the only answer he could give, if the gospel Paul preached was indeed the truth.

The expression, "O wretched man that I am! Who (not what!) will deliver me from this body of death?" is exactly where Paul was when he was on the Road to Damascus (Acts 9), and the answer became obvious, then and now: "Thanks be to God through Jesus Christ our Lord!" His understanding was restored!

Larry Richards' paraphrase continues, "I know that nothing good exists in the old me. The sin nature is so warped that even when I desire good I somehow can't do it. Sin, dwelling in me, is to blame for this situation. It all seems so hopeless! The fact is that when I want to do right, evil lies close at hand. In my inmost self I delight in God's law. But another principle wars with the desire to obey and brings me to my knees, a captive to the principle of indwelling sin."[15] Paul was not able to achieve righteousness by trying to keep the law. His inability to do so led him to despair and to cry out, "Who will deliver me from this body of death?" (Romans 7:24 NKJV). He answers his own question with an expression of thanksgiving, for God through Jesus Christ will deliver him.

God's laws are meant to keep us from harm, sorrow on this earth, and death in eternity. When we learn this, we want to obey God. The psalmists speak of the spiritual man whose "delight is in the law of the LORD, and in His law he meditates day and night" (Psalm 1:2 NKJV). The law is also praised in Psalm 19:

The law of the LORD is perfect, converting the soul;
The testimony of the LORD is sure, making wise the simple;
The statutes of the LORD are right, rejoicing the heart;
The commandment of the LORD is pure, enlightening the eyes;
The fear of the LORD is clean, enduring forever. (verses 7–9
NKJV)

This is what Paul means when he says, "I delight in the law of God" (Romans 7:22 NKJV). The path we are called to walk is often a troublesome one, but we have God's presence and his Word to fill our hearts and minds. This should be our continuous delight.

Saint Augustine

These are the words ["When I want to do good, evil is right there with me"] of one who is now under grace but still battling against his own lust, not so that he consents and sins but so that he experiences desires which he resists.[16]

In Summary of the Struggle

ROMANS 7:25B *So then, with the mind I myself serve the law of God, but with the flesh the law of sin. (NKJV)*

Paul takes a step back to summarize the essence of his struggle. One part of him is a slave to God while another part of him is a slave to sin. He's torn between the two. In the next chapter, we'll look at how Paul puts the resolution of this tension into everyday practice.

There are other interpretations of chapter 7, and some are plausible. Some interpret this passage as Paul describing his unregenerate state, and especially from the Jewish perspective. Some say that Paul is describing a believer who is in an unhealthy spiritual condition—failing to draw upon the grace of God. Or, what has been proposed above: Paul is simply, and honestly, describing himself and Christians in general, although born of the Holy Spirit and free from condemnation, yet we must "grow in the grace and knowledge of our Lord and Savior Jesus Christ" (2 Peter 3:18 NKJV).

Many Christians can relate to what Paul is saying in these verses. We too get frustrated with ourselves. We desperately want to be good, but we can't be. Our hearts hurt. Our minds hurt. Even our bodies hurt because of our own sin. We should find consolation in knowing that the great saint Paul, who wrote more of the New Testament than any other and to whom centuries of Christians are eternally grateful—Paul was in the exact same predicament. He was riddled with his own sin.

Chapter Wrap-Up

- As a widow is no longer bound to her deceased husband, neither are we bound to the law because in Christ's crucifixion we died to the law. (Romans 7:1–3)

- The old nature is stimulated by the law to produce fruit to death. The new nature is stimulated by the Holy Spirit to produce fruit unto God. (Romans 7:4–6)

- The law is holy, righteous, and good in that it shows us our sin, but sin within us is aroused by the law and leads to self-destruction. (Romans 7:7–12)

- Sin uses the law to produce death in us. (Romans 7:13)

- Paul wanted to be godly but failed at every turn. He was vexed and bewildered by his behavior. (Romans 7:14–20)

- Tension arises within us because one part of us is slave to God, while the other is slave to sin. Deliverance is found in Jesus Christ. (Romans 7:21–25)

Study Questions

1. Verse 4 says we died to the law that we might belong to another. What does this mean?

2. What are some of the differences between the old nature and the new nature?

3. How is it that the law is able to show us our sin?

4. How is the law spiritual? What does it mean to be unspiritual?

5. What does Paul mean when he says, "With the mind I myself serve the law of God, but with the flesh the law of sin" (Romans 7:25 NKJV)?

Romans 8 The Triumph of Spirit-Guided Living

Let's Get Started

The great triumph of the Christian's faith is total deliverance from **condemnation**. Paul does not say there is nothing in us that deserves condemnation, because there is, but the truth of the Gospel is that Christ Jesus has released us from condemnation. The believer has been imparted perfect righteousness and lives according to the law of the Spirit, which is the law of God.

We are not only forgiven, we have received the Holy Spirit into our very bodies. He is our source of divine power to bring about our necessary sanctification. Paul speaks of our bodies as God's temple: "Do you not know that your body is the temple of the Holy Spirit who is in you, whom you have from God, and you are not your own? For you were bought at a price; therefore glorify God in your body" (1 Corinthians 6:19–20 NKJV).

Romans 8 is where Paul gathers various strands of thought, starting with the Gospel in chapter 1. He links **justification** with **sanctification**.

Jesus Freedom

> **ROMANS 8:1–2** *There is therefore now no condemnation to those who are in Christ Jesus, who do not walk according to the flesh, but according to the Spirit. For the **law of the Spirit of life** in Christ Jesus has made me free from the **law of sin and death**. (NKJV)*

Here we encounter another of Paul's therefore's. This one takes us all the way back to chapter 3 where Paul said the law's purpose was to silence us before God. Paul has come from pointing out our guilt to there is "now no condemnation" (Romans 8:1 NKJV).

For "no condemnation" to have any meaning we must look at the opposite of condemnation—justification. The idea of justification is foundational to this letter and many other of Paul's writings. It hap-

condemnation
being held responsible for and punished for evil acts

justification
the doctrine of being declared righteous in Christ

sanctification
the process by which God brings the Christian to be the person God created him or her to be

law of the Spirit of life
the normal pattern of a life lived in submission to the Holy Spirit

law of sin and death
the normal pattern of a life lived in sin

pens when we are declared righteous in Christ, but justification goes beyond that. God also accepts us. God not only proclaims us not guilty, he welcomes us to himself with open arms.

The apostle traces the liberating gift of the Spirit back to its ultimate Source: "For what the law could not do in that it was weak through the flesh, God did by sending His own Son in the likeness of sinful flesh"(Romans 8:3 NKJV). Jesus has the power to break the grip of sin in and on all relationships. He is the one who delivers us "from this body of death" (Romans 7:24 NKJV).

God's Gift

> ROMANS 8:3–4 *For what the law could not do in that it was weak through the flesh, God did by sending His own Son in the likeness of sinful flesh, on account of sin: He condemned sin in the flesh, that the righteous requirement of the law might be fulfilled in us who do not walk according to the flesh but according to the Spirit.* (NKJV)

These verses remind us of the anguish in chapter 7. The law makes demands of us, but because of our sinful nature, we are unable to meet those demands. The law is "weak" (Romans 8:3 NKJV) and unable to save us.

God could have let us perish in the wrath that our unrighteousness deserves, but because he loves, he sent Christ to do what the law was unable to do. God became one of us, lived a perfect life, and died for our sins. Through Christ God justly condemned sins of the flesh while offering the gift of righteousness to all who believe. Grace is knowing that God is for us and with us, even in our sinful condition.

The law's purpose is to reveal sin, not to remove it. There is no defect in the law itself. The law was a covenant of works and made no provision for failure if it were to happen. The law leaves us as it finds us, proclaiming with Paul how wretched we are.

what others say

James R. Edwards

The Christian is like a man who has the right tune in his head but cannot remember all the words. Accordingly, when Paul says that love fulfills the law (Romans 13:8; Galatians 5:14), that is not to assert that Christians are perfect, but that they live . . . according to the Spirit. The present tense of the Greek peripatein, "to walk" or live, connotes continued action, forward progress, a pattern of behavior under the Spirit's leading.[1]

Douglas J. Moo

And the law's just demand is fulfilled in Christians not through their own acts of obedience but through their incorporation into Christ. He fulfilled the law; and in him, believers also fulfill the law—perfectly, so that they may be pronounced "righteous," free from "condemnation."[2]

Matthew Henry

It is the unspeakable privilege of all those that are in Christ Jesus that there is therefore no condemnation to them. He does not say, "There is no accusation against them," for this there is; but the accusation is thrown out. He does not say, "There is nothing in them that deserves condemnation," for this there is, and they see it, and own it; but it shall not be their ruin.[3]

Nature and Desire

ROMANS 8:5 *For those who live according to the flesh set their minds on the things of the flesh, but those who live according to the Spirit, the things of the Spirit.* (NKJV)

Paul draws a direct relationship between the essence of one's being and the direction of one's interests. When Paul refers to "those who live according to the sinful nature," he is talking about people who have not accepted the grace of God, non-Christians. The phrase "set their minds on" (Romans 8:5 NKJV) refers to more than what occupies the mind. It refers to one's inner desires. Paul says non-Christians do as their nature dictates. Sadly, they go from one sin to another, destroying themselves along the way.

When Paul refers to "those who live according to the Spirit" (8:5 NKJV), he is talking about Christians who are controlled by the Holy Spirit. Such Christians want with their innermost beings to do as the Holy Spirit directs them.

If we determine by the grace of God to live "according to the Spirit," having our minds set on "the things of the Spirit" (Romans 8:5 NKJV), God's peace and wisdom will reign in our minds and hearts. Because of God's grace, we are able to catch a glimpse of what life was like before sin entered the world and what it will be like when we go to heaven. With Christ, life as it should have been has been partially restored.

Let God Mind Your Business

ROMANS 8:6–8 *For to be carnally minded is death, but to be spiritually minded is life and peace. Because the carnal mind is enmity against God; for it is not subject to the law of God, nor indeed can be. So then, those who are in the flesh cannot please God. (NKJV)*

Paul doesn't beat around the bush when it comes to telling his readers what is in store for the sinful man's mind. He uses one word: *death*. Death is what is in store for people whose minds are focused on sin. In contrast, he says minds controlled by the Holy Spirit will experience life and peace. "Which do you want?" Paul seems to be saying. "Death or life? Pain or peace?"

As the soul is redeemed, the mind must undergo transformation. The Word of God shows high regard for the human mind. Paul told the Corinthians to bring "every thought into captivity to the obedience of Christ" (2 Corinthians 10:5 NKJV). He puts a premium on a properly focused mind. Throughout his writing, Paul is careful to explain how the sin nature can dominate one's thinking, comprehension, and discernment.

You might think as you begin this chapter that Paul is being negative, but sin is not something to be positive about, and Romans is God's definitive word on how God dealt with sin, which has been destroying the human race since the Garden of Eden.

What Paul is sorting out for believers is the difference between flesh and spirit. Here, Paul is not referring to religious do's and don'ts as much as he is pointing to the reality that we are either in the Spirit or in the flesh. We cannot be in both at the same time.

Paul put it this way in his letter to the Philippians, "Whatever things are true, whatever things are noble, whatever things are just, whatever things are pure, whatever things are lovely, whatever things are of good report, if there is any virtue and if there is anything praiseworthy—meditate on these things" (Philippians 4:8–9 NKJV). Paul knew that what a person centered his or her mind on would determine the kind of person one would be.

Your Mind's Focus and the Outcome

Focus on What Is . . .	So That You Can Be . . .
True	Discerning, not easily deceived
Noble	Respectable
Just	Morally upright and just
Pure	Chaste and innocent
Lovely	Delightful
Of good report	Praiseworthy and attractive

key point

Paul is letting the church know in no uncertain terms that anything that the flesh generates is not acceptable to God. Any so-called good works, cultural norms, man's prideful progress are but a stench in the nostrils of God. This includes religious works of people done in an apathetic spirit. John writes that Jesus Christ "will vomit you out of My mouth" (Revevelation 3:15–16 NKJV). His conclusion is unbending: "So then, those who are in the flesh cannot please God" (Romans 8:8 NKJV).

what others say

J. Vernon McGee

This verse reveals how hopelessly incorrigible and utterly destitute the flesh really is. It is a spiritual anarchist. This demolishes any theory that there is a divine spark in man and that somehow he has a secret bent toward God. The truth is that man is the enemy of God. He is not only dead in trespasses and sins but active in rebellion against God.[4]

Adolf Schlatter

Those whom God makes his sons [and daughters] are alive. . . . Paul leaves it to them to determine how to order their physical life in its specifics, in order for the body to remain within its proper bounds. Paul did not formulate ascetic regulations, for he believed in the leadership that the Spirit affords the believers.[5]

James R. Edwards

Left to itself human nature is red in tooth and claw, locked in combat against God. Whether or not the expressions of human egoism are socially acceptable does not change their fundamental enmity from God and others. "Those controlled by the sinful flesh cannot please God" [Romans 8:8].[6]

You Are God's Home

ROMANS 8:9–10 *But you are not in the flesh but in the Spirit, if indeed the Spirit of God dwells in you. Now if anyone does not have the Spirit of Christ, he is not His. And if Christ is in you, the body is dead because of sin, but the Spirit is life because of righteousness. (NKJV)*

Paul now turns to address his readers. "You," he begins. He reminds them of who they are. They are temples of the Holy Spirit. He tells them it is an unadulterated fact they are not controlled by the sinful nature but by the Spirit. Note that he uses "Spirit of God" and "Spirit of Christ" interchangeably (Romans 8:9 NKJV).

He tells them that if they are looking for God, they need look no further than within themselves because "the Spirit of God lives in you" (8:9 NKJV). Note that Paul is not saying, "You are God," and that is not how his readers would have understood him. He is saying God has taken up residence within them because of their faith in Christ. The Holy Spirit dwells within us.

apply it

Christians often forget that God lives within them; the result of this forgetfulness is frustration and lack of contentment. We need people in our lives who remind us that Christ dwells in us. We also need to be as concerned as Paul was for our fellow Christians so that when the need arises we are quick to remind them of who lives in their hearts.

When Paul speaks of having our minds set on "the things of the Spirit" (Romans 8:5 NKJV), he is pointing the church as a body and as individuals to our control center. The Spirit has labored over the church now for two millennia, seeking to fulfill God's will. Indeed, the church exists today only because of the faithfulness of the Holy Spirit.

Just Like New!

ROMANS 8:11 *But if the Spirit of Him who raised Jesus from the dead dwells in you, He who raised Christ from the dead will also give life to your mortal bodies through His Spirit who dwells in you. (NKJV)*

This verse reveals a wonderful truth. The Holy Spirit, who raised Jesus from the dead, can infuse our mortal bodies with resurrection power here and now. We're not helpless victims of sin anymore! The life-giving Holy Spirit can overwhelm the power of sin and empower us to lead holy and godly lives.

It is impossible to appreciate fully what God has done for us in sending his Son. We are promised future perfection when the Spirit raises us from the dead at Jesus' return, and even now we are promised access to his transforming power.

The redemption of our bodies is the crowning act of the redemptive process. The believer's body will be delivered. The effects of sin will no longer be seen on his bride, the church. Jesus will be the only one in heaven with scars. The redemption of our bodies has not yet occurred, so hope is vital to our salvation. We don't hope for what we already possess. Rather, hope points us to that which is yet to be finished.

what others say

Philip Yancey

Alone, a capella, Jessye Norman (at Wembley Stadium) begins to sing, very slowly: Amazing grace, how sweet the sound That saved a wretch like me! I once was lost but now am found—Was blind, but now I see.

A remarkable thing happens in Wembley Stadium that night. Seventy thousand raucous fans fall silent before her aria of grace. By the time Norman reached the second verse, "Twas grace that taught my heart to fear, and grace my fears relieved . . . the soprano has the crowd in her hands. . . . Jessye Norman later confessed she had no idea what power descended on Wembley Stadium that night. I think I know. The world thirsts for grace. When grace descends, the world falls silent before it.[7]

Douglas J. Moo

Christian behavior is the necessary mark of those in whom this fulfillment takes place. God not only provides in Christ the full completion of the law's demands for the believer, but he also sends the Spirit into the hearts of believers to empower a new obedience to his demands. Christians now are directed by the Spirit and not by the flesh.[8]

An Obligation to Live the Good Life

ROMANS 8:12–14 *Therefore, brethren, we are debtors—not to the flesh, to live according to the flesh. For if you live according*

go to

Satan
James 4:7

Holy Spirit
Hebrews 3:7–15

Father
Mark 14:36;
Galatians 4:6

you will die
you will be without
power

put to death
refuse to respond to
sinful inclinations

you will live
you will have power
to live the Christian
life

exhortation
strong encourage-
ment; admonition

*to the flesh **you will die**; but if by the Spirit you **put to death** the deeds of the body, **you will live**. For as many as are led by the Spirit of God, these are sons of God. (NKJV)*

Paul's *therefore* glances back at what he's taught up until now. He has explained the Gospel. He has addressed the differences between Jew and Gentile. He has clearly outlined the need for righteousness and explained how righteousness has been provided for us. He has clarified the principle of justification by faith using Abraham and David as examples, and he has explained that reconciliation has been secured through the blood of Jesus Christ.

Paul moves from instruction to **exhortation**, from what God has accomplished to the importance of our response. He outlines the needed response in one word: *obligation.* In the original text it means, "one who owes a moral debt." We cannot earn or buy our salvation, but we are called by God to follow him. In Christ, we have adequate resources to serve our God, the King of heaven and earth. This is our moral debt, our obligation, and the end result of filling this obligation is life! The good life!

Satan is diametrically opposed to anything that compels us to be submissive to the will of God, but we are called to resist <u>Satan</u> and listen to the voice of the <u>Holy Spirit</u>.

<u>"No Fear" Isn't Just a Brand Name</u>

ROMANS 8:15–16 *For you did not receive the spirit of bondage again to fear, but you received the Spirit of adoption by whom we cry out, "Abba, <u>Father</u>." The Spirit Himself bears witness with our spirit that we are children of God, (NKJV)*

Paul continues to shower his readers with the benefits of being believers. Here he says we are no longer chained to fear—fear of God's wrath, of death, or of where we will end up finally. We are not slaves to fear. We are children of God and as such, Paul encourages us to cry to God as if he were our "Daddy," which is a good trans-lation of *Abba.* Like children with their father, we ought to run to him when we're hurt, ask lots of questions, and trust him when he says everything is going to be okay.

How do we know we are God's children? We feel it deep down. We sense the Holy Spirit's promptings, we feel a new closeness to

God, we are more free in our interaction with him. If you don't feel it, believe it. If you believe it and follow through with action, just be patient, you are bound to feel it eventually. The New Covenant makes God available all day, every day. We have a Father who cares lovingly for his children.

go to

joint heirs with Christ
Philippians 3:10–11;
2 Timothy 2:12

inheritance
1 Peter 1:4

> **what others say**
>
> **Philip Yancey**
>
> God may be the Sovereign Lord of the Universe, but through his Son, God has made himself approachable as any doting human father. In Romans 8, Paul brings the image of intimacy even closer. God's spirit lives inside us, he says, and when we do not know what we ought to pray "the Spirit himself intercedes for us with groans that words cannot express."[9]

Our Inheritance

ROMANS 8:17 *and if children, then heirs—heirs of God and joint heirs with Christ, if indeed we suffer with Him, that we may also be glorified together.* (NKJV)

In Paul's letters, the idea of inheritance is strongly influenced by Roman law. According to Roman law, a person received his or her inheritance rights and was considered co-owner of all his or her parents' tangible and intangible assets from birth, though he or she did not take full possession of the inheritance until the parents' death. Paul's point, therefore, is that as soon as we are "reborn," as soon as we put our faith in Christ, we are joint heirs with Christ in all that God owns. It is God's pleasure to share with his children what is his.

We will not receive the full extent of our inheritance until we enter the full presence of God, but even now God blesses us with the enjoyment of his possessions.

Our precious relationship with "Abba, Father" carries a cost, as all close relationships do. Paul solemnly reminds Christians that they are called as sons and daughters to "suffer with Him, that we may also be glorified together" (Romans 8:17 NKJV).

Esther K. Rusthoi writes in one of her hymns, "It will be worth it all when we see Jesus, life's trials will seem so small when we see Christ; one glimpse of His dear face all sorrow will erase, so bravely run the race 'til we see Christ.'"[10] Being coheirs with Christ implies

fixed on Jesus
Hebrews 12:2

glory
wonder, splendor

creation
all created things

a participation in the fellowship of his sufferings.

The floodgates of God's grace open wide when it comes to our inheritance. We are heirs:

- of the promises God makes to his children
- of righteousness
- of the kingdom of God
- of God
- along with Jesus Christ
- of eternal life

Looking Ahead: A Lesson in Driving

> ROMANS 8:18 *For I consider that the sufferings of this present time are not worthy to be compared with the* ***glory*** *which shall be revealed in us.* (NKJV)

I have a friend, Danny, who owns a driving school. About a year ago, my wife and I took a refresher driving seminar from him to review our driving habits, good and bad. Danny told us the most important thing about driving is using your eyes well. The best way to use your eyes is to look as far ahead as possible.

This is somewhat like Paul's spiritual vision. To stay faithful to the task at hand, to bear the present sufferings and testing, he reminds us to look far ahead into the future. All of the pain, hard work, self-denial, and ridicule we now face is "not worthy to be compared with the glory which shall be revealed in us" (Romans 8:18 NKJV). Once we get to heaven all that we've dealt with here will be insignificant. Also, if our eyes are <u>fixed on Jesus</u> we are more likely to stay out of life's ditches.

Are We There Yet?

> ROMANS 8:19–21 *For the earnest expectation of the* ***creation*** *eagerly waits for the revealing of the sons of God. For the creation was subjected to futility, not willingly, but because of Him who subjected it in hope; because the creation itself also will be delivered from the bondage of corruption into the glorious liberty of the children of God.* (NKJV)

Not only do humans look forward to "the glory which shall be revealed in us" (Romans 8:18 NKJV), all of creation does. As the Fall brought all kinds of affliction to humankind, it injured creation too. Paul says the healing of creation will not take place until the hour of Christ's return.

Have you ever listened to a pastor or teacher whose lesson was so relevant to you that you found yourself leaning forward, hanging onto every word? This is the picture Paul is painting when he uses the words "earnest expectation" (8:19 NKJV). Creation is leaning forward in anticipation of the day of our glorification.

It often seems like society is more interested in saving whales than unborn babies. While there are strict laws regarding whaling procedures, in many places it is legal to kill unborn babies. Respect and love for the earth are a part of God's plan, but worship of nature is not. We can rest assured that one day the earth will be healed.

Noahic flood
Genesis 6;
2 Peter 3:3–7

the whole creation
the entire material universe

adoption
here, God's public acknowledgment of our relationship with him

Noahic
of Noah

<table>
<tr><td colspan="2">what others say</td></tr>
</table>

John Chrysostom

Whatever these sufferings may be, they belong to this present life, but the blessing to come stretches out forever. Since Paul had no way of giving a detailed description of these or of putting them before us in human language, he gives them a name which is used of things we especially desire: glory.[11]

Saint Jerome

When the children of God attain glory, creation itself will be delivered from its slavery.[12]

Creation's Contractions

ROMANS 8:22–23 *For we know that **the whole creation** groans and labors with birth pangs together until now. Not only that, but we also who have the firstfruits of the Spirit, even we ourselves groan within ourselves, eagerly waiting for the **adoption**, the redemption of our body. (NKJV)*

Paul continues his discussion of the yearning of creation. The upheaval in creation—the earthquakes, the famines, the **Noahic flood**, the violent storms—all of these are a result of the Fall. It's obvious that Paul has great compassion for creation, which would not be in its present state of frustration if we had not fallen. He likens creation's groaning to the pains of childbirth. The pains of

go to

fruit
Galatians 5:22–23

fruit
character traits
Christians ought to
exhibit—love, joy,
peace, longsuffer-
ing, kindness, good-
ness, faithfulness,
gentleness, and self-
control

mitigated
made less severe

childbirth are intense, but they are also what tells us new life is on the way. Creation's pain, therefore, is both a consequence of the Fall and a prophecy of redemption.

The creation is groaning, as are we. We have the **fruit** of the Holy Spirit, the grace of God has come our way, yet we are in a waiting cycle. Each generation is in that same cycle, waiting to be adopted.

Paul uses the concept of adoption to describe redemption. The word *adoption* comes from two Greek words, *huios*, meaning "son," and *thesis*, meaning "to place." Thus, adoption literally means "the placing as a son." It means a son or daughter is given to a family to which he or she does not naturally belong.

what others say

John Calvin

When we console ourselves with the hope of a better con-dition, the feeling of our present miseries is softened and **mitigated**.[13]

Pilgrim's Hope

ROMANS 8:24–25 *For we were saved in this hope, but hope that is seen is not hope; for why does one still hope for what he sees? But if we hope for what we do not see, we eagerly wait for it with per-severance.* (NKJV)

Part of our salvation is yet to be given us, namely the redemption of our bodies, so we wait in patient hope. If all the benefits of salvation were ours now, we would have no reason to hope. As it is, we walk the road of life in worship to the God whose full presence we will one day enjoy. We see the dark tunnel of death before us, but we know what awaits on the other side, so we hope. Hope is essential in the battle of waiting. Hope keeps our hearts tender and believing.

What form should our hope take? Should we sit around and twid-dle our thumbs until we go to heaven? Paul answered these ques-tions in one of his letters to the Corinthians. He said, "Always abounding in the work of the Lord, knowing that your labor is not in vain in the Lord" (1 Corinthians 15:58b NKJV). The work we do for God is of eternal value. It doesn't go into some cosmic trash can as soon as we go to heaven. It lasts forever, so we should "abound" to the work of God.

Our Devoted Prayer Partner

ROMANS 8:26–27 *Likewise the Spirit also helps in our weaknesses. For we do not know what we should pray for as we ought, but the Spirit Himself **makes intercession** for us with groanings which cannot be uttered. Now He who searches the hearts knows what the mind of the Spirit is, because He makes intercession for the saints according to the will of God.* (NKJV)

makes intercession
communicates with God on our behalf

God uses both hope and the ministry of the Holy Spirit to support believers in the midst of life's burdens, tests, and disappointments. The Holy Spirit helps us precisely in those places where we are weakest. Paul points out that we do not know what our real needs are, but he assures us that God does and that he will see to those needs. God always does what is best for us no matter what it costs him or us.

The Holy Spirit prays on our behalf with groans. We get the sense from these verses that the groans to which Paul refers are a better form of spiritual communication than words. Perhaps this is because words are limited. Some things cannot be expressed with words. If we take this as true, we may also take it as true that the Holy Spirit's groans are not subject to the same limitation. They may be able to express things that otherwise are inexpressible. In any case, Paul assures us that the Holy Spirit prays for us, and this is for our benefit.

Prayer is a difficult discipline that we all need to develop. Jesus spent a lot of time in prayer and his disciples asked him, "Lord, teach us to pray, as John also taught his disciples" (Luke 11:1 NKJV). The Holy Spirit and the Word of God teach us how to have a faithful prayer life. We find many helpful prayers in the book of Psalms, God's prayer book for the church of the ages.

something to ponder

what others say

Dietrich Bonhoeffer

A Christian fellowship lives and exists by the intercession of its members for one another, or it collapses. . . . How does this happen? Intercession means no more than to bring our brother into the presence of God, to see him under the Cross of Jesus as a poor human being and sinner in need of grace. Then everything in him that repels us falls away; we see him in all his destitution and need. . . . Intercession is a daily service we owe to God and our brother.[14]

God Is a Hard Worker

ROMANS 8:28 *And we know that all things work together for good to those who love God, to those who are the called according to His purpose.* (NKJV)

After reading this verse one might wonder, "Wait a minute. Does this mean that if I fail to love God, he won't work for my good?" Paul seldom talks about believers' love for God. When he does, he does not talk about it as a requirement for God to fulfill his promises. Because love for God is a natural response to God's grace and mercy, when Paul says "those who love God" (Romans 8:28 NKJV), he is referring to all believers. Paul knew very well that as a Christian, he failed to love God in the sense that he struggled to obey God. We saw this back in chapter 7. The fact that he struggled, however, is evidence that he was God's own. God always does what is best for his own.

> **what others say**
>
> **Philip Yancey**
>
> I do not get to know God, then do his will; I get to know him more deeply by doing his will. I enter into an active relationship, which means spending time with God, caring about the people he cares about, and following his commands—whether I spontaneously feel like it or not.[15]

To Paul, love for God meant obedience to God. Many people today think love for God is a feeling. We think if we say, "I love God," God should bend over backwards to make our lives luxurious. When our lives turn out less than luxurious, we begin to doubt God's love, maybe even his existence. Paul's concept of loving God was rooted in the truth that we are sinners, deserving only condemnation, and God is our holy Creator and Judge who in his mercy rescued us from death.

There is an attitude prevalent within our culture that says, "I deserve this. I have a right to that." We see this attitude reflected in billboards and other advertisements that gleam with attractive slogans like, "You deserve a break today" and "Buy this car. You're worth it." These slogans are appealing because we want to believe that we're good people, deserving anything we want, even though we know deep down that we're not good people. Paul knew the only thing we had a right to was condemnation. Our attitude, therefore, should be one of gratefulness and contentment, not entitlement and greediness.

This Is Your Destiny

ROMANS 8:29–30 *For whom He **foreknew**, He also **predestined** to be conformed to the image of His Son, that He might be the firstborn among many brethren. Moreover whom He predestined, these He also called; whom He called, these He also justified; and whom He justified, these He also **glorified**. (NKJV)*

Paul started a discussion about sharing in the sufferings of Christ back in verse 16. He said our sufferings will seem like nothing when we get to heaven. He said all of creation groans under the weight of the Fall and longs for our glorification. He said the Holy Spirit helps us in our weaknesses. He then said God works all things for the good of those who love him.

Continuing in this spirit of encouragement, now Paul says God chose us for himself. He chose us to be saved from sin and death and he chose us to be conformed to the likeness of his Son. He's saying, "Look, God chose you for this. God. The almighty Creator of the universe. And if God chose it, it's as good as done no matter how hard life is. You can count on it." We learn, therefore, that at the end of being with Christ in his sufferings we will be glorified with Christ in heaven.

God in his sovereignty promised Christ's followers that they will take on the character and characteristics of their Master. God's people are predestined by his grace and mercy to be restored into the very image we were originally created to be.

A Done Deal

ROMANS 8:31–32 *What then shall we say to these things? If God is for us, who can be against us? He who did not spare His own Son, but delivered Him up for us all, how shall He not with Him also freely give us all things? (NKJV)*

From here to the end of the chapter Paul explains how secure the position of the Christian is. Nothing is more certain than our glori-

foreknew
to have intimate, accurate knowledge of future events

predestined
preordained, determined beforehand

glorified
perfected, freed of sin and made to be like God

fication. Glorification is when we will enter heaven, experience the full presence of God, and be given new bodies. God has willingly given up his Son for our sins so our place in his kingdom is a done deal.

Wouldn't it be strange if a father gave his son a brand-new Porsche but sold the tires off it and replaced them with cheap tires? If the father went to the trouble of giving his son a new Porsche, wouldn't he give him the tires too?

That's how it is with God, Jesus, and us. God has sacrificed his beloved and only Son. Whatever it costs him to give us anything more is negligible because he has already given us his most precious possession. God gave us his Son. We ought not doubt his willingness to give us every other good thing.

Paul does not deny that we go through hard times, but he wants us to see those hard times in light of the truth that when we enter into heaven, we'll look back and wonder what all the fuss was about. We'll wonder this not because our sufferings are without pain right now but because heaven is going to be that fulfilling!

Q&A

> ROMANS 8:33–34 *Who shall bring a charge against God's elect? It is God who justifies. Who is he who condemns? It is Christ who died, and furthermore is also risen, who is even at the right hand of God, who also makes intercession for us.* (*NKJV*)

Here Paul starts a series of questions and then answers them. His first questions are, "Who shall bring a charge against God's elect?" and, "Who is he who condemns?" (Romans 8:33–34 NKJV). Paul may have been alluding to the fact that Satan is always accusing us. Satan constantly points out the difference between what we profess and how we live (as if Satan were interested in righteousness), but God dismisses Satan's accusations because God has made up his mind to be for us. Because all sin is committed against God, only God has the right to condemn. If God does not condemn us, and he doesn't because our sin has been paid for, no one does.

We Shall Overcome

ROMANS 8:35–37 *Who shall separate us from the love of Christ? Shall tribulation, or distress, or persecution, or famine, or nakedness, or peril, or sword? As it is written:*
"For Your sake we are killed all day long;
We are accounted as sheep for the slaughter."
Yet in all these things we are more than conquerors through Him who loved us. (NKJV)

His second question is, "Who shall separate us from the love of Christ?" (Romans 8:35 NKJV). Again, Paul is trying to convince his readers that come what may, the really important questions have been answered. Nothing will separate us from the love of Christ. Paul quotes from Psalm 44:22 to remind us that suffering is nothing new to godly people. Suffering has been the burden of followers of God since the Old Testament, Paul says.

Jesus said, "In the world you will have tribulation; but be of good cheer, I have overcome the world" (John 16:33 NKJV). Jesus told us in no uncertain terms that we would have trouble so we should not be surprised when we do. He also said, however, that he has overcome the world. In other words, the world has tried to beat him, but it failed. Jesus prevailed over the world and because we are linked to Christ, we too will overcome the world.

key point

Love Keeps Hangin' On

ROMANS 8:38–39 *For I am persuaded that neither death nor life, nor angels nor principalities nor powers, nor things present nor things to come, nor height nor depth, nor any other created thing, shall be able to separate us from the love of God which is in Christ Jesus our Lord. (NKJV)*

The apostle seems to pull out all the stops in these last verses of Romans 8. God's love and provision for his own are presented in exalted and passionate language. The apostle speaks of God's purpose in calling out a people who would love him.

Paul emphasizes the certainty of our sanctification. If we are in Christ Jesus, we will be in heaven one day with Christ. He puts the emphasis on the fact that "we know" this. This is a hope that is certain, even though we are in a posture of waiting.

We need to ask ourselves, do we love him? A yes to this question will solve most of the schisms and factions that Satan has created in the church.

You might be eloquent in discussing predestination, you might have solved the so-called free will issue, but if you "have not love, [you] have become sounding brass or a clanging cymbal" (1 Corinthians 13:1 NKJV). The church Jesus came to build needs to rededicate her efforts to living in Christ's love and proclaiming the Gospel.

Chapter Wrap-Up

- Christ set us free from the law of sin and death. Therefore, there is no condemnation in our future. (Romans 8:1–4)

- Our mind's focus is essential to becoming the people God created us to be. (Romans 8:5–8)

- The Holy Spirit is within us and is giving us life. He helps us pray and is with us in our weaknesses. (Romans 8:9–11)

- We have an obligation to live according to the Holy Spirit, which will bring us blessings. (Romans 8:12–17)

- Suffering is a very real part of living in a sin-sick world. God wants us to get a biblical view of suffering. Hope sustains us while we wait for God's transforming grace to mold our character. (Romans 8:18–25)

- We have been predestined to be conformed to the image of the risen Christ. God has promised that there is no "created thing" (verse 39 NKJV) that will be able to separate us from the love of God. (Romans 8:29–39)

Study Questions

1. Why is the law powerless to save a person who sincerely seeks to keep it?

2. How does our mindset influence our spiritual journey?

3. What does it mean to be controlled by the Holy Spirit? Isn't this another form of bondage?

4. We are coheirs with Christ. What does this mean?

5. What does the Holy Spirit do?

Part Four
JEWS AND GENTILES

Romans 9 God Is in Charge

Chapter Highlights:
- Paul's Pain
- Election
- The Necessity of Faith
- Passionate Compassion
- Glorious Patience

Let's Get Started

In chapters 1 to 8 Paul explained the details of the New Covenant. The New Covenant was different from the Old Covenant. The Old Covenant, which came through Moses, said God would reward Israel if the nation obeyed God, and punish Israel if it disobeyed God. Israel failed on their part of the deal. The New Covenant, Paul explained, imparted righteousness to all those who believed in Christ, Jew and Gentile alike. The Jews, therefore, might have made the accusation that God was being unfair to the Jews by changing his mind and being inconsistent. It is this accusation that Paul addresses in chapters 9 to 11.

It is critical that we take chapters 9, 10, and 11 together, as a whole, not coming to a premature conclusion about Paul's argument until one has heard the whole discussion. We shall surely misinterpret, thereby misunderstand, these chapters if we fail to recognize that at the center of Paul's discussion is the careful unveilings of God's mercy.

It hardly seems accidental that the verb *eleein* (mercy) occurs only one other time in Romans, five times in the whole of Paul's other epistles, but occurs seven times in these three chapters. C. E. B Cranfield writes: "Paul is here concerned to show that the problem of Israel's unbelief, which seems to call into question the reliability of God Himself, is connected with the nature of God's mercy as really mercy and as mercy not just for one people but for all people."[1] It appears that the Apostle wants to bring home to the church community in Rome that it is by God's mercy alone that it lives, i.e. exists!

what others say

C. E. B. Cranfield

These chapters vigorously resist our speaking of the Church as having once and forever taken the place of Israel, God's Covenant people. Apart from understanding and receiving the mercy of God, the non-Jewish members of this fellowship

go to

the prophetic message
Amos 9:13–15;
Zechariah 14:1–9

God's chosen people
Genesis 12:1–3;
15:1–21

the prophetic message
the Old Testament promises concerning Israel

could consider (give voice to) the unscriptural notion that God has cast off His people Israel. He has not and he will not! (Even Barth said, "I confess with shame" that he used replacement language when it came to Israel.)[2]

Paul points out that God has not been inconsistent. He has always imparted righteousness on the basis of faith. Moreover, God is sovereign, which means he has always been free to deal with any people as he chooses. He is not bound by what humans think of him. In other words, God's in charge.

In chapter 9 Paul demonstrates that even though the Jews had failed to accept God's promises, the Word of God had not failed. A great many Jews fell away because they did not seek righteousness by faith as Abraham had.

No Lie

ROMANS 9:1–4A *I tell the truth in Christ, I am not lying, my conscience also bearing me witness in the Holy Spirit, that I have great sorrow and continual grief in my heart. For I could wish that I myself were accursed from Christ for my brethren, my countrymen according to the flesh, who are Israelites,* (NKJV)

Paul was about to say something that he knew his readers would find outlandish so he starts with a preface. He says he is speaking the truth, but not only that, he says he is speaking the truth "in Christ" (Romans 9:1 NKJV). He says he is not lying. He says his conscience confirms it, but not only that, he says his conscience confirms it "in the Holy Spirit" (9:1 NKJV). By this time his readers may have been thinking, "Okay, okay, we believe you. Out with it already."

He does come out with it, and what he says is quite sobering. Paul is tormented over the failure of his people to receive Jesus Christ. He says he would take condemnation on himself if it would save his fellow Jews. By this time in his life Paul knew enough about Jesus to believe he was the fulfillment of **the prophetic message**, and he desperately wanted his fellow Jews to believe the same.

Paul was a Jew. He loved his Jewishness and never strayed from his Jewish heritage. What he is attempting to do in Romans 9 is explain how and why the Jews—<u>God's chosen people</u>—had rejected their Messiah. A number of questions needed to be answered:

1. Had God abandoned the Jewish people?

2. What further role did Israel as a nation play in God's plan?

3. In the face of human rejection, does God abandon his promises?

4. Can man foil the sovereign workings of God?

he wept
Luke 19:41–44

sons
Jeremiah 31:9;
Hosea 11:1

In time Paul answers all of these questions for the Jewish believers.

Paul said if it was possible for his own condemnation to bring salvation to the Jews, he would wish condemnation upon himself. When we remember that hell is a place completely absent of God, full of torture and pain forever, it is obvious Paul had extraordinary compassion for his unbelieving brothers and sisters. It is similar to the kind of love Jesus demonstrated when he wept over Jerusalem.

Not many of us would wish condemnation on ourselves in exchange for the salvation of others. Not many of us cry over people who do not know God. How is it that Paul and Jesus had this much compassion for lost people? Perhaps it was a combination of knowing how much unbelievers were missing and what they were doomed for. They were missing the everlasting joy of God. They were doomed for eternal separation from God. There was one thing, and only one thing, that would grant them one and save them from the other: faith in Christ. Paul and Jesus were in agony because they could not force the Jews to believe. That was something the Jews had to do on their own.

A Listing of Blessing

> ROMANS 9:4B–5 *to whom pertain the adoption, the glory, the covenants, the giving of the law, the service of God, and the promises; of whom are the fathers and from whom, according to the flesh, Christ came, who is over all, the eternally blessed God. Amen. (NKJV)*

In the midst of his grief and reflection, Paul reviews Israel's God-given blessings. These blessings were designed by God to support and affirm his people in their spiritual journey. Paul lists seven spiritual privileges that belonged to the Jewish people:

1. *They were adopted as sons.* Moses was to tell Pharaoh "Thus says the LORD: 'Israel is My son, My firstborn'" (Exodus 4:22 NKJV). Who else could claim adoption as sons?

go to

theophanies
Exodus 3:2; 24:10

covenants
Genesis 5:18;
Exodus 19:5;
Deuteronomy 29:1;
2 Samuel 7:21

law
Deuteronomy
5:1–22

temple
2 Chronicles 7:11;
Psalm 11:1

theophanies
visible manifesta-
tions of God

2. *They saw the divine glory.* The Israelites experienced the very presence of God in <u>theophanies</u>.

3. *They had the covenants.* God entered into <u>covenants</u> with Abraham, Moses, and David.

4. *They received the <u>law</u>.* God gave Moses the law on Mount Sinai.

5. *They had <u>temple</u> worship* (*latreia,* "the sacred place"). The Temple was ordained and pleasing to God as a place of worship, praise, and spiritual fellowship.

6. *They had the promises* (especially the promise of Messiah). Hundreds of promises fill their sacred writings.

7. *They had the Patriarchs.* Abraham, Isaac, Jacob, David, and all the prophets that God lists in Scripture belong to the nation of Israel.

What a heritage! The Jews had been given an array of spiritual treasures, yet in the end they rejected God their king and the blessings of his kingdom. Paul was bearing the burden of their foolishness, but the same God whom the Jews rejected was the God who sustained Paul in his grief.

There is what we might call a comprehensive Israel: all who are Israelites according to natural birth. There are also the called, the selective Israel: all those who respond to the love of God in Jesus, the Messiah. But it takes both groups to speak of God's elect people. The children of the flesh "are not the children of God; but the children of the promise are counted as the seed" (Romans 9:8a NKJV). Throughout the history of the Jews this has always been the same. It is the same in the Gentile world: there are believing Gentiles and there are the unbelieving Gentiles, but they are all Gentiles, that is, non-Jews. This must not be interpreted that they are excluded from the embrace of God's mercy, for Paul explicitly writes in 10:13: "For whoever calls on the name of the Lord will be saved" (NKJV). So not to call on the name of the Lord sets us in opposition to God and his Word. But in mercy, he extends the invitation.

The Real Israel

ROMANS 9:6–7A *But it is not that the word of God has taken no effect. For they are not all Israel who are of **Israel**, nor are they all children because they are the seed of Abraham;* (NKJV)

Pastor Mark Driscoll writes, "On the surface it appears that God had attempted to redeem Israel and had failed."[3] But Paul goes beneath that surface mentality and says, "It is not as though God's word had failed." Paul's primary emphasis is on God's purposes, not Israel's failures. To build a strong argument for the truth, Paul first dispels all false presumptions.

Though it seemed safe to assume that if you were from Israel, you were then a child of promise, that simply was not the case:

"For they are not all Israel who are of Israel, nor are they all children because they are the seed of Abraham" (Romans 9:6–7 NKJV). Here Paul establishes that there is a distinction between ethnic Israel and the "Israel of God" (Galatians 6:16 NKJV).

Paul has been preparing to say this since chapter 2 where he confronted those who called themselves Jews. He made it very clear: "He is not a Jew who is one outwardly . . . But he is a Jew who is one inwardly" (Romans 2:28–29 NKJV). Here the apostle reaches the core of the matter: It's not the natural born who are the children of God, but the spiritually born who are the children of God through promise.

what others say
James D. G. Dunn
The depth of the feeling expressed here would be almost melodramatic were it not for the strength of the oath introducing it. . . . Paul would insist, he is being true to his heritage in taking the gospel to the Gentiles. And it is precisely the misunderstanding of that claim which causes him such continuous and painful anguish, for it means that most of his fellow Jews are failing to enter into their own heritage.[4]

A Promise Kept

ROMANS 9:7B–9 *but, "In Isaac your seed shall be called." That is, those who are the children of the flesh, these are not the children of God; but the children of the promise are counted as the seed. For this is the word of promise: "At this time I will come and Sarah shall have a son."* (NKJV)

Israel
God's chosen people

dead
Ephesians 2:1–3;
Romans 5:12–21

family
Genesis 25:19–26

His primary evidence is God's word to Sarah: "At this time I will come and Sarah shall have a son" (Romans 9:9 NKJV). God had promised Abraham and Sarah that even though they were well beyond childbearing age, they would have a son, born of promise, to bless all people. Then Sarah got pregnant and Isaac, the son of promise, was born.

We are not naturally spiritual. We are <u>dead</u> in trespasses and sins. To be children of Abraham, called "children of God," we must be "born of the Spirit of God." Salvation is of God, totally apart from what we do. Augustine put it succinctly, "God does not choose us because we believe, but that we may believe."[5] Works may follow, which goes back to Paul's discussion in chapter 8 where he addresses moral obligation, but they don't earn us any favor either before salvation or after. If we serve in God's kingdom, we are simply doing what we should be doing as members of the family of God.

> ### what others say
>
> ### D. Martyn Lloyd-Jones
>
> Paul refers to the fact that Jews, in contrast with Gentiles, had not obtained the righteousness of God. This was because of their unbelief. So if a man is saved, it is because God has saved him. But if a man is lost, that is to be attributed to his own rejection of the gospel and his rebellion against God's way of salvation.[6]

Jacob: God's Choice

ROMANS 9:10–13 *And not only this, but when Rebecca also had conceived by one man, even by our father Isaac (for the children not yet being born, nor having done any good or evil, that the purpose of God according to election might stand, not of works but of Him who calls), it was said to her, "The older shall serve the younger." As it is written, "Jacob I have loved, but Esau I have hated." (NKJV)*

Paul goes beyond God's word to Abraham and Sarah to the <u>family</u> of the son of promise. Isaac and his wife Rebekah gave birth to twin boys named Jacob and Esau. Paul was responding to the possible objection that Ishmael was not Abraham's child and therefore Paul's argument that God elects certain people and not others didn't hold any water. Paul is careful to explain that Jacob and Esau had the same father; God chose Jacob, not Esau.

God was creating a line that would one day bring forth the promised Messiah. The arrival of twins proposed a potential problem. According to customary human experience, the boys should stand on equal terms before God and man.

Due to God's sovereign will, that could not be. God made a distinction between Jacob and Esau before the twins arrived. This was a sovereign decision. The boys' characters had not been shaped, and they had performed no deeds that could form a basis for evaluation. Moreover, God decreed that the older of the two brothers would serve the younger, something contrary to the custom of the day.

As the boys grew into their manhood, they were both in need of the typical kinds of correction that take place in childhood. One was not necessarily any more spiritual than the other.

The passage is not talking about hatred in the sense of antagonism or fierce anger toward another person. God bestowed many blessings on Esau and his descendants, a manifestation of grace and love. In the biblical world this was legal language. A person would say, "I hated so-and-so" in his or her will to indicate which people had been written out of the estate. The passage is saying God decisively rejected any claim that Esau might have had to the covenant. History proved that God had chosen one of the twins and rejected the claim of the other twin.

what others say

Larry Richards

The verse does not mean God condemned Esau before his birth. In its O.T. context ["Esau I hated"] means that God decisively rejected Esau's claim to the covenant promises which would be his as older son.[7]

God's grace is unfettered. His love, his covenants, his promises, and his Son are demonstrations of his unconditional commitment to his people. A God who could be manipulated by the will of his creatures would be a dangerous God. We can see this negative attribute in Satan, who is the god of this world, causing evil wherever he can manipulate willing subjects.

what others say

Peter Stuhlmacher

But Sarah's pregnancy is only the first example of God's free elective grace in Israel's history. It is no different with Isaac's

go to

tent meeting
Exodus 33:7–9

predestination
in Greek, *proorizo*,
to mark out ahead
of time, to predeter-
mine

election
an exercise of God's
free choice of some
for his own special
purposes

Yahweh
name for God,
meaning "I am"

tent meeting
Moses met with
God at the entrance
of a special tent

wife Rebecca. When she became pregnant (by Isaac) and the twins Esau and Jacob were still not yet born, God documented the freedom of his providence, which acts according to the principle of **predestination**, in that his creative word of promise determined that the older must serve the younger.[8]

Passionate Compassion

ROMANS 9:14–15 *What shall we say then? Is there unrighteousness with God? Certainly not! For He says to Moses, "I will have mercy on whomever I will have mercy, and I will have compassion on whomever I will have compassion." (NKJV)*

Here Paul anticipates an objection from the Romans which is not unlike an objection we commonly hear today. Many feel the principle of **election** makes God unjust or unfair. No matter how much grace and blessing people have experienced, this attack on God's character surfaces generation after generation.

But God has a right to be God. It's not wrong to try and understand these deep truths, but we need to be humble and respectful in that learning process. We should also remember that God did not have to save anybody. We all deserve death. In his great mercy he decided to save some.

Paul takes his readers back to Exodus 33 where Moses and **Yahweh** had a **tent meeting**. It was during one of these conversations that God said to Moses, "I will make all My goodness pass before you, and I will proclaim the name of the LORD before you. I will be gracious to whom I will be gracious, and I will have compassion on whom I will have compassion" (Exodus 33:19 NKJV). God does not need our permission to do what he wants to do. He is God, we are not.

How does mercy differ from grace? How are they partners? Mercy is God's compassionate response to man's need. Grace is God's determination to have mercy on all because of Christ, despite the fact that mercy is not merited.

A Heart Like Granite

ROMANS 9:16–18 *So then it is not of him who wills, nor of him who runs, but of God who shows mercy. For the Scripture says to the Pharaoh, "For this very purpose I have raised you up, that I may show My power in you, and that My name may be declared in all the earth." Therefore He has mercy on whom He wills, and whom He wills He hardens. (NKJV)*

For an example of God's sovereign will, Paul takes readers back to the days of Pharaoh in Egypt. God was merciful to Pharaoh, but Pharaoh's pride kept him from seeing the glory of God in God's servant Moses.

Pharaoh is introduced as the type of person, Jew or Gentile, who resists God; here he is a prefiguration of Israel, who in her disobedience shows strong opposition to the gospel. In this way, Pharaoh, too, became a witness—albeit an unbelieving, unwilling, and indeed ungrateful witness—to the saving power and the personal intervention of God in the affairs of man. God's will is always "good and acceptable and perfect" (Romans 12:2b NKJV). His will is shaped by his absolute righteousness, his boundless mercy, and his nature of love, leaving man, his creation, one path to understanding: Jesus.

God did not change Pharaoh's nature or manipulate Pharaoh's will. God revealed more and more of himself through the **judgments**, and Pharaoh reacted to God's self-revelation by rejecting God and his will. This is called "revelatory hardening," when God reveals himself to a human and the human's reaction is to harden his or her heart toward God. An analogy for this is what the sun does to wax or clay. When wax is heated by the sun it softens because of the nature of wax. When clay is heated by the sun it hardens because of the nature of clay. In the same way, when God revealed more and more of himself to Pharaoh, Pharaoh's heart hardened because of Pharaoh's essential nature.

After the final judgment when Pharaoh began to pursue the Jews and entered the <u>Red Sea</u>, God hardened Pharaoh's heart again. This was "judicial hardening." Judicial hardening is when a person is already hard-hearted and God hardens his or her heart even more. Judicial hardening is a punishment for being totally committed to rebellion against God.

In neither case did God cause Pharaoh to act against his essential nature. God permitted Pharaoh to become Pharaoh ("raised [him] up" [Romans 9:17 NKJV]) because he knew full well who he was and how he would behave. Pharaoh chose to rebel against God. God used his rebellion to accomplish his own purposes.

Red Sea
Exodus 14:17

judgments
punishments from God

what others say

James R. Edwards

Desire and effort were in fact very much part of Paul's commitment to Christ (Philippians 3:12–16), but they had nothing to do with his (or Israel's) choosing by God. Human effort is a necessary response of gratitude and commitment to God for his grace in Christ Jesus, but it neither merits nor maintains grace. With regard to election God remains totally free, not to employ arbitrary (or worse, malevolent) designs, but to express mercy.[9]

Martin Luther

["God will have mercy on whom he wants to have mercy"] is a harsh answer for the proud and those who think they know everything, but for the meek and the humble it is sweet and pleasing, because they despair of themselves; and thus God takes them up.[10]

Yakkety Yak, Don't Talk Back

ROMANS 9:19–21 *You will say to me then, "Why does He still find fault? For who has resisted His will?" But indeed, O man, who are you to reply against God? Will the thing formed say to him who formed it, "Why have you made me like this?" Does not the potter have power over the clay, from the same lump to make one vessel for honor and another for dishonor? (NKJV)*

We want the final word. It's human nature. We feel we have the right to challenge God and even think it's smart or cute. The old nature, as we learned earlier in this letter, will always resist the truth. It is only the new nature that begins to trust in the wisdom and grace of God.

The accusation behind the questions "Why does He still find fault? For who has resisted His will?" (Romans 9:19 NKJV) is this: God is unfair because he blames us for his own decisions. This accusation assumes that we are innocent to begin with, and we are not. God never condemns innocent people; he condemns sinners. He is under no obligation to save anyone, yet he does save those whom it pleases him to save.

We know that God, who is both righteous and **omniscient**, always makes wise choices. The problem is that we disagree with his will and fail to discover his wisdom and love, while living in the old-nature rebellion.

Paul uses a metaphor to explain further. He presents God as a potter. Just as the potter makes decisions about his creation, doesn't the God who made all things have the same prerogative? And just as it would be ridiculous for a lump of clay to talk back to the potter, it is ridiculous for us to talk back to our Creator.

apply it

what others say

James R. Edwards

Right is not right because God does it; rather, God does it because it is right. God's righteous will, as revealed in the Ten Commandments and in the rules of fairness and justice associated with them, is ultimate, and not even God can transcend it. . . . There is a moral code in creation only because there is a corresponding moral order in the Creator. This passage does not depict or defend a cosmic bully. God is perfect love and perfect justice.[11]

Gracious Patience

ROMANS 9:22–24 *What if God, wanting to show His wrath and to make His power known, endured with much longsuffering the vessels of wrath prepared for destruction, and that He might make known the riches of His glory on the vessels of mercy, which He had prepared beforehand for glory, even us whom He called, not of the Jews only, but also of the Gentiles?* (NKJV)

An important thing to remember is that every human on the planet will glorify God, willingly or not, in heaven or in hell. Either people will glorify God as objects of his mercy and glory, or they will glorify God as objects of his wrath and power.

The phrase "prepared for destruction" (Romans 9:22 NKJV) might imply that God makes up his mind to send people to hell even before he creates them, but this is not likely. The preparation refers to what unbelievers do despite what their consciences tell them. Such people are "preparing" themselves for destruction.

Paul points out the patience of God in that God tolerates the sins of the wicked for a time. He says he tolerates wickedness "to make known the riches of His glory on the vessels of mercy" (9:23 NKJV). He does this in two ways. One was already mentioned in reference to Pharaoh. Pharaoh was raised up, his heart was hardened, and his sins accumulated so God could more fully display his wrath in judging him in the end. The second way he shows his glory is in delaying his wrath to give sinners a chance to repent.

Come On In

ROMANS 9:25–26 *As He says also in Hosea:*
"I will call them My people, who were not My people,
And her beloved, who was not beloved."
"And it shall come to pass in the place where it was
said to them,
'You are not My people,'
There they shall be called sons of the living God." (NKJV)

Aren't those wonderful words? When someone says "come on in," we feel included. We feel like our company is desired. None of us wants to be alone or left on the outside. With Christ's death and resurrection, God stood at the threshold of his kingdom, looked at the Gentiles, and said, "Come on in."

Paul was fond of quoting Scripture to prove his points. Here he uses Scripture to prove that Gentiles will be part of God's kingdom. He quotes Hosea 2:23 and Hosea 1:10, both of which refer to when Israel fell from God's favor and was later restored. Here Paul is using the first quote (Hosea 2:23) to refer not to Israel, but rather to the Gentiles. Paul wasn't the only one to do this. Peter did it too in 1 Peter 2:10.

Paul may have been using the second quote from Hosea 1:10 to refer to the Gentiles also, but it's possible he was referring to the Jews. In any case, Paul's point is that God's kingdom would be made up of both Jews and Gentiles and that God's choice to include people he previously excluded is not an innovation. In fact, it is in the Jews' best interest not to scorn God for this. If it were not for God's willingness to welcome those who were previously on the outside of his kingdom, yes the Gentiles would be on the outside, but so would the Jews!

Faithful Remnant

ROMANS 9:27–29 *Isaiah also cries out concerning Israel:*
"Though the number of the children of Israel be as the sand
of the sea,
The remnant will be saved.
For He will finish the work and cut it short in righteousness,
Because the LORD will make a short work upon the earth."

And as Isaiah said before:
  "Unless the LORD of Sabaoth had left us a seed,
  We would have become like Sodom,
  And we would have been made like Gomorrah." (NKJV)

Remember that beginning with chapter 9 Paul is answering the accusation that God was being unfair to the Jews in establishing the New Covenant. Another question Paul wanted to answer was whether God's purpose for the Jews had failed because not all Jews were believing in Christ. Throughout chapter 9 Paul has been explaining that God's purpose did not fail because God never intended to save every Jew. In the verses quoted previously, however, Paul quotes from Isaiah to point out that God has always had a faithful **remnant** of Jews. This was true in Paul's time as well.

The remnant idea goes back to Romans 2 when Paul explained the difference between those who had been circumcised outwardly and those who had been circumcised inwardly. "The remnant" (Romans 9:27 NKJV) to which Paul refers is the number of Jews who had come to Christ. Paul understood this at a very personal level because he himself was one of the remnant.

Someone steeped in the Old Testament might raise the charge that God had abandoned the people whom he foreknew, the Jews, but Paul says otherwise. God provided a way for all people, including Jews, to be saved.

In many ways Paul can be compared to Christians who come from non-Christian families. Such Christians may be tempted to turn their backs on their families, thinking only of how their parents or siblings wronged them. When he became a Christian, Paul did not ignore his fellow, unbelieving Jews. He was in anguish because many of the Jewish race, the race from which Jesus came, did not put their faith in Christ. Paul knew that if they did not repent and believe, they faced eternal destruction—just like the people in Sodom and Gomorrah. Christians who come from non-Christian families should follow Paul's example.

People who may look like God's favorites, because of how joyful they are, are not his favorites. They are simply more humble and more honest about sin and are always ready to seek forgiveness. Moreover, joyful Christians are joyful because they have found out that in the long run, righteousness is more fun than sin!

key point

something to ponder

Stumbling Stone

shadows
the promises of God
which point to Christ

substance
the Christ who came
as Jesus of Galilee

ROMANS 9:30–33 *What shall we say then? That Gentiles, who did not pursue righteousness, have attained to righteousness, even the righteousness of faith; but Israel, pursuing the law of righteousness, has not attained to the law of righteousness. Why? Because they did not seek it by faith, but as it were, by the works of the law. For they stumbled at that stumbling stone. As it is written:*

"Behold, I lay in Zion a stumbling stone and rock of offense, And whoever believes on Him will not be put to shame." (NKJV)

Paul concludes this section like a true orator: "What shall we say then?" (Romans 9:30 NKJV). It's as if he's looking for a way to put a period at the end of this sentence before he enters the next phase of the dialogue.

key point

He finds an apt way. He points out the difference between the two peoples, the reason God receives the Gentiles and rejects the Jews. The Gentiles found that by embracing Jesus Christ by faith they could attain righteousness. But the Jews chased after righteousness by trying to keep the law, not by faith, but by religious works. They continued to embrace the **shadows** and reject the **substance**. They rejected the merits of their Messiah for their own supposed good works.

To articulate his point, Paul quotes Isaiah 28, a passage which depicts Christ as the Rock. Instead of a stepping stone to raise them up, he becomes a stumbling stone. But those who "[believe] on Him will not be put to shame" (Romans 9:33 NKJV).

what others say

F. F. Bruce

It is sadly ironic that the goal which the Jews missed the Gentiles have reached without trying. The Jews had been going the wrong way about it. They sought to get right with God by their works, basing their hope of salvation upon the law, which they could not keep. The Gentiles now in the Church had made no such attempt but accepted the ready-made faith-righteousness offered by God through the work of the Cross. To the Jews a crucified Messiah was a stumbling-block (I C. I: 23), but to those who read the OT with Christian eyes this comes as no surprise since Isa. 8:14 envisages this very situation. Christ is the Stone, as He Himself claimed.[12]

One of the greatest promises in all of Scripture is located in Romans 9:30–33. If our trust is in Jesus, God's Messiah, we will never be put to shame. We might have to walk through the fire, but he will be with us, bearing our pain and shame.

We ought to pursue righteousness by having faith in Christ, not by running after the law. We will never catch up with the law because the law is beyond our reach. But Christ is a different story. He raced with the law side-by-side and came out the winner. The law fell over dead, and Christ was given the gold medal. He is our righteousness now, and he does not challenge us to race him. He <u>walks</u> toward us. Will we embrace him, or run hopelessly after the law?

go to

walks
Revelation 3:20

what others say

W. Burrows

The Stone laid by God in Zion becomes a stumbling-stone and rock of offence. This is not the divine design. This Stone was chosen by God out of the eternal quarry as being most fitted for the erection of a spiritual temple. The Stone was selected by infinite wisdom, prepared by divine power, and was the expression of eternal love; and though the Stone was rejected by the foolish builders, the scribes and priests of this world, it was accepted by God, crowned with glory and honour. And God never placed this Stone in Zion to be a stumbling-block to any. Men stumble because pride sets itself against divine love and wisdom.[13]

Chapter Wrap-Up

- Paul's heart was in anguish over Israel's rejection of their Messiah. His pain was for them, for the shame it brought upon God, and for the despair it brought to his heart. (Romans 9:1–5)

- God chose a line through which the messianic hope would be carried. God used this to demonstrate the principle of election. For God's plan to remain infallible, it has to remain God's plan. Man can add nothing to the purposes of God. (Romans 9:6–21)

- How we pursue righteousness has serious consequences. God will not accept man's works as a substitute for faith in Jesus Christ. Only those who choose to put their faith in Christ will be saved. They are called "the remnant." (Romans 9:22–33)

Study Questions

1. Why does Paul begin this chapter with a preface?

2. The Jews had been given a rich heritage. Paul names seven characteristics that made the people of Israel different. What are they?

3. Why are people offended by the election concept?

4. What two historical events does Paul use to discuss the sovereignty of God in election?

5. What does Scripture mean by "remnant"?

Romans 10 Faith Avenue

Chapter Highlights:
- Real Zeal
- Two Kinds of Righteousness
- The Source of Faith
- A Lesson in Contrasts

Let's Get Started

There are times when our hearts feel like they are going to break. A divorce, the death of a loved one, an accident that leaves a friend crippled for life—events like these make our hearts heavy and our spirits downcast. The apostle Paul was going through such a time. When loved ones do not embrace the truth, it hurts. Often anxiety and feelings of estrangement set in.

Another way of being downcast comes from compromising on that which you know in your heart and mind to be true. When we compromise the truth of God's Word—exactly what Satan wants us to do—we become hypocrites.

Paul felt deeply the rejection of his Jewish brothers, yet he remained faithful to the Jewish Messiah that brought him the message of God's mercy and grace. Though Paul was in pain because many Jews were lost, his spirit was free.

The Zeal Deal

ROMANS 10:1–2 *Brethren, my heart's desire and prayer to God for Israel is that they may be saved. For I bear them witness that they have a zeal for God, but not according to knowledge.* (NKJV)

Paul addresses his readers as "brethren" (Romans 10:1 NKJV). Here he is addressing the Jews, his natural brothers, not his Christian brothers. It is obvious that Paul identified with his fellow Jews. He cared for them inexpressibly.

It was not long before Paul wrote his letter to the Romans that he was zealously seeking a righteousness by the law. He had been where the Jews were. At one time Paul thought Jesus and his followers were traitors of his beloved Judaism because they did not seek righteousness the same way he and other Pharisees did.

What Paul sought, however, he sought in ignorance, thus he says the Israelites' zeal for God is not based on knowledge. This is

zeal
John 2:17;
Psalm 69:9

carnal
fleshly

because in many cases the Israelites refused to know anything about the righteousness God offered through Christ.

Note that Paul acknowledges the Israelites' zeal for God. He is not accusing the Jews of laziness. He's saying their zeal is in the wrong direction. This should remind us that being passionate for God is not enough. First we must be willing to admit that our own agenda may not be God's agenda. Then we must be knowledgeable about how God wants us to be passionate for him.

False Zeal vs. Real Zeal

Usually <u>zeal</u> is necessary for communicating what you feel deeply. In Romans 12:10–11 Paul exhorts, "Be . . . not lagging in diligence, [but] fervent in spirit, serving the Lord" (NKJV). Obviously there's a valid place for zeal. But paradoxically, it is Israel's zeal that created their greatest historical blunder. Their zeal created a mob mentality. Theirs was a zeal built on emotions, not God's will.

In his commentary on the Book of Romans, D. Martyn Lloyd-Jones offers a number of indicators for false or inappropriate kinds of zeal.

First, "zeal must always be tested and examined." The Jews' zeal was not according to knowledge. They needed to carefully examine what they were doing and encouraging others to do. Second, a zeal that "has been whipped up or organized" may well be a false zeal.

Third, a zeal that "puts greater emphasis upon doing than upon being" always alerts caution.

Fourth, in a "false zeal it is the activity, rather than the truth" which is at the center.

Fifth, "when methods, organization and the machinery are very prominent" you have evidence of a false zeal.

Sixth, when the zeal has a CARNAL sense about it, it is a false zeal.

Seventh, "false zeal dislikes being questioned. It resents inquiry." It has no patience with any examination.[1]

The above addresses some of the characteristics of false zeal, but what about true zeal? True zeal is a natural expression of one's emotions and convictions. It's a demonstration of who we are. Godly zeal reflects grace and maturity, not manipulation, for true righteousness does not seek to beguile. Finally, knowledge is the decisive

factor in the litmus test between true and false zeal. The presence of knowledge indicates true zeal; the absence of it signals false zeal.

The Law's End

ROMANS 10:3–4 *For they being ignorant of God's righteousness, and seeking to establish their own righteousness, have not submitted to the righteousness of God. For Christ is the end of the law for righteousness to everyone who believes.* (NKJV)

The Jews had no idea that righteousness could be a gift. They knew it was an attribute of God. In fact, they prided themselves on knowing their God was righteous whereas pagan gods were not, but if you had said to a Jew, "Righteousness is a gift," he or she would have looked at you like you belonged in a straitjacket.

As for human righteousness, the Israelites thought the way to be righteous was by keeping the Mosaic law and Rabbinic traditions. As long as a Jew observed the holy feasts and the Sabbath, he or she assumed all was fine. Because of (1) how ignorant they were, and (2) how preoccupied they were with their own self-made ideas of human righteousness, the Jews did not even look for the gift of "God's righteousness" (Romans 10:3 NKJV). They did not know such a thing existed.

Of course, the Jews were not righteous. Their righteousness and

Damascus
Acts 9:1–19

recalcitrant
defiant, unruly

God's righteousness were as different as monopoly money is from real greenbacks issued by the U.S. Treasury.[4]

So, what was the solution? Christ. Christ, Paul explained, was "the end" of the law in at least three ways.

1. The law leads us to Christ.

2. Christ lived the perfect life that the law required.

3. Christ caused the law to disappear from the scene ("We are not under law but under grace" [Romans 6:15 NKJV]).

Christ fulfilled the requirements of the law, and Christ's righteousness is credited to the believer's account.

As a result of the Jews' **recalcitrant** wills, "their foolish hearts were darkened" (Romans 1:21 NKJV). This is a serious warning for all who confess faith in God, as did the Jews, but refuse to submit to the righteousness of God as revealed in Christ. Such an attribute is evidence of a false, nonbiblical zeal.

Paul speaks plainly about Israel's failure, but not in a reproachful manner. He speaks out of a sense of duty to declare the truth. As we observed in Romans 9 and here again in this chapter, the apostle feels a deep love for his native heritage. He has a Jewish heart and appreciates his Jewish roots. Yet Paul knew their spiritual condition, because their condition was his own prior to his <u>Damascus</u> road experience.

Paul is up front about his desire for Israel. He wanted them to be saved. His pre-Calvin doctrines (this was nearly 1700 years before Calvin and the other Reformation fathers) did not prevent him from believing, praying, and going to the lost. The doctrines of election and predestination were never barriers to Paul; they were open windows from heaven. He knew God loved the world and that he was called by God to go and preach God's love to the world. He felt this intimately when preaching to his Jewish countrymen.

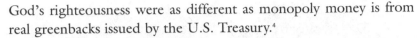

what others say

C. E. B. Cranfield

Luther, referring to Paul's use of Deuteronomy 30 in this chapter, says: "It is as if he wanted to give us an impressive proof of the fact that the whole Scripture, if one contemplates it inwardly, deals everywhere with Christ, even in so far as it is a sign or a shadow, it may outwardly sound different. This is why he says: 'Christ is the end of the law' (Romans 10:4); in other words: every word in the Bible points to Christ."[5]

The Nearness of God

ROMANS 10:5–8 *For Moses writes about the righteousness which is of the law, "The man who does those things shall live by them." But the righteousness of faith speaks in this way, "Do not say in your heart, 'Who will ascend into heaven?' " (that is, to bring Christ down from above) or, "'Who will descend into the abyss?' " (that is, to bring Christ up from the dead). But what does it say? "The word is near you, in your mouth and in your heart" (that is, the word of faith which we preach):* (NKJV)

Once again Paul goes back to the Old Testament to show his fellow Jews where they've gone wrong. He refers to Moses, the man through whom the Jews received the law. First Paul shows the Jews what is Moses' definition for a "righteousness which is of the law" (Romans 10:5 NKJV). In short, Moses said that righteousness by the law is attained by keeping the law. The person who keeps the law will live. The only snag is that anyone who does not keep the law—and none of us does—is condemned.

Paul then moves on to another passage from Moses, but this one is used to describe a "righteousness of faith" (10:6 NKJV). Here is the passage from which he quotes:

"The LORD your God will circumcise your heart and the heart of your descendants, to love the LORD your God with all your heart and with all your soul, that you may live . . . This commandment which I command you today is not too mysterious for you, nor is it far off. It is not in heaven, that you should say, 'Who will ascend into heaven for us and bring it to us, that we may hear it and do it?' Nor is it beyond the sea, that you should say, 'Who will go over the sea for us and bring it to us, that we may hear it and do it?' But the word is very near you, in your mouth and in your heart, that you may do it" (Deuteronomy 30:6, 11–14 NKJV).

This passage starts with a heart devoted to God and proceeds to point out that following God is not something out of our reach. We do not need to reach for heaven because in Christ, heaven has come to us. If we submit our lives to God, his will is near to us—as close

go to

boast
Ephesians 2:9–10

patriarchs
Abraham, the
founder of the
Jewish people, his
son Isaac, and
grandson Jacob

prophets
spokespersons com-
missioned by God
to communicate his
words

confess
publicly express

carnal
worldly, non-
Christian

as our mouths that praise him and as close as our hearts that lodge a desire to please him.

Lest someone suppose God used Paul because he did such a great job at keeping the law, here is what Paul wrote to his missionary-friend, Timothy, "Christ Jesus came into the world to save sinners—of whom I am chief. However, for this reason I obtained mercy, that in me first Jesus Christ might show all longsuffering, as a pattern to those who are going to believe on Him for everlasting life" (1 Timothy 1:15–16 NKJV). Paul had no illusions about his own sin. He knew that it was God's mercy, not his own merit, that had snatched him out of the self-destruction of his depravity.

Many throughout the generations were humbled and had a wonderful walk of faith with God. Among the outstanding ones were the **patriarchs** and the **prophets**. But there were many others also. In short, the concept of a "righteousness that is by faith" was not a new one, but it hit a major snag among the nation's leaders when Jesus came on the scene.

The law gave Israel God's moral requirements, which they couldn't fulfill, and which God used to show them their need for repentance. The continuation of his love was in bringing Jesus the Messiah. The promise of his coming is throughout the whole Old Covenant. One who believes a promise has faith in the promise giver.

<u>Mouth and Heart</u>

> ROMANS 10:9 *that if you **confess** with your mouth the Lord Jesus and believe in your heart that God has raised Him from the dead, you will be saved.* (NKJV)

It's one thing to say the words, it's another thing to confess them and to show what's in your heart by acting accordingly.

The path to faith always seems like a bad choice to the **carnal** mind. Works make us feel significant, like we have a right to something. They make us feel like we have something to <u>boast</u> about. But the path of faith leads us to the truth, which is that we are sinners, have nothing to boast about, and are infinitely blessed by God.

In his other letters, Paul said something very interesting to the Philippians about confessing Jesus as Lord. He said, "God also has highly exalted [Christ] and given Him the name which is above every name, that at the name of Jesus every knee should bow, of those in heaven, and of those on earth, and of those under the earth, and that every tongue should confess that Jesus Christ is Lord, to the glory of God the Father" (Philippians 2:9–11 NKJV). In other words, each and every person who ever lived will eventually confess that Jesus is Lord. Paul is not saying everyone will be saved. He's saying both saved people who go to heaven and lost people who go to hell will acknowledge the lordship of Christ. Christians will acknowledge it in joy, non-Christians will acknowledge it in despair.

key point

what others say

D. Martyn Lloyd-Jones

[regarding the battle with intellectualism and the Gospel] I say once more that the most ignorant, the most illiterate, and the most benighted can believe this message and be saved by it in a second . . . you are not saved by a knowledge of doctrine! You are saved by the Lord Jesus Christ and what He has done on your behalf . . . thank God! We do not have to drag Him down or lift Him up. He has done it all! He has come; He has done the work; He has risen again . . ."Only believe"![6]

James R. Edwards

What is humanly impossible—to scale the heights or descend the depths—has been revealed by God in the law, but ultimately in Christ. All noble, pious, and heroic attempts to demonstrate human righteousness are only active unbelief. It is not we who bring Christ to people, but Christ who sends us to them with his saving word.[7]

Charles Hodge

They were not to regard the resurrection and the ascension of Christ as impossible. But the whole context shows that the purpose of the apostle is to contrast the legal and the gospel methods of salvation—to show that the one is impracticable, the other easy. By works of the law no flesh living can be justified; whereas, whosoever simply calls on the name of the Lord shall be saved.[8]

A person who is saying the same kinds of things today that Paul said nearly two thousand years ago is Billy Graham. For a number of years, I've served as chair of the Billy Graham Phone Center in Seattle, Washington. I've participated in over forty of the telecasts. I've watched God use Billy Graham to present the Gospel in each of these crusades. He always presents this apostolic message with grace and clarity. The Spirit of God comes upon the hearts of thousands of people, and they come forward to "confess with [their] mouth, 'Jesus is Lord.' " It is the power of the Gospel through the faithful preaching of a man who was himself saved by that Gospel. It always blesses my heart to listen to the Gospel being preached.

You Are Invited

> ROMANS 10:10–13 *For with the heart one believes unto right-eousness, and with the mouth confession is made unto salvation. For the Scripture says, "Whoever believes on Him will not be put to shame." For there is no distinction between Jew and Greek, for the same Lord over all is rich to all who call upon Him. For "whoever calls on the name of the LORD shall be saved." (NKJV)*

Here Paul explains how the Gospel manifests its power: "With the heart one believes unto righteousness" (Romans 10:10 NKJV). God changes your heart to be ready to receive the Gospel. The Holy Spirit causes you to be born again. He comes to live with you and in you. It is by God's grace and mercy that this occurs.

Further, "with the mouth confession is made unto salvation" (10:10 NKJV). Believe and confess are two inseparable aspects of coming to faith in Jesus Christ. Conversion is not an intellectual show-and-tell, but an intentional and public witness of your faith in the risen Christ.

The way the apostle presents this explanation of the Gospel's power shows the Christian two very essential things: First, to say you believe without confession hints at betrayal; and second, to confess without really believing is self-deception, resulting in hypocrisy. These are two of Satan's best shots. Avoid them at all cost.

Paul writes, "For there is no distinction between Jew and Greek" (Romans 10:12 NKJV). What does he mean? There is no difference when it comes to the necessity of salvation. We are all sinners. Earlier in his letter, Paul reminded the church that "the righteousness of God, through faith in Jesus Christ, to all and on all who believe. For there is no difference; for all have sinned" (3:22–23 NKJV).

There is no difference because God said there isn't: "The same Lord over all is rich to all who call upon Him. For 'whoever calls on the name of the Lord shall be saved' " (Romans 10:12–13 NKJV). God has spoken and we need to listen for his voice. Obedience to the truth is evidence that you love God and respect his Word.

Douglas J. Moo

Central to the Reformers' teaching about salvation was their distinction between "law" and "gospel." "Law" is whatever God commands us to do; "gospel" is what God in his grace gives us to do. The Reformers uniformly insisted that human depravity made it impossible for a person to be saved by doing what God commands; only by humbly accepting, in faith, the "good news" of God's work on our behalf could a person be saved.[9]

Adolf Schlatter

Believing is the effort of the heart and confessing that of the mouth. If faith is accomplished by the heart, righteousness is the result, and if confession is made with the mouth, salvation is its fruit . . . righteousness liberates from guilt, and salvation from death. The former orders the inner life, hence Paul attributes it to the heart. The latter renders the believer part of the community that is destined to life.[10]

D. Martyn Lloyd-Jones

What I am trying to say was put in a pithy phrase by one of the great Puritans who went out from this country to New England in the 1630's, a man called Thomas Hooker, who lived and preached in Cambridge, Massachusetts. He put it like this: "If a man hath faith within, it will break forth at the mouth." And that, I believe, is exactly what the Apostle is saying here: that this true, heartfelt, sincere belief in the context of saving faith will inevitably give expression to itself.[11]

Dirty Feet Are Beautiful to God

ROMANS 10:14–15 *How then shall they call on Him in whom they have not believed? And how shall they believe in Him of whom they have not heard? And how shall they hear without a preacher? And how shall they preach unless they are sent? As it is written:*

"How beautiful are the feet of those who preach the gospel of
    peace,
Who bring glad tidings of good things!" (NKJV)

Apollos
an early Christian leader, mentioned in Acts 18:24–28

evangelism
sharing the Gospel with others

In this passage, Paul transitions from proclaiming that all who call on the Lord will be saved to exploring the nuts and bolts of how this is done. He introduces five how's into his discourse.

1. His first how is this: "How then shall they call on Him in whom they have not believed?" (Romans 10:14 NKJV). Paul moves from what is required of the seeker to the role of the believer. He addresses this again in his letter to the Corinthians: "As it is written: 'Eye has not seen, nor ear heard, nor have entered into the heart of man the things which God has prepared for those who love Him.' But God has revealed them to us through His Spirit. For the Spirit searches all things, yes, the deep things of God. For what man knows the things of a man except the spirit of the man which is in him? Even so no one knows the things of God except the Spirit of God" (1 Corinthians 2:9–11 NKJV). Thus, the Holy Spirit participates in the communication of the Gospel and in the conversion of the soul. Paul is serving God by giving God the glory and declaring his truth. He goes on to reveal God's method in assigning each his task: "I planted, **Apollos** watered, but God gave the increase. So then neither he who plants is anything, nor he who waters, but God who gives the increase" (1 Corinthians 3:6–7 NKJV).

We see from these two passages that God sent out servants to plow and cultivate the soil and to plant the seeds of the Gospel. It is the mission of the church to do the work of **evangelism**—to prepare the way and to spread the good news. It takes the grace of God to make the seeds take root. The Spirit of God touches people's hearts, making them open to hearing the Gospel message. We need to trust the Holy Spirit for his grace to move hearts.

2. The second how is closely linked to the first: "How shall they believe in Him of whom they have not heard?" (Romans 10:14 NKJV). Here Paul reminds believers that faith depends on knowledge. The Gospel has to be communicated, and preaching is God's primary method. One must hear the Gospel before receiving or rejecting the Lord. This is an important truth to bring with us as we go about our lives.

There are many wonderful ways to sow the seed of God's love. One way is simply by showing love toward others—this will lead people to inquiry in a world filled with pain and loneliness.

herald
to proclaim or announce important news

incarnational
represented in human flesh

3. Paul's third how is this: "How shall they hear without a preacher?" (Romans 10:14 NKJV). This is God's call to the church to be a servant people. We are called to serve, to do the work of the kingdom for the glory of God and for the fulfillment of the great commission. Our service is to bear witness to the saving power of Jesus Christ.

4. Paul's fourth how is this: "How shall they preach unless they are sent?" (Romans 10:15 NKJV). Here Paul addresses the need for order, discipline, and organization. Being sent suggests one should operate under an appointed mentor or authority or society that has a vision from God. Being sent addresses accountability on the part of the one going and the one staying. Our message does not originate with us, but with God. He and his Word are the final authority. God has appointed leaders to do his bidding.

5. The apostle turns his final how into a statement: "How beautiful are the feet of those who preach the gospel of peace" (Romans 10:15 NKJV). This was the message that was **heralded** when Israel began to return from her captivity in Babylon. It announces the favor of the Lord to the Holy City of Jerusalem. It was a proclamation of peace—good tidings after years of servitude. Paul's emphasis on "the feet of those who preach the gospel of peace" (10:15 NKJV) points to the need for servants who will go forth in the name of God to make the message of love personal, therefore **incarnational**.

If the proclamation of peace was considered good news—and indeed it was—how much more is the promise of eternal life through Jesus Christ our Lord. The Gospel is not merely a philosophy or an idea, though it does significantly influence one's worldview. The Gospel is a life-transforming message that tells people how to be who they were created to be.

what others say

John F. Walvoord and Roy B. Zuck

Carrying God's gracious offer involves human beings who God has brought to Himself and then uses as His heralds. They share God's message of salvation because He will save everyone who calls on His name.[12]

William S. Plumer

All the ecclesiastical authorities in the world cannot impart to men the gift of preaching aright. They must have an unction to teach them all things. They must be called and sent by the Lord himself. There is much cause to fear that some refuse to preach who are duly called; and that others obtrude themselves into the sacred office without any divine mission. [13]

Douglas J. Moo

He (Paul) has asserted a universally applicable principle: that salvation is granted to all who call on the Lord. But people cannot call on the Lord if they do not believe in him. They cannot believe in him if they do not hear the word that proclaims Christ. And that word will not be heard unless someone preaches it. But a preacher is nothing more than a herald, a person entrusted by another with a message. Thus preaching, finally, cannot transpire unless someone sends the preachers. [14]

A Lesson in Contrasts

ROMANS 10:16–21 *But they have not all obeyed the gospel. For Isaiah says, "LORD, who has believed our report?" So then faith comes by hearing, and hearing by the word of God. But I say, have they not heard? Yes indeed:*

"Their sound has gone out to all the earth,
And their words to the ends of the world."

But I say, did Israel not know? First Moses says:

"I will provoke you to jealousy by those who are not a nation,
I will move you to anger by a foolish nation."

But Isaiah is very bold and says:

"I was found by those who did not seek Me;
I was made manifest to those who did not ask for Me."

But to Israel he says:

"All day long I have stretched out My hands
To a disobedient and contrary people." (NKJV)

Paul makes it very clear that the Father's offer of righteousness by faith was extended to all, Jews and Gentiles alike. But unfortunately not everyone accepted the offer. And it was the official rejection by the Jewish leaders that caused Paul so much anguish. He knew what this would ultimately mean to the nation.

The Jews had ample opportunity to hear the Word of God, both by **general revelation** and by **special revelation**. They heard, but they did not accept God's invitation. Paul uses Old Testament Scripture to point out the sad reality that the Gentiles, who for a long time were ignorant of God, were in the end more accepting of God's invitation than the Jews, whom God actively pursued over and over again throughout history. The idea is that while God sought after the Jews, they rejected him. The Gentiles, who were not even looking for God, found and believed in him.

The phrase "all day long" (Romans 10:21 NKJV) is an expression of how long-suffering God is in his love for people. His invitation is still open. He is still holding out the gift of his eternal presence.

go to

general revelation
Psalm 19:1–4, 7–11;
Romans 1:19–20

special revelation
1 Corinthians
2:10–13

general revelation
what can be deduced about God from the natural universe

special revelation
information given to human beings by God, especially in the Scriptures

what others say

Saint Augustine

The preaching of predestination should not hinder the preaching of perseverance and progress in faith, so that those to whom it has been given to obey should hear what they ought to hear. For how will they hear without a preacher?[15]

Charles Hodge

The universal revelation of God in nature, was a providential prediction of the universal proclamation of the Gospel . . . the manifestation of God in nature, is, for all his creatures to whom it is made, a pledge of their participation in the clearer and higher revelations.[16]

Chapter Wrap-Up

- Israel had a zeal for God, but their zeal wasn't based on knowledge. They had rejected the Gospel. (Romans 10:1–5)

- The law has no saving potential. It helps us see ourselves more clearly, more honestly. Righteousness by the avenue of faith is the only sure way of securing a relationship with God. (Romans 10:6–13)

- Faith comes from hearing the message. And the message is heard through the Word of Christ. This makes the Christian faith a personal faith, grounded in daily experience, and a faith that will last eternally. (Romans 10:14–21)

Study Questions

1. What was wrong with the Jews' zeal for God?

2. How does "righteousness . . . of the law" differ from "righteousness of faith" (Romans 10:5–6 NKJV)?

3. How does one receive the Lord Jesus as his or her Lord and Savior?

4. When Paul says in Romans 10:12, "There is no distinction between Jew and Greek" (NKJV), what does he mean?

5. What's Paul's point in saying, "How beautiful are the feet of those who preach the gospel of peace" (Romans 10:15 NKJV)?

Romans 11 Israel's Destiny

Chapter Highlights:
- Paul the Jew
- The Remnant
- Mercy for the Gentiles
- Grafted In
- God's Promise
- God Be Praised

Let's Get Started

In chapter 9 Paul emphasized God's sovereignty in choosing Israel to be his people. In chapter 10 Paul pointed out that Israel had consistently been reluctant to accept God's gift of "righteousness of faith." Chapter 10 ended with the sobering charge that Israel is a "disobedient and contrary people."

So, we have God's sovereign choice of Israel on the one hand and Israel's obstinance on the other. Will God give up on Israel? Will he find a way, despite Israel's disobedience, to preserve and enact his purpose? These are the questions Paul addresses in chapter 11.

No Rejection for the Remnant

> ROMANS 11:1–2A *I say then, has God cast away His people? Certainly not! For I also am an Israelite, of the seed of Abraham, of the tribe of Benjamin. God has not cast away His people whom He foreknew.* (NKJV)

Paul is determined to help the Romans rightly understand Israel's fall. He was determined to do so not because of a selfish desire for his own peace, though surely this was a motivating factor. Rather, Paul sought God's will and wanted to state it accurately.

When Paul says "His people" (Romans 11:1 NKJV), he has in mind the remnant he referred to in Romans 9:27–29. Though most Jews were disobedient throughout the Old Testament and when Paul was teaching,

God had not given up on "His people." We remember that "they are not all Israel who are of Israel" (Romans 9:6 NKJV).

Paul includes himself in the discussion for at least two reasons. One was to present himself as evidence that God had not rejected the Jews. If God had rejected the Jews, he would not have given Paul such a prominent role in spreading the Gospel. A second reason was to remind the Jews that he was one of them. He was therefore qualified to speak with fairness about their situation.

go to

King Ahab
1 Kings 16:29–33

Baal
Judges 2:13;
1 Kings 19:18

Sidonian
from Sidon, a
Phoenician kingdom
near Israel

King Ahab
king of Israel's
Northern Kingdom

Baal
a Canaanite term
for "god"

D. Martyn Lloyd-Jones

But in chapter 11 he (Paul) goes further. He looks into the future and shows how this great and grand purpose of God is going to be carried out in its glorious fulness, both as regards Gentiles and Jews. So there is a new theme here. The present has been explained but the question now is, What of the future? The Jews are outside, are they always to be there?[1]

God's Track Record

ROMANS 11:2B–6 *Or do you not know what the Scripture says of Elijah, how he pleads with God against Israel, saying, "LORD, they have killed Your prophets and torn down Your altars, and I alone am left, and they seek my life"? But what does the divine response say to him? "I have reserved for Myself seven thousand men who have not bowed the knee to Baal." Even so then, at this present time there is a remnant according to the election of grace. And if by grace, then it is no longer of works; otherwise grace is no longer grace. But if it is of works, it is no longer grace; otherwise work is no longer work. (NKJV)*

In this passage, Paul takes his readers back to 1 Kings 19 where we find the account of Elijah fleeing from Jezebel, who was the **Sidonian** wife of **King Ahab**. This pagan woman had been promoting **Baal** worship throughout the land.

Elijah had just had a whale of a victory on Mount Carmel (see Illustration #6) against 450 prophets of Baal. When Ahab informed Jezebel of Elijah's astounding victory, she sent a threatening note to Elijah telling him she would have his head in the next twenty-four hours.

Elijah buckled. He fled out into the desert south of Beersheba to hide and pray. While there, "the word of the LORD came to him, and He said to him: 'What are you doing here, Elijah?' " (1 Kings 19:9 NKJV). Elijah was feeling like the battle was over and he was the only faithful servant left in the land. He was ready to give up because he thought he was alone. But God informed him, "I have reserved seven thousand in Israel, all whose knees have not bowed to Baal, and every mouth that has not kissed him" (1 Kings 19:18 NKJV). In this case, seven thousand does not mean an exact head count; rather, it suggests that which is complete, maybe even more than one can count. The "seven thousand" of Israel were the remnant. In

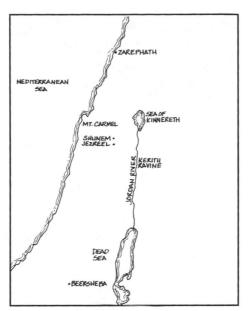

Illustration #6
Elijah's Triumph and Trial—This map shows Mount Carmel where Elijah fought the prophets of Baal. After learning that the queen wanted to have him killed, Elijah fled south of Beersheba.

battle
2 Chronicles 20:15

Scripture there is a special significance attached to seven and to multiples of seven; it is a symbol of completeness or perfection (see Matthew 18:21–22). In Revelation there are the seven churches (1:4), seven seals (5:1), seven trumpets (8:2), seven thunders (10:4) and seven golden bowls (15:7). In creation there are seven days. Seven is a significant part of God's prophetic language. In referencing the seven thousand men of Elijah's day, Paul is giving the church a picture of God's faithfulness to his divine purpose, a purpose that will go unchanged, uninterrupted by the sovereign will of God.

Paul brings up this Old Testament story as a way of saying God has always had a faithful remnant of Jews. It was true in the dark days of Elijah, and it's true now. God has not and will not reject Israel.

In the battle against the forces of evil, it's easy to get overwhelmed. We feel like we're the lone sentinel on a hill. In those moments, we forget that the <u>battle</u> is God's to fight, not ours. Paul was reminding the Jews who were faithful to Jesus Christ that "at this present time there is a remnant according to the election of grace" (Romans 11:5 NKJV), just as God had reserved a godly number in Elijah's day.

We can only rightly understand God's elective purposes when we understand that God is sovereign. We do not become part of God's remnant through our efforts; it is a gift of God. The larger lesson in this context is this: Since the remnant has been secured by the grace

works

merit earned by
what an individual
does

of God, the remnant stands as a pledge that God will continue to show favor toward Israel as a whole.

Paul is reminding Israel, as well as the Gentiles, that salvation has always been a matter of God's grace. Israel was called into existence by the grace of God. The Church was called into existence by God's grace. And the future heavenly reward of both groups rests on God's grace.

Romans 11:6 says, "And if by grace, then it is no longer of <u>works</u>; otherwise grace is no longer grace" (NKJV). He's clarifying his reference to "a remnant according to the election of grace" (11:5 NKJV). Grace and works are opposites. Like oil and water, grace and works due to their diverse characteristics cannot mix, and when we do mix them, we spoil both.

---

what others say

Joseph Shulam

Paul begins the climax to the argument which he begins in 9:30 and finally resolves in 11:11–36; that far from God having rejected His people because of their unfaithfulness, their transgression is in fact part of God's purpose to include all mankind in His kingdom.[2]

John Calvin

The grace of God and the merit of works are so opposed to one another that if we establish one we destroy the other. If, then, we cannot allow any consideration of works in election without obscuring the unmerited goodness of God . . . those fanatics, who make the worthiness which God foresees in us the cause of our election, must consider what answer they are to give to Paul.[3]

Israel Goes Bad

ROMANS 11:7–10 *What then? Israel has not obtained what it seeks; but the elect have obtained it, and the rest were blinded. Just as it is written:*
"God has given them a spirit of stupor,
Eyes that they should not see
And ears that they should not hear,
To this very day."
And David says:
"Let their table become a snare and a trap,

A stumbling block and a recompense to them.
Let their eyes be darkened, so that they do not see,
And bow down their back always." (NKJV)

"Don't pity the Israelites," Paul says. They sought God in the wrong way. Recall in Romans 9:31 when the apostle reminded us that Israel pursued "the law of righteousness" (NKJV). They did not seek God by faith. Now we find out more about the consequences of those actions.

In their vain attempt to establish their own adequacy—their own standing before God—they refused, knowingly and unknowingly, to receive the righteousness that comes from God. Rejection of God starts with one act, and it snowballs from there. Each rejection of God afterward gets easier and easier. The result was that God hardened the unbelieving Jews' hearts. He gave them a "spirit of stupor" (Romans 11:8 NKJV).

Grace is the sign of the elect, for **the elect** obtain righteousness by trusting in divine grace, not in the works of the flesh—no matter how sincere they are. Though there is a "remnant according to the election of grace" (Romans 11:5 NKJV), most people in Israel failed to attain divine righteousness.

Earlier Paul told the Roman believers that God "has mercy on whom He wills, and whom He wills He hardens" (Romans 9:18 NKJV). We can only resist his will so long, and then the hardening takes place. When hearts are hardened, they resist the grace of God, and people without grace are people under judgment.

Judgment is such a serious matter that the apostle throws the weight of Scripture behind his argument for God's truth. The Jews had **the Law**, **the Prophets**, and **the Writings**. Paul quotes from all three—Deuteronomy 29:4, Isaiah 29:10, and Psalm 69:22–23—to make sure his hearers understand. Paul knows if you mess with the truth, you undermine all of what's best in life.

The Route of Resistance

Two things happen to those who continue to resist when God holds out his hands of grace, mercy, and love.

First, they become hardened, making it difficult to receive truth in the future. This hardening produces a **flinty** heart and permanent bluntness. It's like a spiritual tattoo—nearly impossible to reverse.

go to

righteousness
Romans 1:17

the elect
one of Paul's terms
for Christians

the Law
first five OT books

the Prophets
writings of the
prophets

the Writings
Psalms and the
wisdom literature

flinty
rocklike, inflexible,
or inert

Second, God removes blessings from their lives. In the biblical world the table was a symbol of prosperity that represented the pleasures of life. So when the psalmist prayed, "Let their table become a snare before them, and their well-being a trap" (Psalm 69:22 NKJV), he was asking God to take pleasure out of the lives of those who rejected God.

In his second letter to the Corinthians Paul answered the question of how he and his ministry partner, Apollos, should be viewed. He wrote, "Not that we are sufficient of ourselves to think of anything as being from ourselves, but our sufficiency is from God" (2 Corinthians 3:5 NKJV). Paul's statement reflects how indebted he felt toward God. He knew that his salvation, even his competence as a minister of Christ, came not from himself but from God. We cannot mock the grace of God and hope to be at peace in our heart, spirit, soul, or body.

Israel Is Green with Envy

ROMANS 11:11–12 *I say then, have they stumbled that they should fall? Certainly not! But through their fall, to provoke them to jealousy, salvation has come to the Gentiles. Now if their fall is riches for the world, and their failure riches for the Gentiles, how much more their fullness!* (NKJV)

church
Matthew 16:17–20

Paul now turns his attention from the remnant to Israel as a whole. He asks if there is any hope. Will Israel ever get back up? Are they doomed forever? "Certainly not!" Paul answers (Romans 11:11 NKJV). He explains that while the Jews are rejecting God, God will sow the gospel seed among the Gentiles to make the Jews envious. Paul is saying the Jews will see God's blessing upon the Gentiles and they'll get jealous. He goes on to say if the "failure" (11:12 NKJV) of the Jews brings riches to the Gentiles, their return to God will bring even greater riches to the Gentiles!

Because Israel did not welcome Christ, God opened his gift of salvation to the Gentiles. Prior to Christ the only way for a Gentile to identify himself or herself as a follower of Yahweh was to identify with God's covenant people and submit to God's law as a Jew. With Christ Gentiles no longer had to convert to Judaism. If they put their faith in Jesus, they were not Jews, they were Christians!

Here we see a real hint of the future salvation of Israel. God in his grace and power is bringing great good out of the foolishness of Israel. They were offered the righteousness of God, but rejected it for the old way of the law. The consequence has been enormous—centuries of testing and grief. But all is not lost.

The glory of God is clearly revealed in this unusual process of making good out of failure. Gathering people from among the nations, Jesus created the very <u>church</u> that he said he would build. Christianity became reality, but not without hope for Israel. Today's remnant from Israel is secured in that they come into God's kingdom through their Messiah, the Lord Jesus Christ.

absolute rejection of Israel. He comes to the conclusion that it does not . . . further, he is confident that, as the Jews have led to the conversion of the Gentiles, so the Gentiles will be the agents of the conversion of the Jews.[7]

Adolf Schlatter

Israel's fall is God's work, as the Scripture declared it; yet God's action is always goal-oriented. Did Israel stumble in order to fall? If so, only wrath would be at work in its destiny and God's grace would not be seen. Israel's fall denotes guilt; it is a **paratoma** and therefore what Israel suffers has been prepared for them by wrath. But grace will be made manifest even in what it suffers, because its fall brings about the salvation of those who are of the nations.[8]

Holy Branches, Batman!

ROMANS 11:13–15 *For I speak to you Gentiles; inasmuch as I am an apostle to the Gentiles, I magnify my ministry, if by any means I may provoke to jealousy those who are my flesh and save some of them. For if their being cast away is the reconciling of the world, what will their acceptance be but life from the dead?* (NKJV)

Paul links this paragraph with the preceding one. He wants to make certain that the Gentiles are paying attention. It's important for the unity and the growth of the church that the Gentiles catch the full importance of what Paul is saying and doing. He emphasizes that he's the apostle to the Gentiles.

It is good that they understand him to be the "apostle to the Gentiles" (Romans 11:13 NKJV), but he doesn't want them to forget that he's a witness to the Jews as well. Christ doesn't have two bodies of people. The Church he is building is "one body and one Spirit, just as you were called in one hope . . . one Lord, one faith, one baptism; one God and Father of all" (Ephesians 4:4–6 NKJV). It is made up of Jews and Gentiles. Paul pays close attention to his ministry because he knows that the more the Gentile world responds to the Gospel, the more the Jews will be aroused to action.

God's work is being carried out even if the Jews continue to reject their Messiah. Paul has been given spiritual eyes to see exactly what the Father is doing.

A Down Payment with More to Come

ROMANS 11:16 *For if the firstfruit is holy, the lump is also holy; and if the root is holy, so are the branches.* (NKJV)

Paul uses two analogies—the lump of dough and the root—to teach a significant concept without making a prophetic announcement. "The lump" is the present number of Jews that have bowed to Jesus as their Lord; they are the "firstfruit," the elect (Romans 11:16 NKJV).

The second analogy—"the root" (Romans 11:16 NKJV)—addresses their beginning or the source of their life. Covenantally, their root goes back to Abraham whose place in their history and theology is beyond dispute.

Paul is pointing to the future restoration of the nation of Israel to God. He did not expect this to happen in his own lifetime, though he hoped his work would help to convert "some" (Romans 11:14 NKJV). He expected the nation's restoration to happen sometime in the indefinite future.

Prepare to Be Pruned

ROMANS 11:17–18 *And if some of the branches were broken off, and you, being a wild olive tree, were grafted in among them, and with them became a partaker of the root and fatness of the olive tree, do not boast against the branches. But if you do boast, remember that you do not support the root, but the root supports you. (NKJV)*

The olive tree (see Illustration #7) is a familiar and beautiful part of the landscape in Israel. It's a symbol of both strength and blessing. David penned in Psalm 52:8: "I am like a green olive tree in the house of God; I trust in the mercy of God forever and ever" (NKJV).

Paul uses the branch of an olive tree to picture what God has done in grafting the Gentiles, the "wild olive tree" (Romans 11:17 NKJV), into the cultivated olive tree, Israel. In Paul's metaphor, some of the olive tree's branches were broken off and wild shoots were grafted into the tree.

Illustration #7
Olive Tree—A slow-growing olive tree such as this one was a common sight in Israel during New Testament times. Its fruit was crushed and the oil was extracted and used for cooking, lighting, and mixing ointments and perfumes. One tree could produce twenty gallons of oil. The wood was hard and had many uses as well.

God was turning the Gentiles into a fruit-bearing people. This left no room for boasting. Paul told the Gentiles, "If you do boast, remember that you do not support the root, but the root supports you" (Romans 11:18 NKJV). Paul is pointing them to the very source of their lives: God. God is the Keeper of the vineyard, the ultimate Gardener.

what others say

A. T. Robertson

Ramsay (*Pauline Studies*, pp. 219ff) shows that the ancients used the wild-olive graft upon an old olive tree to reinvigorate the tree precisely as Paul uses the figure here and that both the olive tree and the graft were influenced by each other, though the wild olive graft did not produce as good olives as the original stock.[11]

You See the Hole, Now Step Around It

ROMANS 11:19–21 *You will say then, "Branches were broken off that I might be grafted in." Well said. Because of unbelief they were broken off, and you stand by faith. Do not be haughty, but fear. For if God did not spare the natural branches, He may not spare you either.* (NKJV)

The Gentiles were now recipients of all the blessings of belonging to God. Many Jews had rejected God and therefore did not receive these blessings. The Gentile temptation to boast must have been enormous.

Paul warns the Gentile Christians not to repeat the sins of the Jews. The Jews did not depend on God for their salvation, but their own works. Paul tells the Gentiles to remember that the only reason they were grafted into the tree of God's kingdom was because they depended on God. If they now let go of their dependence on God, God could just as easily break them off of the tree as he broke off the self-reliant Jews.

key point

what others say

Saint Jerome

Whenever I see a synagogue, the thought of the apostle always comes to me—that we should not boast against the olive tree whose branches have been broken off but rather fear. For if the natural branches have been cut off, how much more we who have been grafted on the wild olive should fear, lest we become like them.[12]

Stern Kindness

ROMANS 11:22–24 *Therefore consider the goodness and severity of God: on those who fell, severity; but toward you, goodness,*

parable
a story that teaches
a lesson

**ten thousand
talents**
approximately
twelve million
dollars

**one hundred
denarii**
about eighteen
dollars

*if you continue in His goodness. Otherwise you also will be cut
off. And they also, if they do not continue in unbelief, will be
grafted in, for God is able to graft them in again. For if you
were cut out of the olive tree which is wild by nature, and were
grafted contrary to nature into a cultivated olive tree, how
much more will these, who are natural branches, be grafted into
their own olive tree? (NKJV)*

In this passage, we see Paul holding out hope for the Jews, who,
if they "do not continue in unbelief, will be grafted in, for God is
able to graft them in again" (Romans 11:23 NKJV). Unbelief is what
kills. Belief is what gives life. If the Jews simply give up persisting in
their unbelief, Paul says, then the kindness and power of God will
reestablish them in the kingdom of God.

Paul had the heart to perceive what was on the horizon for his fellow Jews. The phrase "how much more will these, who are natural
branches, be grafted into their own olive tree?" (Romans 11:24b
NKJV) shows that Paul had hope for the Jews. The apostle sees that
God's original plan for the Jewish nation will unfold naturally when
unbelief is out of the way.

In this passage we see the vastness of the character and personhood
of God. He is able to be kind in his sternness and stern in his kindness, all while remaining righteous. This is a feat that is difficult for
humans. We are usually mean in our sternness and permissive in our
kindness.

God Commands Kindness

In the **parable** of the unmerciful servant, a servant was unable to
repay his master **ten thousand talents** he owed him and begged for
mercy. The master "was moved with compassion, released him, and
forgave him the debt" (Matthew 18:27 NKJV).

Then the forgiven servant met one of his fellow servants who
owed him **one hundred denarii** (see Illustration #8). The forgiven
servant refused to forgive the fellow servant and had him thrown in
prison.

When the master of the servants heard what happened he said,
"You wicked servant! I forgave you all that debt because you begged
me. Should you not also have had compassion on your fellow ser-

vant, just as I had pity on you?" (Matthew 18:32–33 NKJV). The servant was sent off to prison until he had paid the ten thousand talents. Jesus concluded his parable, "So My heavenly Father also will do to you if each of you, from his heart, does not forgive his brother his trespasses" (Matthew 18:35 NKJV).

Once we have learned the grace of kindness, we are **accountable** to distribute that same kindness to others. This is an unconditional condition in God's kingdom.

accountable
obligated

mystery
an aspect of God's plan not revealed in the Old Testament

what others say

Frederick L. Godet

Unhappy is the believer for whom grace is no longer grace on the hundredth or the thousandth day, as it was on the first! For the slightest feeling of self-exaltation which may take possess of him on occasion of grace received or of its fruits, destroys in his case grace itself and paralyzes it. There is nothing more for him to expect in this condition than to be himself cut off from the stem.[13]

The Defeat of Conceit

ROMANS 11:25–27 *For I do not desire, brethren, that you should be ignorant of this **mystery**, lest you should be wise in your own opinion, that blindness in part has happened to Israel until the fullness of the Gentiles has come in. And so all Israel will be saved, as it is written:*
"The Deliverer will come out of Zion,
And He will turn away ungodliness from Jacob;
For this is My covenant with them,
When I take away their sins." (NKJV)

Illustration #8
Denarius—One denarius, pictured here, was one day's wage for the average worker at the time Paul wrote Romans.

Paul wants the Gentiles to be knowledgeable of the "mystery" (Romans 11:25 NKJV). By "mystery" Paul is referring to the future salvation of the bulk of Israel. He wants the Gentile Christians to know this so they won't be conceited about their own part in God's plan. They did not permanently replace the Jews as God's chosen people. They were not the be all and end all of God's activity throughout history. Paul says part of the reason Israel experienced a hardening was so the full number of Gentiles could enter God's kingdom. In other words, the Gentiles are on very shaky ground when they look down on hardened Israel because if it were not for Israel's hardening, many Gentiles would not have been saved!

Furthermore, Paul says when the full number of Gentiles are saved, Israel as a nation will be saved. This will happen at the return of Christ (when "the Deliverer will come out of Zion" [Romans 11:26 NKJV]). We do not need to interpret the passage to mean every living Jew will be saved at the return of Christ, only that Israel as a nation will turn to him.

Paul may have mentally compared Israel's future conversion to his own conversion. Paul was not converted until Christ appeared to him and confronted him with the question, "Saul, Saul, why are you persecuting Me?" (Acts 9:4 NKJV). To this very day the nation of Israel has not turned to Christ, and Paul knew two millenia ago that their conversion would not take place until Jesus came back. When at last Jesus does come back, Israel will likely have an experience that is comparable to that of Paul's encounter with Christ on the Damascus Road.

what others say

C. E. B. Cranfield

Paul wants the Gentile Christians in the Roman church to know the mystery which he is about to state, because it is the solemn confirmation of what he has just said, which at the same time goes beyond anything which he has already said.[14]

Beloved Enemies

ROMANS 11:28–29 *Concerning the gospel they are enemies for your sake, but concerning the election they are beloved for the sake of the fathers. For the gifts and the calling of God are irrevocable.* (NKJV)

Paul explains a two-sided truth to the Gentiles. He says the unbelieving Jews are God's enemies in the sense that they have rejected God's gift of righteousness by faith. God will use the Jews' unbelief to bring the "fullness of the Gentiles" (Romans 11:25 NKJV) into his kingdom.

On the other hand, Paul says God loves the unbelieving Israelites because ever since the faith of Abraham, Israel has been God's specially chosen people.

Paul insists that God's gifts and God's call are irrevocable. Nothing can defeat or even frustrate the promises of God. God promised that the sins of the nation of Israel would be taken away in Isaiah 59:20–21, and God always makes good on his promises.

God has not given up on the Jewish race "for the sake of the fathers" (Romans 11:28 NKJV), which is to say that somehow there is a connection between the faith of the founders of Judaism and the Jews of today. This truth should remind us that the things we say and do, good or bad, have an effect on the generations that follow us. Children whose mothers and fathers make prayer a priority are more likely to pray themselves, children whose parents are abusive are more likely to be abusive later in life. This is simply the God-created order of things.

The Pendulum Swings Both Ways

ROMANS 11:30–32 *For as you were once disobedient to God, yet have now obtained mercy through their disobedience, even so these also have now been disobedient, that through the mercy shown you they also may obtain mercy. For God has committed them all to disobedience, that He might have mercy on all. (NKJV)*

go to

committed them all
Romans 3:9–20

Paul reminds the Gentiles that they too were once disobedient. God used the disobedience of the Israelites to show mercy to the Gentiles. Many Gentiles left their disobedience to embrace God's mercy. Now it was the Jews who were in disobedience, and God would eventually use the mercy he showed to the Gentiles to bless Israel.

The emphasis here is on *mercy*, a word that appears four times in these three verses. Only God's mercy can save people. In chapter 9 Paul quoted God as saying, "I will have mercy on whomever I will have mercy" (verse 15 NKJV), implying that God will not have mercy on everyone. Here, Paul points out how inclusive God's mercy is by saying, "For God has committed them all to disobedience, that He might have mercy on all" (Romans 11:32 NKJV). It does not follow that God is obligated to save each and every person on the planet. It does follow, however, that God will show mercy to all groups of people. He will not show mercy to one race at the expense of another.

something to ponder

We also learn from this passage that to appreciate mercy, we must see it against the dark background of our *disobedience*, another word that appears four times in these three verses. We are tarnished with our sin, but God's mercy burns away our impurities and leaves us brilliant with his glory.

---

what others say

James Montgomery Boice

Sin abounds! But it is precisely in that context and against that dark and tempestuous background that the mercy of God flashes forth like lightning.[16]

James R. Edwards

The Greek word for "bound over" means to "shut up" or "imprison" and is a close parallel of Galatians 3:22. Gaugler [another commentator] likens verse 32 to a master key which opens all the doors to Paul's gospel. . . . That may be an overstatement, but it certainly is the master key to Romans 9–11. What a breathtaking conclusion: God goes so far as to hand over all peoples to disobedience.[17]

God took the common thread that runs through all humanity—sin—and did something beautiful with it: "For God has <u>committed them all</u> to disobedience, that He might have mercy on all" (Romans 11:32 NKJV). In showing mercy to sinful people, God proves how superhuman he is.

To God Be the Glory

ROMANS 11:33–36 *Oh, the depth of the riches both of the wisdom and knowledge of God! How unsearchable are His judgments and His ways past finding out!*
"For who has known the mind of the LORD?
Or who has become His counselor?"
"Or who has first given to Him
And it shall be repaid to him?"
For of Him and through Him and to Him are all things, to whom be glory forever. Amen. (NKJV)

Paul's understanding and explanation of God's righteous dealings with all humankind bring him to a new height of spiritual joy. He bursts forth in song, quoting from Isaiah 40:13 and Job 41:11! Paul's doxology expresses his bewilderment at the superiority of God. Specifically, Paul mentions the wisdom, knowledge, judgments, paths (or ways), and mind of God.

Paul also points out that God does not owe us anything because whatever we give God came from him. We can't even praise God without his assistance.

In our sinfulness and finiteness, it is often difficult to see and understand the wisdom of God: "Oh, the depth of the riches both of the wisdom and knowledge of God! How unsearchable are His judgments and His ways past finding out!" (Romans 11:33 NKJV). We cannot fully understand God's plan, but worship is a godly response when the glory of God reaches our hearts. Simple praise is a way to honor and adore our Savior. Blaise Pascal, a great servant of God in the seventeenth century, taught that what the mind cannot know the heart may know by other reasons.

God decides what to do without the assistance of counselors. It is impossible for us to lay hold of him. He is God, the only God, Father, Son, and Holy Spirit.

what others say

James Montgomery Boice

The reason we do not see great periods of revival today is that the glory of God in all things has been largely forgotten by the contemporary church. It follows that we are not likely to see revival again until the truths that exalt and glorify God in salvation are recovered. Surely we cannot expect God to move among us greatly again until we can again truthfully say, "To him [alone] be the glory forever! Amen."[18]

Chapter Wrap-Up

- Paul explains that he was from the tribe of Benjamin and also a descendant of Abraham. He presents himself as Exhibit A, showing that God has not rejected his people. (Romans 11:1–2)

- A second matter that needs clarification is the remnant "according to the election of grace" (verse 5 NKJV)—those who believe in Jesus as the Messiah of God. (Romans 11:3–6)

- Israel's fall has opened the door for the Gentiles to enter into the kingdom of God. Paul calls this "riches for the world" and "riches for the Gentiles" (Romans 11:12 NKJV). As the apostle to the Gentiles, he is seeking to arouse his own people to envy, hoping to make some breakthrough in their hearts. (Romans 11:7–16)

- Paul presents an olive tree metaphor. The branches that were broken off made room for the Gentiles to be grafted in. But the fact that they were broken off portrays the unbelief of the Jews. This bothered Paul greatly. (Romans 11:17–24)

- Paul knows that we cannot have complete insight, but ignorance is not acceptable in the Christian community. When God gives, he doesn't turn back. His gifts and call are irrevocable. This speaks of God's faithfulness and mercy. (Romans 11:25–31)

- For Paul, worship is a result of careful study and a love for God. Paul's doxology is an expression of worship and praise. (Romans 11:33–36)

Study Questions

1. Why was Paul so concerned about Israel's rejection of God?

2. In Romans 11:7–10, what does Paul mean by "a spirit of stupor" (verse 8 NKJV)?

3. Was Israel's fall permanent?

4. In Romans 11:25–32, what mystery is Paul seeking to explain?

5. How were the unbelieving Jews God's enemies and yet at the same time loved by God?

6. Against what should we see God's mercy and why?

Part Five
A GRACE-FILLED CHURCH

Romans 12 How to Do Church

Chapter Highlights:
- Living Sacrifice
- Mind Renewal
- God-given Gifts
- Sincere Love
- Good Government

Let's Get Started

Now Paul changes the topic of discussion. He has spent the better part of the preceding chapters discussing how sinful humans can come into a right relationship with God. Having addressed this matter thoroughly, in chapter 12 he moves on to discuss how having a right relationship with God should affect our everyday lives, especially within our church community.

go to

sacrifice
Leviticus 4:1–12;
Hebrews 8;
1 Peter 2:4–10

sacrificial blood
Hebrews 9:14

High Priest
Hebrews 4:14–16

Sacrifice Your Body

> ROMANS 12:1 *I beseech you therefore, brethren, by the mercies of God, that you present your bodies a living sacrifice, holy, acceptable to God, which is your reasonable service. (NKJV)*

The use of *therefore* is the apostle's way of signaling a transition and an important summary of all that's gone before. You can find this same method used in Romans 3:20, 5:1, and 8:1.

The Temple in the Old Covenant was a building. In the church, the body of the believer is the Holy Spirit's temple. In the Old Covenant the blood of bulls, goats, and calves was the <u>sacrifice</u>, but under the blessing of the New Covenant, the <u>sacrificial blood</u> is Christ's. In the Old Covenant the priests handled the sacrifices and were permitted to enter the Holy of Holies only once a year (see Illustration #9). In the New Covenant believers became priests with direct access to the Holy of Holies—God's presence—at all times.

Christians are believer-priests and are identified with Christ, our great **High Priest**. The church is a kingdom of **priests**—called, gifted, and sent into the world to serve the Savior. The priesthood is not an office that you attain by doing good works, going to seminary, or being ordained. Christ solemnly bestowed the title of priest on us when we accepted his blood as atonement for our sins. Our gifts will help determine how we exercise our priestly duties.

High Priest
one who offered a sacrifice atoning for all sins

priests
represent God to others, communicate with God on behalf of themselves and others

Illustration #9
Floor Plan of the Temple—This illustration shows the layout of the Temple. The High Priest could enter the Holy of Holies only once a year. Because of Christ, believers now have unrestricted access to God.

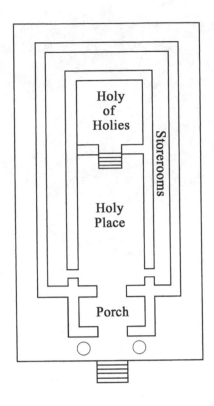

Old and New Covenants Compared and Contrasted

Old:	New:
Old Covenant Priests: human, imperfect, sinners, mortal	New Covenant Priests: human, redeemed, representing Christ our High Priest
Temple: actual, physical building, God's presence in the Holy of Holies	Temple: believers' bodies, in which the Holy Spirit resides
Animal Sacrifices: repeated, outward, reminder of sin; could not perfect sinner	Jesus the Sacrifice: brought once-for-all cleansing from sin for all who believe in God's Son
Who benefits? A select group of people; called to be God's people of promise	Who benefits? Every tribe, tongue, people, nation . . . all people

key point

Presenting our bodies as living sacrifices is an essential part of godly worship. There is nothing inherently evil about the human body. Our bodies are capable of sin or righteousness, evil or good. Because God created our bodies, we need to bring them under God's control. If our attitudes and actions are right, we become an offering "acceptable to God" (Romans 12:1 NKJV).

go to

mind
1 Peter 3:1–2;
Philippians 4:7

Mind Bath

ROMANS 12:2 *And do not be conformed to this world, but be transformed by the renewing of your <u>mind</u>, that you may prove what is that good and acceptable and perfect will of God. (NKJV)*

conformed
squeezed into the world's mold

transformed
changed from the inside out

We are either being **conformed** or **transformed**. God calls us to a life of transformation. A transformed life requires renewal of the mind. We ought to think differently as Christians than we thought as non-Christians. Often Paul writes about having the mind of Christ. We must begin to think about our circumstances and goals the way Christ would think about them. We must use a new perspective, a perspective that takes practice and self-discipline to develop.

When Paul says "Present your bodies as a living sacrifice," he is saying that the sacrifice is living because your body has eternal life dwelling in it, which is Christ the Lord. Another way of speaking this great mystery is this: the Logos, the Word, desires that we offer our flesh to God in absolute purity through the power of the Holy Spirit. Paul uses the word *present* because this is a divine work, yet a work that is reasonable because we have the mind of Christ (see 1 Corinthians 2:16).

what others say

Robert Haldane

It is not the conduct merely, but the heart itself, of the Christian that is changed; and it is from the renewal of the mind that the conduct is also renewed.[2]

Adolf Schlatter

The believer does not fall prey to the servitude of the body and does not draw his thinking and action from the wisdom of this world, but differs from the world because of a new character, and for this he is indebted to God's mercy that does not reckon his sins to his account.[3]

sin nature
Romans 7:14–20

John Chrysostom

How is the body to become a sacrifice? Let the eye look on no evil thing, and it has already become a sacrifice. Let the tongue say nothing filthy, and it has become a sacrifice. Let your hand do nothing evil, and it has become a whole burnt offering. But even this is not enough, for we must have good works also.[4]

In other letters, Paul said this to the Philippians about having a Christ-like perspective: "Let this mind be in you which was also in Christ Jesus, who, being in the form of God, did not consider it robbery to be equal with God, but made Himself of no reputation, taking the form of a bondservant, and coming in the likeness of men. And being found in appearance as a man, He humbled Himself and became obedient to the point of death, even the death of the cross" (2:5–8 NKJV). Renewing our minds so that we have the perspective of Christ is a matter of humbling ourselves to the extent that we become servants to those around us.

The Body Shop

> ROMANS 12:3–5 *For I say, through the grace given to me, to everyone who is among you, not to think of himself more highly than he ought to think, but to think soberly, as God has dealt to each one a measure of faith. For as we have many members in one body, but all the members do not have the same function, so we, being many, are one body in Christ, and individually members of one another. (NKJV)*

Paul was able to address issues that hindered the growth of the church. What he said was relevant to all believers.

apply it

Paul thought too highly of himself before he converted, which is one of the reasons he persecuted the church, but later he became aware of how destructive pride is. He exhorts believers to be sober in their judgments as an act of faithfulness to God. We are not to promote ourselves because to do so is to act out of our sin nature. When our <u>sin nature</u> drives our attitudes and actions we "cannot please God" (Romans 8:8 NKJV).

The grace that Paul received was the gift of apostleship. This gift, in serving the kingdom and overseeing the church, gave him a godly authority that was unique to his calling. As members of the Body of Christ, we all serve different functions. We are not all called by God to be apostles. We all have different jobs to do.

The Christian body is a bit like an orchestra. Different instruments play different notes, but all the sounds blend harmoniously into beautiful music. Imagine if the violins refused to play. The symphony would be missing an important melody. Similarly, if one group of believers within the Body of Christ refused to perform its function, the church would not work right. This is why Paul reminds his readers to think soberly, "as God has dealt to each one a measure of faith" (Romans 12:3 NKJV). Humility is not thinking little of yourself, but thinking nothing of yourself.

gifts
Ephesians 4:7–8, 11–16;
1 Corinthians 12:1–11

gifts
Holy Spirit–given abilities to minister to others

> ### what others say
>
> **John F. Walvoord and Roy B. Zuck**
>
> God has given each believer some faith by which to serve Him. . . . Paul emphasized that human pride is wrong partly because all natural abilities and spiritual gifts are from God. As a result every Christian should have a proper sense of humility and an awareness of his need to be involved with other members of Christ's body. As Paul explained, a parallelism exists between a believer's physical body which has parts with differing functions and the community of believers in Christ as a spiritual body.[5]
>
> **John Chrysostom**
>
> Paul addresses these words not to one group of people only but to everyone. The governor and the governed, the slave and the free, the ignorant and the wise, the woman and the man, the young and the old—all are included.[6]

Spread the Wealth

*ROMANS 12:6–8 Having then **gifts** differing according to the grace that is given to us, let us use them: if prophecy, let us prophesy in proportion to our faith; or ministry, let us use it in our ministering; he who teaches, in teaching; he who exhorts, in exhortation; he who gives, with liberality; he who leads, with diligence; he who shows mercy, with cheerfulness. (NKJV)*

Paul knows that gifts come from God to help Christians do ministry. He wants believers in Rome to be useful to each other, and he knows that right actions grow out of right attitudes.

Eugene Peterson's *The Message* renders the passage this way: "So since we find ourselves fashioned into all these excellently formed and marvelously functioning parts in Christ's body, let's just go ahead and be what we were made to be, without enviously or pridefully comparing ourselves with each other, or trying to be something we aren't.

"If you preach, just preach God's Message, nothing else; if you help, just help, don't take over; if you teach, stick to your teaching; if you give encouraging guidance, be careful that you don't get bossy; if you're put in charge, don't manipulate; if you're called to give aid to people in distress, keep your eyes open and be quick to respond; if you work with the disadvantaged, don't let yourself get irritated with them or depressed by them. Keep a smile on your face."

apply it

We will help each other most if we focus on whatever task God has set before us. We will become ineffective members of the body if we compare ourselves to other members or if we grumble about our role. God created us with certain gifts for certain jobs. Each job is absolutely crucial to our overall task of being Christ to the world. Every gift is a spiritual endowment from God meant to make and keep the Body of Christ healthy.

Spiritual Gifts in Romans 12

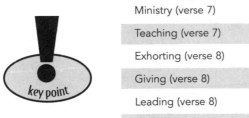

key point

Gifts	Paul's Admonition	The Gift's Effect
Prophesying (verse 6)	Prophesy in proportion to your faith.	People are built up.
Ministry (verse 7)	Minister.	God's work is accomplished.
Teaching (verse 7)	Teach.	Spiritual growth occurs.
Exhorting (verse 8)	Exhort.	Emotional needs are met.
Giving (verse 8)	Give liberally.	Physical needs are met.
Leading (verse 8)	Lead with diligence.	Things run in an orderly way.
Showing mercy (verse 8)	Show mercy with cheerfulness.	Burdens are borne thoughtfully.

yourselves more highly than you ought," he says. Instead believers are to see themselves as part of a body, to which they each contribute. . . . The focus is on relationships within the body, rather than on the relationships of individual believers or of the body to the larger community.[7]

Mark Driscoll

In the church community we discover that we belong to others, and that God has given each of His children gifts and abilities to be a means of grace to others. As we discover this gift and God's will for its use we then know how to glorify God.[8]

James R. Edwards

Some gifts appear to be natural talents strengthened by the Spirit, whereas others are unique abilities following conversion. They are and remain gifts, however. True to their name, they are spiritual endowments for ministry within Christ's body; they are not our possessions or status-builders.[9]

Love Will Keep Us Together

ROMANS 12:9–10a *Let love be without hypocrisy. Abhor what is evil. Cling to what is good. Be kindly affectionate to one another with brotherly love,* (NKJV)

The apostle uses two forms of the word *love* to communicate his message, *agape* and *philadelphia*. Agape is used in 1 John 4:8: "God is love [agape]" (NKJV). It is also used in John 3:16, "For God so loved the world that He gave His only begotten Son" (NKJV). This love is a description of God's attitude toward the human race.

Paul says "Let love [agape] be without hypocrisy" (Romans 12:9 NKJV). In other words, if love is not sincere, it is not love.

The second word for love used in this text is *philadelphia*. It literally means, "love for man." It suggests tender affection. In Jesus' dialogue with Peter in John 21:15–17 (NKJV), we see these two words used in a context that helps us to understand the difference in their meaning. When Jesus asked Peter, "Do you love [*agape*] Me?" Peter responded, "Yes, Lord; You know that I love [*phileo*] You." Peter used the more general word for love, expressing his affections; whereas, the Lord used agape, a love that is centered in the will, not in the emotions. God's love [*agape*] will produce emotional responses, but it is a love that goes beyond feelings. It is a love based on commitment. God is capable of loving the unlovely. Christ within

us makes our love real and complete. Due to the Fall, we are not inclined to be sincere. When our love is tested and life gets hard, we are likely to give up on a person and look for someone nicer to love. Paul says, "No way! Don't do that. Love as Christ loved—with complete commitment and brotherly feeling."

Be a Determined Disciple

ROMANS 12:10B–13 *in honor giving preference to one another; not lagging in diligence, fervent in spirit, serving the Lord; rejoicing in hope, patient in tribulation, continuing steadfastly in prayer; distributing to the needs of the saints, given to hospitality.* (NKJV)

Our love for one another is to be lived out as we see Christ expressed individually through Christians around us. It is not meant to be locked up between our ears as a mere concept or good idea. Love for fellow Christians is not based on how attractive or useful they are to us. It is based on the truth that because other Christians are now in a very real sense our family, we are obligated to look after them. We are to shoulder one another's burdens.

apply it

Paul says never to be lagging in diligence and to keep our spiritual fervor. What he means is don't let yourself get bored with Christ. Think of when Jesus called to Peter and Andrew in their fishing boat. There they were, going about their workaday business, when Jesus showed up and said, "Follow me." Peter and Andrew could have said, "Naw, we've got work to do, but thanks anyway," but they didn't. "They immediately left their nets and followed Him" (Matthew 4:20 NKJV). Now Jesus is asking us to follow him. Will we stay in our boats or will we follow? Paul is saying, "Keep making the decision to follow Christ. Don't get lazy."

Hospitality means, literally, having a love for strangers, and practice means to pursue. So, Paul is telling his readers to pursue a love for strangers. Without hospitality, the spread of the Gospel during the days of the infant church would have been significantly hindered.

Jesus encouraged his disciples to depend on the kindness and hospitality of their countrymen when he <u>sent them</u> out on missions. Godly hospitality is a powerful way to build your spiritual walk.

go to

sent them
Matthew 10:11

what others say

Dietrich Bonhoeffer

The first service that one owes to others in the fellowship consists in listening to them. Just as love to God begins with listening to His Word, so the beginning of love for the brethren is learning to listen to them. It is God's love for us that He not only gives us His Word but lends us His ear. So it is His work that we do for our brother when we learn to listen to him.[11]

Billy Graham

We fail to overcome temptation when we forget to trust the Lord or when we are too lazy or too proud to call on His strength. . . . The natural, easy, pleasing way is self-indulgence and moral softness. The hard way is self-denial and self-discipline, which incidentally, is commanded in the Word of God. We have too many soft Christians today! One of the best ways to overcome temptation is to keep busy for the Lord. Find something to do for Him. Seek to serve Him. Once you are willing, He will open innumerable doors of service for you.[12]

Charles R. Swindoll

Fortunately, grim, frowning, joyless saints in Scripture are conspicuous by their absence. Instead, the examples I find are of adventurous, risk-taking, enthusiastic, and authentic believers whose joy was contagious even in times of painful trial. Their vision was broad even when death drew near. Rules were few and changes were welcome. The contrast between then and now is staggering. The difference, I am convinced, is grace.[13]

Put Down Your Big Stick

ROMANS 12:14 *Bless those who persecute you; bless and do not curse. (NKJV)*

Jesus said, "Love your enemies, bless those who curse you, do good to those who hate you, and pray for those who spitefully use you and persecute you" (Matthew 5:44 NKJV) and, "To him who

go to

persecution
Acts 12:1–4

Herod
king of Judea,
AD 37–44

Nero
Nero Claudius
Caesar, Roman
emperor, AD 37–68;
notoriously cruel

strikes you on the one cheek, offer the other also" (Luke 6:29a NKJV). Here, Paul is saying something very similar.

Persecution can come in many different forms. Someone may mock your values, laugh when you mention the name Jesus, or call you unintelligent for believing in God. The way to be a follower of Jesus when someone persecutes you is to respond with blessing. Our tendency is to get angry and to act out of that anger.

We might yell at our persecutor or call him or her names. We might feel so wounded that all we can do is cry. We may even want to take up arms against our persecutors. Paul says to bless your persecutors. In other words, when someone shows hatred for you or God, respond by showing that person love. This is perhaps the most difficult part of Christian living.

Keep in mind Paul and his readers were living in a time of great <u>persecution</u>. James the son of Zebedee was beheaded by command of King **Herod**. At that same time, Peter was put into prison, all before the year AD 44. Andrew, Philip, and Jude all died through persecution in the years following the death of James. In AD 44 persecution under **Nero** was swift and massive. The blood of the martyrs stained the soil of the entire Roman Empire. We have no record of the final stages of Paul's trial in Rome, but we do know it ended in martyrdom in AD 67 or 68. Records indicate he died of decapitation.

Paul lived by the word that God wrote on his heart, and he died because of that word. He was free to live for God, and he was free to die for God. He had one motive: to glorify God.

what others say

Ambrosiaster

God makes Christians new people in every respect, so that here too he wants to take away from us the habits of anger which are common to everyone, so that instead of cursing others in anger, which we once did so easily, we might rather overcome our anger and bless them, so that the Lord's teaching might be praised.[14]

Be an All-Around Companion

ROMANS 12:15–16 *Rejoice with those who rejoice, and weep with those who weep. Be of the same mind toward one another.*

Do not set your mind on high things, but associate with the humble. Do not be wise in your own opinion. (NKJV)

To rejoice with those who are being blessed is easy if we too are being blessed. When someone is rejoicing while we are going through a tough time, it is much more difficult to rejoice. Yet, the mature Christian can and will respond to Paul's admonition.

The other side of this spiritual theorem is also a challenge: "Weep with those who weep" (Romans 12:15 NKJV). This is how Jesus loved. He did not run from people in grief. He wept with them. Think of Mary and Martha who were grieving over the loss of their dear brother, Lazarus. Jesus wept with them.

Jesus also associated with people of low position, as Paul encourages us to do. He called Matthew, for example, to be his disciple. Matthew was a tax collector, which in that culture meant that he was the lowest of the low, lower even than a prostitute. The reason for this was because as a tax collector, Matthew had turned on his own people (the Jews) to collect taxes for the Roman Empire and pocket some for himself. The Jews would have thought very little of Matthew, yet he became one of Jesus' biographers when he wrote the Book of Matthew.

All Together Now

This set of admonitions has that everyday kind of feeling about it. Living harmoniously with one another can be hard work; in fact, it usually is. It seems that our likes and dislikes are forever bumping into one another.

But the truth is, we need to seek to live in a way that our personality quirks and our personal oddities don't create tension and division in the fellowship. We should never seek to cause emotional trauma.

apply it

The word translated "of the same mind" (Romans 12:16 NKJV) is *phroneo*, and it means "to think, to be mindful of." It does away with unreasoned opinions. Leaders must treat opinions with grace, and at the same time test them against the facts and against the Word of God.

For the sake of godly harmony, if an opinion is not in accord with the truth, we need to disregard it, while seeking to walk with the one who espouses it.

Positive Charges for a Negative World

ROMANS 12:17 *Repay no one evil for evil. Have regard for good things in the sight of all men. (NKJV)*

In this group of charges, Paul gives explicit counsel on how to face hostility and indifference. His instruction stems from a lifetime of studying God's Word and experience on the mission field. Paul never talked nonsense.

When we meet Jesus and his grace brings us under the shelter of his love, that is only the beginning point. **Sanctification** takes a lifetime. We bring our bad habits, our lack of understanding, and our lack of control with us when we join the community called church.

Paul exhorts, "Repay no one evil for evil" (Romans 12:17 NKJV). This admonition is obviously on the mark, but most of us are not ready to obey it in those early years of our spiritual journey. The Holy Spirit has to burn it on our souls so that a right response will happen when we are touched by evil and want to get revenge.

The apostle takes us a step further when he says, "Have regard for good things in the sight of all men" (12:17 NKJV). Someone once asked me, "Does all men mean everybody? My wife? My neighbor? The guys I work with?"

I asked him what he thought. After a moment of silence, he responded, "It's not possible!"

I know only one person who has fulfilled this charge, and that is Jesus. But his fulfillment of this charge is sufficient, for Jesus gives us the wisdom, grace, and desire to seek this kind of righteousness.

what others say

Frederick L. Godet

He (Paul) returns to this subject to treat it more thoroughly; here is the culminating point in the manifestations of love. He has in view not merely the enmity of the unbelieving world. He knows only too well from experience, that within the church itself one may meet with ill-will, injustice, jealousy, hatred.[15]

Joseph Shulam

Paul develops the concept of non-retaliation (cf. verses 9ff) into the full-blown view that restraint and love for one's neighbor is not only proper behavior, but can also influence one's

The Smart Guide to the Bible

opponents towards better, more righteous behavior . . ."love your neighbor as yourself" in Leviticus 19:18, which was interpreted to mean that if you overwhelm the sinner by a human approach, you can make him better.[16]

go to

peace
Romans 5:1–2

Your Right to Revenge Has Been Revoked

ROMANS 12:18–21 *If it is possible, as much as depends on you, live peaceably with all men. Beloved, do not avenge yourselves, but rather give place to wrath; for it is written, "Vengeance is Mine, I will repay," says the Lord. Therefore*
"If your enemy is hungry, feed him;
If he is thirsty, give him a drink;
For in so doing you will heap coals of fire on his head."
Do not be overcome by evil, but overcome evil with good. (NKJV)

Paul knows what living in the world is like when he says, "If it is possible, as much as depends on you, live peaceably with all men" (Romans 12:18 NKJV). For peace to be a reality, all parties must want peace and seek it. We have watched the peace negotiations between Israel and Palestine over the past thirty years, and we have yet to see a real, lasting, secure peace. We don't have the power nor do we have divine permission to manipulate other people's motives or hearts. It took a divine work in our soul to bring us to the place where we have <u>peace</u> with God. We have to be patient while we wait for God to work in the hearts of others.

One of the great destroyers of the peace process at the human level is the spirit of revenge. Knowing this, the apostle concludes his instruction with a negative and a positive: (1) Don't take revenge, and (2) Be kind to your enemy.

key point

Paul says that by showing kindness to our enemies, we will heap burning coals on their heads. What does he mean? Larry Richards writes, "Most suggest kindness induces a stinging sense of remorse in those whose actions merit punishment. It may be that remorse will only be felt on judgment day and unrequited kindness shown to the wicked and rejected will be the cause of even more severe judgment."[17]

Only God is qualified to avenge our enemies, though our feelings say otherwise. The cross is how God handled revenge. He took on man's sin as the only way to destroy the need for revenge. In so doing, he demonstrated how to overcome evil with good. The cost was tremendous, but the results are stupendous.

Revenge is a doctrine in several world religions. They have a perverted view of God, according to this text. But Jesus is our Savior and our model of righteousness. In the resurrection he literally overcame evil with good. Revenge is a doctrine of Satan, and that is exactly why we feel so strongly tempted to make things right in whatever fashion we might choose.

what others say

James R. Edwards

God is not complacent in the face of evil, but his just wrath is of a wholly different character from human vengeance, which often and easily is fueled by self-interest, excess, and vindictiveness. The early church broke ground at this point, for in Judaism revenge was permissible against non-Israelites or in cases of personal injury. Paul categorically excludes revenge: Do not take revenge, my friends, but leave room for God's wrath (v. 29). "The anger of man does not work the righteousness of God" (James 1:20, RSV).[18]

Martin Luther

Do not be overcome by evil. That is, see to it that he who hurts you does not cause you to become evil like him and that his iniquity does not overcome your goodness. For he is the victor who changes another man to become like himself while he himself remains unchanged. But rather by your well-doing make him to become like you. Let your goodness overcome his wickedness and change him into you.[19]

Saint Augustine

The evil man who is overcome by good is set free, not from an exterior, foreign evil but from an interior, personal one, by which he is more grievously and ruinously laid waste than he would be by the inhumanity of an enemy from without.[20]

Chapter Wrap-Up

- God does not want animal sacrifices under the New Covenant. He wants us to be living sacrifices by following him daily. (Romans 12:1)

- Sin has marred our thoughts so we need to renew our minds in order to live transformed lives. (Romans 12:2)

- Humility is a character trait that both Jesus and Paul stress as essential if our service is to be useful to God. (Romans 12:3)

- Gifts are an important part of God's plan to reach the world in Jesus' name. Paul lists seven essential gifts in the building of the church as a community. (Romans 12:4–8)

- Love must be sincere. God's love enables believers to walk in a world full of sinful people. We must not be overcome with evil. We must contend for the faith in such a manner that our opponents will have to respect our way of living and being. (Romans 12:9–21)

Study Questions

1. How is offering our bodies as living sacrifices an act of worship?

2. We are to be transformed by the renewal of our minds. How do the mind and the Spirit interact?

3. What is the meaning of Paul's statement in Romans 12:3 that no one should "think of himself more highly than he ought to think" (NKJV)?

4. Paul lists seven key gifts that have been graciously given. What is the purpose of these gifts?

5. A key principle in this chapter is "Let love be without hypocrisy" (Romans 12:9 NKJV). How might you check the sincerity of your love for God and for your fellow man?

Romans 13 God and Country

Let's Get Started

The situation between the church and the government was tense in Paul's day. How could the Roman Christians entrust themselves and their families to a government that persecuted them and denied them civil rights, and later had them executed simply for their allegiance to Jesus Christ? How could this government be **ordained** by God?

ordained
established

Nevertheless, the church leaders consistently upheld the New Covenant teaching that civil authorities were ordained by God and had every right to exercise restraint on a person's body but not the soul.

Christians were to obey the law of the land, respect the civil authorities, and pay their taxes whether they agreed with the authorities or not. If secular rulers violated their own authority, it was the duty of Christians to testify to the truth, but only by using peaceful means.

Undergirding the New Covenant teaching is the knowledge that God is in control and that we should respect the government whether we like it or not. In Proverbs 8:15–16 God says, "By me kings reign, and rulers decree justice. By me princes rule, and nobles, all the judges of the earth" (NKJV). God is the final authority regardless of who sits in the authority seat on earth.

President of the Universe

ROMANS 13:1 *Let every soul be subject to the governing authorities. For there is no authority except from God, and the authorities that exist are appointed by God. (NKJV)*

Paul talked a lot about how to be righteous before God in Romans 1–12 and about how to live out that righteousness in different areas of one's life on earth. The believer's relationship to the government, or state, is one of those areas. In chapter 13 Paul talks about how Christians should conduct themselves in relation to a government that often contradicts God's nature and values. God doesn't want the rotten barrel to spoil the good apples, but his preservation plan is not what we might expect.

We must remember the historical context of the Roman people. Jews had been kicked out of Rome by Claudius and had only recently been allowed to reenter when Paul wrote his letter. The Jewish Christians who returned might very well have felt hostility for the Roman government because of the way they had been treated previously.

key point

Paul's words are unswerving. Those in authority are under God's sovereign control, whether they realize it or not. God gives the authorities that exist, Christian or non-Christian, permission to rule. There is no authority, regardless of how it seems, except that which God has established. All government authorities are established by God.

In God We Trust

Paul's admonition in Romans 13 has puzzled many and caused concern among some biblical scholars. Some have suggested that we eliminate these verses from Paul's letter. Such scholars think these verses were interpolated because there is nothing quite like this teaching anywhere else in Paul's writings.

But let's go back to the starting point of Paul's argument. First, note that it states, categorically, "Let every soul be subject" (13:1 NKJV). It is not only the Christian community, but the entire society. This is a universal law in every nation, among all people, everywhere!

Why such a dogmatic stand? Paul understood history, he understood the heart of man; it is not simply that society would get into trouble (and it would), but he answers his own rhetorical question— we must obey because "there is no authority except from God" (verse 2 NKJV). In other words, the authorities that exist, great and small, do so because God—we must listen carefully—God is the One who has established all authority, in heaven and upon earth.

So with Paul, we must take God's sovereignty authority and will seriously. Paul's argument, it seems to me, is the doctrine and teaching of the sovereignty of God, that's Paul starting point. If we miss this great truth, a cloud comes over the entire chapter. You ask, what about evil rulers such as Stalin, Hitler, and Osama bin Laden and his late emir Abu Musab Zarqawi in present-day Iraq? Men who show no impression of guilt or shame as they murder and maim and disfigure their fellow man? The answer is found in the sovereign hand of God. They will face the Judge one day, and that day is never far away for any of us.

God confronts the world with evil to bring us to that place where the word of truth, "Do you want to be unafraid of the authority?" (verse 3 NKJV), brings all mankind to our knees. Rebellion against authority is in some way in the hearts of all people. So Paul makes it very clear: "Therefore whoever resists the authority resists the ordinance of God, and those who resist will bring judgment on themselves" (verse 2 NKJV).

This is a universal precept with the apostle Paul.

The writer of Psalms struggled with submitting to the government because it was doing wrong. Examining what the psalmist said helps us to gain a biblical perspective about civil submission. The psalmist prayed, "The kings of the earth set themselves, and the rulers take counsel together, against the LORD and against His Anointed [Christ]" (2:2 NKJV). Then the psalmist heard God's answer: "He who sits in the heavens shall laugh; the LORD shall hold them in derision" (2:4 NKJV). The psalmist understood that God had nothing to fear from earthly government. He laughed at their puny attempts to fight against him. We need to realize the same thing. No matter how bad our governments are, no matter how much they go against God, God is not afraid of them. He will have the final word.

what others say

F. F. Bruce

Generally speaking, to subject oneself to the civil authorities is but an indirect way of obeying God Himself. At bottom the issue is in a sense not "either God or state" nor "both God and state" but "God via the state." . . . In that respect the Christian should instinctively view the government not as an enemy but as an ally and helper towards his own moral endeavours. In fact the civil power is God's servant, doing God's work positively and negatively by encouraging virtue and discouraging vice.[1]

Everyone Means EVERYone

To understand Paul's sternness when he says, "Let every soul be subject to the governing authorities" (Romans 13:1 NKJV), we can go to the Greek *pasa psucha*, which is best translated "every soul." Paul was referring to each and every individual on earth.

Paul is explaining a spiritual law that we are all subject to in principle just as we are to the Ten Commandments. There is no authority except those that God ordains, so to oppose a government when its laws are not in contradiction with God's law is equivalent to opposing God himself.

Rebel with a Cause

ROMANS 13:2–3 *Therefore whoever resists the authority resists the ordinance of God, and those who resist will bring judgment on themselves. For rulers are not a terror to good works, but to evil. Do you want to be unafraid of the authority? Do what is good, and you will have praise from the same.* (NKJV)

What about Christians who rebel against the authority? We are in the world to shine as <u>lights</u>. When we disobey the rules of our society, we are punished. That too is God's sovereign will! Our freedom in Christ does not free us from society's laws and if we break them, from traffic tickets to prison, we will feel the consequences.

In a democracy or a republic we have certain power through the ballot box, but once the ballot is cast and the tally is in, we still must live under the appointed authorities.

The apostle follows up his teaching on rejecting authority with a forthright statement: "Do you want to be unafraid of the authority? Do what is good, and you will have praise from the same" (Romans 13:3 NKJV). He means, for example, "Do you wish not to worry when you see a policeman in an unmarked car? Well, drive the speed limit, stop at all the stop signs, and you won't have to be afraid of getting a ticket. You might even receive a compliment for good driving."

To Obey or Not to Obey

There are two ways that a person upholds the law. One way is by obeying it. The other way is to disobey the law when it is unjust, but to accept the consequences. In both ways a person upholds the law.

Whenever we have to decide whether or not to obey a law of man that contradicts a law of God, we must have faith. It is our duty to speak out against injustices done by our government and our bosses, but we will likely face consequences.

Sadducee
first-century liberal, religious, political party

Zealot
first-century religious, political party that called for armed rebellion against Rome

Pharisee
first-century religious, political party that called for strict observance of OT law

what others say

Pelagius

The ruler is set up by God to judge with righteousness, so that sinners might have reason to be afraid should they sin.[4]

James R. Edwards

Paul thus approached the relation of church and state not as a **Sadducee** who lived from the advantages of the state, nor as a **Zealot** who lived to overthrow the state, nor as a **Pharisee** who divorced religion from the state, nor as a Roman citizen for whom the state was an end in itself. Paul wrote as a free man in Christ, and he appeals to the church to be equally free in obedience to the state, but not conformed to it.[5]

John Calvin

"Render then to all what is due" . . . Now this passage confirms what I have already said—that we ought to obey kings

anarchy
complete absence
of government

and governors, whoever they may be, not because we are constrained, but because it is a service acceptable to God; for he will have them not only to be feared, but also honoured by a voluntary respect.[6]

Good Government

ROMANS 13:4A *For he is God's minister to you for good.* (NKJV)

Paul says the function of government is to be God's agent for good in that government provides a rule of law that guards against **anarchy** and the excesses associated with it. Even bad governments protect its citizens to some extent from injustices like murder and robbery. Even bad governments provide roads and streetlights.

By implication Paul is saying that if a government is truly evil, it is bound to fall. If a government fails to maintain order and respect its citizens to the extent that uncontainable masses of people turn against that government, the only possible outcome is that the government will fall. The government is an agent for good.

Two examples of governments that fell are that of German leader Adolf Hitler and Iraqi dictator Saddam Hussein. Hitler's government fell because of external pressure, while Pinochet's government caved in on itself because of internal pressure. Both governments were too evil to sustain themselves.

Count on Consequences

ROMANS 13:4B–6 *But if you do evil, be afraid; for he does not bear the sword in vain; for he is God's minister, an avenger to execute wrath on him who practices evil. Therefore you must be subject, not only because of wrath but also for conscience' sake. For because of this you also pay taxes, for they are God's ministers attending continually to this very thing.* (NKJV)

When Paul says the government "bear[s] the sword" (Romans 13:4 NKJV), what he means is that the government has the power to coerce people to do things. Governments coerce behavior in many different ways, from creating laws to imposing taxes to using police force.

Paul is addressing the moral consequences that are linked with the issue of authority. He gives two reasons why we should obey author-

insurrection
rebellion against
established authority

unequivocally
without doubt

ity: to avoid punishment and because our conscience demands it.

The responsibilities associated with authority move in both directions, from subjects to their authorities and from authorities to their subjects. In a family children are under the authority of their parents from day one, but parents are ultimately subject to the Lord's authority. Paul told parents in his letter to the Ephesians, "Fathers, do not provoke your children to wrath, but bring them up in the training and admonition of the Lord" (6:4 NKJV).

In the business world owners have the responsibility of overseeing the work of employees, to treat them with respect, to create safe working conditions, and to pay them fairly for their service. On the other hand the employees are responsible to God to give a day's working for a day's pay.

In the political realm those who are appointed or elected into office are to be genuinely concerned with the lives of the people they are called to serve, showing compassion and acting in good faith. Those of us who live under their authority are to show respect and honor, even when we disagree with a particular political philosophy. Paul points out that we should pay our taxes.

Did Jesus Pay His Taxes?

Jesus showed respect for the government of his day when he answered the question, "Is it lawful to pay taxes to Caesar, or not?" (Matthew 22:17 NKJV). Jesus knew his questioners were trying to trick him and charge him with **insurrection** so he asked to see one of the coins used to pay taxes. There was an inscription of Caesar on the coin (see Illustration #8). Jesus said to his questioners, "Render therefore to Caesar the things that are Caesar's, and to God the things that are God's" (Matthew 22:21 NKJV). Jesus' submission to civil authorities, concerning money or death on a cross, was perfect.

what others say

Ravi Zacharias

How do you come to terms with what the human nature essentially is? Jesus taught **unequivocally** that the self-will within each life, which seeks absolute autonomy and bends to no higher law than one of its own, is in rebellion of the highest order, inevitably descending to the lowest level of indignity and indecency. No good can come if the will is wrong. as

doctrinaire
person who tries to put abstract theory into effect without regard for practical problems

impediment
hindrance, road-block

This teaching of Jesus is often dismissed as **doctrinaire** and as an **impediment** to human creativity. Yet in the proverbial wisdom of every culture it is sustained and proven again and again.[7]

Billy Graham

Every Christian in every nation—totalitarian, democratic, or somewhere in between—decides daily to be loyal to Christ and the kingdom He is building or to give in to this age and its values.[8]

Won't You Be My Neighbor?

ROMANS 13:7–10 *Render therefore to all their due: taxes to whom taxes are due, customs to whom customs, fear to whom fear, honor to whom honor. Owe no one anything except to love one another, for he who loves another has fulfilled the law. For the commandments, "You shall not commit adultery," "You shall not murder," "You shall not steal," "You shall not bear false witness," "You shall not covet," and if there is any other commandment, are all summed up in this saying, namely, "You shall love your neighbor as yourself." Love does no harm to a neighbor; therefore love is the fulfillment of the law.* (NKJV)

Thus far, Paul's main admonition is, "Render therefore to all their due." Owe nothing to anyone. Make sure you meet all your obligations. The only exception is our debt of love that we owe one another. We are never paid up on our debt of love. Every day we go deeper and deeper in debt on that account.

Paul says, "He who loves another has fulfilled the law" (Romans 13:8 NKJV). In other words, by loving we fulfill "the righteous requirement of the law" (Romans 8:4 NKJV). We do this not by striving after the law but by doing what the Holy Spirit prompts us to do.

Paul sums up all of the commandments that are about relating to others with one principle: "Love your neighbor as yourself" (Romans 13:9 NKJV). The Greek for "neighbor" here is derived from "one who is near." In other words, we should not decide who our neighbor is on the basis of race, socioeconomic status, or political affiliation. Our neighbors are those who are near to us—our families, our friends, people at church, our coworkers, the person who rings up our groceries, and the people who live with us in our city or town.

key point

"Render therefore to all their due" is a universal spiritual law. As Christians, it's our duty to do this. Paul isn't just talking about books or money you borrowed and forgot to return or repay, although these are important. We owe more than just money and things. It is our debt to bring Christ to the world. It is our debt to be loving to our neighbors.

Sometimes we may be unaware of our debts to others. Ask God to reveal to you what you owe and to whom. When he does, waste no time in reconciling those debts. No matter what kind of debt is in question, the best thing a debtor can do is repay the debt as soon as possible.

When we are told to love our neighbor as ourselves, we discover the burden of God's heart. He is asking us to do as he is doing. The debt of love is unqualified, and it grants no exceptions. The Greek word for love in this context is *agape*. This isn't an abstract concept. Agape love seeks out people who are ready to receive love. Just as God searches for and finds us so that he may show love to us, we are to do the same with people around us.

Real love rarely happens without conscious effort. Ask yourself how you might show love to those around you. An unexpected card or gift can work wonders. Maybe you need to sit down and have a long talk with someone you've been in conflict with. Think carefully how those around you would best feel loved by you, and then take action. Those who actively love often receive far more than what they give.

what others say

Origen

In many cases debt is equivalent to sin. Paul therefore wants us to owe nothing on account of sin and to steer clear of debts of this kind, retaining only the debt which springs from love, which we ought to be repaying every day.[9]

Saint Augustine

This law [love your neighbor as yourself] is not written on tables of stone but is shed abroad in our hearts through the Holy Spirit who is given to us.[10]

W. Burrows

Christians are not to neglect the laws of social life, or overlook the fact that distinction of rank is highly necessary for the

nearer
1 Corinthians
7:29–31;
1 Peter 4:7–10;
1 John 2:18

final judgment
Revelation 20:11–15

salvation
total deliverance
when Jesus returns

final judgment
last reward, or
punishment, at
history's end

> economy and safety of the world . . . Love will not permit us to injure, oppress, or offend our brother; it will not give us leave to neglect our betters or despise our inferiors. It will restrain every inordinate passion, and not suffer us to gratify our envy at the expense of our neighbour's credit and reputation; but it will preserve us harmless and innocent.[11]

Wake Up and Smell the Coffee

ROMANS 13:11 *And do this, knowing the time, that now it is high time to awake out of sleep; for now our **salvation** is nearer than when we first believed. (NKJV)*

Paul tells the Roman Christians to love while on earth but to do so with the knowledge that the fulfillment of their salvation is always drawing closer. Christ was not afraid to touch lepers and dead people. His love within us compels us closer to people who do not know him. But as Christ's focus on following his Father put him at a distance from the degenerate world, so should our hope in God's promises keep us far from the temporary and self-destructive pleasures of the world.

Paul says the reason we need to be awake is because "our salvation is <u>nearer</u> than when we first believed" (Romans 13:11 NKJV). Salvation is pictured a number of ways in Scripture: (1) Salvation is that moment we are saved, when Jesus becomes our Savior and Lord, (2) salvation is progressively unfolding in our lives as we become more like Christ, and (3) salvation sometimes refers to the **final judgment** when there will be complete deliverance from all that pollutes and condemns.

Paul is saying be aware of who you are and what your mission is. Are you living a fruitful life while you're waiting for that heavenly moment? The apostle wants to make certain God's people are not lulled to sleep by the sweet talk of the world. None of us knows when our call home will come, but we do know the call will come. Paul is saying, "Be ready!"

While Paul is speaking to a particular people—the church in Rome—he's presenting a universal subject, a message for the whole church. When he says, "knowing the time" (Romans 13:11 NKJV), he isn't referring to clock time, but to the interval between Christ's first and second comings. When Paul calls the church to "awake out of sleep" (13:11 NKJV), he's asserting what must be our constant attitude if we are concerned about a faithful walk with God. We must stay alert and not be lured away from God by the petty indulgences of this world.

go to

stay alert
Ephesians 5:14

Move Over, Armani

> ROMANS 13:12–14 *The night is far spent, the day is at hand. Therefore let us cast off the works of darkness, and let us put on the armor of light. Let us walk properly, as in the day, not in revelry and drunkenness, not in lewdness and lust, not in strife and envy. But put on the Lord Jesus Christ, and make no provision for the flesh, to fulfill its lusts.* (NKJV)

Paul continues to expand his closing exhortation by using images of slumber and night. Both night and slumber are times when the mind becomes less active and we feel our weaknesses—tiredness, fatigue, fearfulness, weariness, dullness, indifference. We want to be left alone.

This imagery suggests vulnerability or evil, as in the time just before the Flood. Jesus comments on this event saying, "As the days of Noah were, so also will the coming of the Son of Man be. For as in the days before the flood, they were eating and drinking, marrying and giving in marriage, until the day that Noah entered the ark" (Matthew 24:37–38 NKJV). The picture is one of people who are focused not on eternal matters but on matters of this world. Paul wants us to have eyes to see what is important for eternity.

God calls us to put away our nighttime clothing, to wear clothing fit for the day. Our behavior is to be appropriate to our calling. Listen carefully to God's call: "Let us cast off the works of darkness, and let us put on the armor of light. Let us walk properly, as in the day, not in revelry and drunkenness, not in lewdness and lust, not in strife and envy" (Romans 13:12–13 NKJV). This sounds like downtown San Francisco, Chicago, L.A., or any other metropolis around the world. Orgies, drugs, drunkenness, and debauchery were the scene in Paul's day, and they're the scene in our day too. Humanity hasn't improved, culture hasn't made things better, and the twenty-first century will surely repeat the errors and sins of the twenty centuries preceding it.

apply it

Paul's solution is for people to "put on the armor of light" (Romans 13:12 NKJV). This armor is an interior armor. He tells the church in Ephesus to "take up the whole armor of God, that you may be able to withstand in the evil day, and having done all, to stand" (Ephesians 6:13 NKJV). Light is a powerful metaphor throughout Scripture. Light scatters darkness. Light makes God's path visible. To put on the "armor of light" is to put on Jesus Christ. Christians are to be alert, dressed in spiritual armor, and ready to fight the powers of darkness.

Instead of participating in the **debauchery** of this sick world, Paul says to "put on the Lord Jesus Christ, and make no provision for the flesh, to fulfill its lusts" (Romans 13:14 NKJV). By the grace of God we can do this. Christ works in the hearts of believers, scattering our darkness, healing our woundedness, putting up barricades against the evil one, inspiring the use of our gifts, strengthening our weak limbs, and preparing us for the battle on today's front, as well as for our journey home.

If our relationship with Jesus is truly honest, it will have the edge of adventure that keeps the mind directed toward righteousness and away from the lust of the flesh.

---

what others say

John Calvin

Now to put on Christ, means here to be on every side fortified by the power of his Spirit, and be thereby prepared to discharge all the duties of holiness; for this is the image of God renewed in us, which is the only true ornament of the soul.[12]

Robert Benson

The culture we live in teaches us to get what we can, outsmart the other guy, vote for the folks who will protect our interests, buy everything that is not nailed down, and rent a storage facility if you cannot hold it all in the house you can barely afford. The **Teacher** calls us to give ourselves away, to stop worrying about tomorrow, to do good to the ones that hate us, to seek only the kingdom.[13]

Saint Augustine

Provision for the flesh is not to be condemned if it has to do with the needs of bodily health. But if it is a question of unnecessary delights or luxuries, a person who enjoys the delights of the flesh is rightly chastised. For in that case he makes provision for the desires of the flesh, and he who sows in the flesh will reap corruption in the flesh.[14]

Chapter Wrap-Up

- It is sin if a believer fails to submit to the governing authorities. God has established the need and the rule of authority. (Romans 13:1)

- Fear of authority is unnecessary. If we do what is right, the authority will do right by us. God is the author of all authority and will be with us when we are tested. (Romans 13:2–7)

- God wants us to extend love to one another, giving witness to the love and grace of God, which makes salvation possible. (Romans 13:8–14)

Study Questions

1. Is submission to governing authorities necessary for everyone or just for some?

2. Identify five areas of your life in which you live under authority.

3. How can we free ourselves from the fear of those in authority?

4. How does conscience work against or with authority?

5. According to Paul's analysis, why do we pay taxes?

6. We are to leave no debt outstanding except the debt of love. What is the debt of love?

7. How does one put aside the deeds of darkness?

Romans 14 Keeping Peace

Chapter Highlights:
- Disputable Matters
- Live for God
- Strong and Weak
- You Are What You Eat
- Our First Loyalty

Let's Get Started

Have you ever argued with fellow Christians about the right way to baptize people or about whether or not it's okay for Christians to smoke or drink alcohol? These and other issues have traditionally been referred to as doubtful things about which Christians disagree because Scripture does not speak decisively about them. Issues like adultery and theft are not doubtful things, of course, because Scripture is clear about such matters.

The doubtful things to which people pay attention may change throughout history, but the existence of doubtful things is nothing new. In chapter 14 Paul begins a discussion about the doubtful things of his own day. We do not know how much Paul knew about the inner workings of the Roman church so it is difficult to tell whether he is responding to information he had somehow gathered from the Roman church or if he is merely addressing issues that were what he considered generally important at the time. Regardless, Paul obviously thought the issues found in Romans 14 were worth discussion.

receive
Romans 15:7

unclean
animals, which, according to Mosaic law, were unfit to eat

Catch the Little Foxes

> **ROMANS 14:1** *Receive one who is weak in the faith, but not to disputes over doubtful things. (NKJV)*

The person of weak faith in Paul's day was the person who thought that some foods were **unclean**. The weak believed, for example, it was wrong to eat meat that had been offered to idols. Paul says, "Receive one who is weak" (Romans 14:1 NKJV). To "receive" in Greek literally means, "keep on taking to yourselves." We are responsible for maintaining fellowship with those who are weak of faith. Ungracious handling of disputable matters creates stress and disintegration in Christian communities.

Wise Solomon wrote, "Catch us the foxes, the little foxes that spoil the vines, for our vines have tender grapes" (Song of Solomon 2:15

go to

eat kosher
Exodus 23:19;
34:26;
Leviticus 17

eat kosher
follow strict dietary
rules, including not
mixing meat and
dairy items

NKJV). It was the little things, such as what one ate and how one observed special religious days, that created tension in the Body of Christ. Little things are the little foxes that keep the vineyard from bearing fruit for God's glory. These matters create much negative, useless discussion that causes division and grief.

"Receive one who is weak in the faith, but not to disputes over doubtful things" is Paul's admonition to this body of believers. Charles Hodge writes: "This verse contains the general direction that weak and scrupulous brethren are to be kindly received, and not harshly condemned."[1] Hodge also suggests that *faith* in this context means "persuasion of the truth." This particular weakness is not inconsistent with an earnest commitment to Jesus Christ—it's simply a doubtful thing.

In God's Kingdom, We're All the Same Height

ROMANS 14:2–3 *For one believes he may eat all things, but he who is weak eats only vegetables. Let not him who eats despise him who does not eat, and let not him who does not eat judge him who eats; for God has received him. (NKJV)*

We don't know all the details of the dispute, but Paul does give us enough of them to speculate. The believers in Rome may have been arguing about whether or not it was okay to eat meat that had been offered to idols. If believers thought eating such meat was wrong and could not be certain that the meat sold at market had not been offered to idols, they may have become vegetarians. Jewish believers may have been concerned about whether or not they should continue to **eat kosher** foods. The Gentile believers may have believed Christians should live an ascetic lifestyle, becoming vegetarians and drinking only water. Paul commands each individual to follow his or her own conscience.

Mind Your Master

ROMANS 14:4 *Who are you to judge another's servant? To his own master he stands or falls. Indeed, he will be made to stand, for God is able to make him stand. (NKJV)*

It's easy to judge others and look down on them as having weak faith. But Paul says, "Give it up! Let God be the judge. It's not your job to judge others. God has already accepted those people." When it comes to disputable matters, each individual is to be responsible to God, not to pastors, not to the pope, not to elders, not to boards, not to the general feeling of a congregation, not to anyone but God.

By careful control of our <u>thoughts</u>, we can help build a fellowship where judgment on "disputable matters" is under the control of the Holy Spirit. He gives us the grace necessary to nurture each other despite our differences.

Believers are at different levels of spiritual maturity. We come from diverse backgrounds that affect our attitudes and behaviors. One of the first lessons we need to learn in order to live harmoniously is to stop judging each other.

The Jews were used to following certain dietary laws of the Old Covenant that were no longer necessary when Christ came because Christ was the fulfillment of the law. The Jewish Christians had a difficult time making this transition, and the Gentiles needed to be sensitive.

Neither the one "who is weak in the faith" (Romans 14:1 NKJV) nor the one who eats "all things" (14:2 NKJV) is free to condemn the other. Here is where Paul pulls the rug out from under both parties. God accepts both as long as neither passes judgment on the other.

Paul asks the Roman believers, "Who are you to **judge** another's servant?" (14:4 NKJV). We all agree that it's silly for someone to give orders to another person's servant or household worker. And that's the point Paul is making. We are all servants of God and only God. He's our boss. When we try to tell others how to act in disputable matters, we are wrong. To act as a judge when it comes to disputable matters is to perform duties that belong to God alone. To do so is arrogant and sinful.

thoughts
2 Corinthians 10:5;
1 Corinthians
10:23–24

judge
condemn

Follow the Leader

> ROMANS 14:5–8 *One person esteems one day above another; another esteems every day alike. Let each be fully convinced in his own mind. He who observes the day, observes it to the Lord; and he who does not observe the day, to the Lord he does not observe it. He who eats, eats to the Lord, for he gives God thanks; and he who does not eat, to the Lord he does not eat, and gives God thanks. For none of us lives to himself, and no one dies to himself. For if we live, we live to the Lord; and if we die, we die to the Lord. Therefore, whether we live or die, we are the Lord's.* (NKJV)

Paul continues to explain how people of differing opinions or preferences can still live in harmony with one another. Paul knows how important it is to have harmonious relationships within the family of God. He knows that disunity is the surest way to destroy the work of God. Paul addresses sacred days and eating meat, the subjects that were important to his readers. He urges each person to seek God's will earnestly for himself or herself.

key point

He tells them to learn to live with whatever they are fully convinced is true, but not to be the judge of those who disagree. God's grace freed Paul to accept the differences of fellow believers without doing violence to the Word of God. This was a lesson that both Jew and Gentile had to learn if harmony was to exist between them.

To the Colossian church Paul wrote, "So let no one judge you in food or in drink, or regarding a festival or a new moon or sabbaths, which are a shadow of things to come, but the substance is of Christ" (Colossians 2:16–17 NKJV). Here again we find Paul pointing to Christ, whose coming caused a shift from Old Covenant thinking to New Covenant thinking. If the Roman Christians were successful at making that shift, the result would be the apprehension of true righteousness and the defeat of worthless legalism.

When you are convinced that your own position on any given disputable matter is not in contradiction to the will of God, you are free to live out your faith, but this freedom is not without obligation.

As we grow in grace and in the knowledge of Christ, we will discover from time to time that we need to reevaluate our position. We need to be humble when such times come because we serve one who is infinite in love, knowledge, wisdom, and holiness. He demands growth.

judge
James 4:11–12

what others say

William S. Plumer

We belong to God, our life and our death are ordered by him; we are accountable to him for the use we make of our liberty, in things uncommanded; and if we make a right use of that liberty, we do glorify God living or dying, and are the property of the Lord, not of one another.[4]

Peter Stuhlmacher

The mutual acceptance which Paul here commends thus has its model in Jesus' own conduct toward sinners . . . but the strong, who eat everything, as well as the weak, who renounce the consumption of meat, should both abstain from reacting toward one another with disdain or condemnation.[5]

Who Are You to Judge?

ROMANS 14:9–12 *For to this end Christ died and rose and lived again, that He might be Lord of both the dead and the living. But why do you judge your brother? Or why do you show contempt for your brother? For we shall all stand before the judgment seat of Christ. For it is written:*
"As I live, says the LORD,
Every knee shall bow to Me,
And every tongue shall confess to God."
So then each of us shall give account of himself to God. (NKJV)

Paul is still concerned with the spirit of judgment that exists in the assembly and continues to discuss it with them. He has let them know that both groups will answer to God in the coming day.

There is a huge difference between discerning what is right and wrong for oneself and imposing those standards on others. It is Christ's responsibility to be our judge. The Lord's death and resurrection makes him both the Lord of the dead and of the living. His qualifications are impeccable and eternal. Christ is God's measuring rod. Paul says to all Christians: How do you measure up? Are you really qualified to be a judge?

Christ is the only person qualified to determine who is right and who is wrong in disputable matters. This is why Paul told the folks in Corinth, "Therefore judge nothing before the time, until the Lord comes, who will both bring to light the hidden things of darkness and reveal the counsels of the hearts. Then each one's praise will come from God" (1 Corinthians 4:5 NKJV). Instead of using our ability to discern right from wrong on others, we should use it on ourselves, remembering that there will come a day when God will judge us.

apply it

We all need daily cleansing from the bad habit of judgmentalism, which surfaces in gossip, in harsh language, in disrespect, and in convenient hearsay. Paul concludes this passage, "So then each of us shall give account of himself to God" (Romans 14:12 NKJV). Let us become accountable now, so on the judgment day we can give glory to God.

In becoming more accountable to him, God makes gracious provision for the changing of our hearts and minds. Here are some tips to keep you accountable:

1. Place yourself under the leadership of godly leaders who will disciple you.

2. Develop a relationship with two or three people who will hold you accountable. These are friends that walk with the Lord and keep **close accounts**.

3. Get into the habit of Bible reading; listen to the voice of the Holy Spirit.

4. Pray for ways to share your faith in Christ; stay humble and real.

5. Develop a regular habit of worship and praise where the Word is taught.

6. As you get your footing, reach out to others and build relationships.

John Chrysostom

It is not the law which will demand an account from us but Christ. You see how Paul has released us from the fear of the law.[6]

Charles R. Swindoll

What a wonderful future [and present] God has for people who accept grace. It is almost too good to be true. When George MacDonald, the great Scottish preacher, was talking with his son about the glories of the future, his little boy interrupted and said, "It seems too good to be true, Daddy." . . ."Nay, laddy, it is just so good it must be true!"[7]

You Are What You Eat

ROMANS 14:13–14 *Therefore let us not judge one another anymore, but rather resolve this, not to put a stumbling block or a cause to fall in our brother's way. I know and am convinced by the Lord Jesus that there is nothing unclean of itself; but to him who considers anything to be unclean, to him it is unclean.* (NKJV)

Paul uses the better part of what remains in this chapter to address the "strong" Christians—the Christians of Paul's time who believed no food was unclean. Paul is candid about his own position concerning the food issue. As a Jew, he confesses that he sees no food as unclean. This places Paul among the "strong" believers, but the possible division that could result over food is far more important to Paul than bringing everyone around to his own way of thinking.

The question Christians need to ask is not, "Do I have freedom to do this?" but "If I do this, will I offend another brother or sister?"

Paul Roots for Reconciliation

Paul is determined to bring this clash between believers to a godly conclusion. There were two issues to confront:

1. They disagreed about what to eat.

2. They were passing judgment on one another.

Paul reasons with his readers. He exhorts them to think of each other.

The best solution was for both parties to lay down their swords and continue toward an enlightened dialogue. Sword wielding, if it continued, could lead to deeply felt divisions that lasted for years, if not forever.

Too often believers are driven by emotions rather than logic. In this case the emotions of Paul's readers were likely blocking the way to a real solution. Paul had to address their situation like a referee breaking up a hockey fight.

Paul was able to see the Romans' situation from at least three different angles.

1. He saw the difficulty the Jews were going through because he was a Jew himself and had for most of his life lived by the laws of the Old Covenant.

2. He saw the Gentiles' temptation to look down on the Jews because he shared their belief that no food was unclean.

3. He saw the situation from a Christ-like perspective because Paul's first loyalty was to God and God's kingdom.

what others say

Stanley K. Stowers

The weak hold to false beliefs about things like food and special days that they would use as criteria for not accepting others in the community who act more in line with the boldness and freedom of Jesus' faithfulness. The strong are inclined to accept the weak only in order to attack their superstitious beliefs with rational arguments, acting like philosophers subjecting the foolish to therapy of the passions of reason.[8]

Food Isn't Worth It

ROMANS 14:15 *Yet if your brother is grieved because of your food, you are no longer walking in love. Do not destroy with your food the one for whom Christ died. (NKJV)*

Paul tells the strong believers to forgo their freedom in front of weak believers. Selfish insistence on freedom can destroy the spiritual development of others, and obviously the spiritual development of fellow Christians is more important than our own exercise of certain freedoms. Paul points out that the principle to follow is the principle of love. Let love make your decision about whether or not to eat meat or observe holy days. Let love guide your relationships with other Christians.

In his second letter to the Corinthian church, Paul clearly speaks to this matter. He says God "made us sufficient as ministers of the new covenant, not of the letter but of the Spirit; for the letter kills, but the Spirit gives life" (2 Corinthians 3:6 NKJV). Arguments over disputable matters are hopelessly rooted in a strict adherence to the letter of the law, either an old law that tells people things like, "Don't eat these foods," or an invented law that tells people things like, "Because we are free to eat all foods, that freedom must never be sacrificed even if it brings ruin to the spiritual growth of a fellow Christian." Following the letter of a law, whether it be a new law or an invented one, ultimately brings death.

what others say

F. F. Bruce

Love takes precedence over knowledge. If the "strong" do not care about the sensitivities of the "weak" but openly fly in the face of them, what will the result be? Will the "weak" be distressed, ruined, for example by their being led to act against their consciences? Will they be put off and made to backslide as a result of the example of the "strong," which to them is sin? If so, the overall loss is surely far, far greater than the net gain.[9]

Peter Stuhlmacher

The freedom of the strong to eat whatever they want can confuse the weak concerning faith in Christ, and this is precisely what ought not to happen in the body of Christ. In order not to offend one's (weak) fellow believers, it is imperative to renounce meat, wine (which has been dedicated to foreign gods . . .) and every other form of nourishment which to the weak can become a hindrance to their faith.[10]

Karl Barth

No triumphant freedom of conscience, no triumphant faith to eat all things justifies me, if, at the moment of my triumph, I have seated myself on the throne of God and am myself preparing stumbling blocks and occasions of falling instead of making room for God's action.[11]

From Good to Bad

> ROMANS 14:16 *Therefore do not let your good be spoken of as evil;* (NKJV)

The "good" (Romans 14:16 NKJV) spoken of here is the liberty to eat. Persisting in the exercise of one's freedom at the expense of the spiritual formation of others can result in our Christian freedom being "spoken of as evil" (14:16 NKJV). The word *evil* the apostle Paul uses is *blasphemeistho*, meaning "to blaspheme, to defame, to slander." This is one of the most serious charges in the New Testament.

If we allow that which we know to be good to be blasphemed because of our own stubborn hearts, we have committed a serious evil against God and one another.

key point

Keep First Things First

> ROMANS 14:17–18 *for the kingdom of God is not eating and drinking, but righteousness and peace and joy in the Holy Spirit. For he who serves Christ in these things is acceptable to God and approved by men.* (NKJV)

The argument about what foods were appropriate and what days were more holy had become an obsession with destructive overtones. Paul brings the discussion to a higher level here. He's taking the focus off externals and zeroing in on what really matters in the kingdom of God.

"Righteousness and peace and joy" (Romans 14:17 NKJV) characterize the lives of those in whom Christ reigns. The Holy Spirit is always with believers, teaching them righteousness. The result is peace and joy, both of which are fruits of the Spirit.

The apostle directs them to higher and deeper levels of thought. Paul graciously reminds them of their kingdom and of what should be important to them.

what others say

James R. Edwards

The reduction of the "kingdom of God" to "eating and drinking" is like playing a Mozart piano concerto with one finger. The reign of God confounds all attempts to reduce it to caricatures and formulas. These are human contrivances designed to serve human ends, but the gospel is a matter of serving Christ.[12]

Adolf Schlatter

But when fellowship results in the destruction of the other's life, there is no upbuilding. This eliminates food from the concerns that are important for the community, for the right to eat meat dare not give rise to an attack on God's work. The work of God is peace and the community's upbuilding. God's work is the individual who is able to believe. To motivate him to sin is to destroy God's work.[13]

Douglas Moo

By insisting that they [the strong] exercise their liberty in these matters, they are causing spiritual harm to fellow believers and are thereby failing to maintain a proper focus on what is truly important in the kingdom of God. Theirs, paradoxically, is the same fault as that of the Pharisees, only in reverse: where the Pharisees insisted on strict adherence to the ritual law at the expense of "justice, mercy, and faith," the "strong" are insisting on exercising their freedom from the ritual law at the expense of "righteousness and peace and joy in the Holy Spirit."[14]

upbuilding
Ephesians 4:11–16

upbuilding
nurturing, maturing

Fostering Fellowship

ROMANS 14:19–21 *Therefore let us pursue the things which make for peace and the things by which one may edify another. Do not destroy the work of God for the sake of food. All things indeed are pure, but it is evil for the man who eats with offense. It is good neither to eat meat nor drink wine nor do anything by which your brother stumbles or is offended or is made weak.* (NKJV)

Paul is concerned about the peace and **upbuilding** of all believers. His experience has taught him that fellowship is fragile. It takes time and effort to create an environment where fellowship can grow naturally, where the Holy Spirit is free to minister, and where trust abounds so that everyone is comfortable being themselves.

Paul directs his readers' thoughts to principles that could bring about the resolution of the problem. He says, "It's your job to do your best to bring peace and help build up other people" (see Romans 14:19). It's our vocation as believer-priests to help each other grow in this holy faith.

go to

lasting peace
Psalm 34:14;
Isaiah 26:3;
Ephesians 2:14

liberty
Ephesians 5:13–18;
Galatians 5:1

One could take the word *peace* to mean a number of different things. In our modern world, peace is a state of mutual tolerance—the result of a universal attitude that says, "I won't mess with you if you don't mess with me." The peace of Christ, however, is quite different from these. The peace of Christ is the result of Christians actively pursuing the edification of other Christians. This is a much more profound, active, and <u>lasting peace</u>.

"One may edify another" (Romans 14:19 NKJV) implies that the strong may learn something special from the weak, and the weak will be lifted in their spirits and renewed in their faith when they experience acceptance and love from their stronger brethren.

<u>Liberty</u> becomes a dangerous license when we refuse to show honor to our brothers and sisters in Christ. At times when we must make a decision about doing or not doing something, the Holy Spirit will whisper counsel to us. We must be quiet enough to listen.

what others say

Leon Morris

Paul exhorts his readers to pursue (a verb which indicates more than a slight interest; it means earnest application) *what leads to peace* (more literally "the things of peace). In the New Testament the most important thing about peace is that Christ has brought about peace with God, but in passages like this one the thought is rather that of peace with one another . . . it is the responsibility of those at peace with God to pursue the kind of conduct that will promote peace with people.[15]

Paul's Beatitude

> ROMANS 14:22 *Do you have faith? Have it to yourself before God. Happy is he who does not condemn himself in what he approves.* (NKJV)

Chapter 14 ends with a word of clear instruction first for the strong, then for the weak. To the strong he says exercise freedoms associated with disputable matters in privacy. The strong are not to go around setting everyone straight.

Some things need to be kept between us and God. We are not required to go against our convictions if it is not a matter of sin, but we are not to flaunt our freedom either.

Consistency between one's beliefs and one's behavior falls in the area of conscience. When believers are free of condemnation in how they carry out their walk with God, Paul says they are "happy" (Romans 14:22 NKJV). It is possible, by behavior that is contrary to the will of God, to destroy the work of God.

what others say

Charles Hodge

Paul presents in 14:22, more distinctly than he had before done, the idea that required no concession of principle or renunciation of truth. He did not wish them to believe a thing to be sinful which was not sinful, or to trammel their own conscience with the scruples of their weaker brethren. He simply required them to use their liberty in a considerate and charitable manner.[16]

From Faith

ROMANS 14:23 *But he who doubts is condemned if he eats, because he does not eat from faith; for whatever is not from faith is sin. (NKJV)*

Verse 23 is for the weak. "Faith" should be understood here not as that which saves us from hell but as that which guides us in our daily walk with God. When we do something because we are confident that it is right and good, we are acting "from faith" (Romans 14:23 NKJV). When we are not confident about whether or not a certain behavior is right and we do it anyway, what we are doing is "not from faith" (14:23 NKJV). We ought to be certain that a behavior is right before participating in it.

Doubt in Greek means "to be without a way." It means a person does not have the resources to think a matter through. So doubt is like a red flag. It is a warning, and we need to heed our consciences until we have time for further prayer and research.

apply it

what others say

Pelagius

What is good is our freedom, which we have in the Lord, so that everything is clean to us. We should not use our freedom in such a way that we appear to be living for the stomach and for feasts.[17]

William S. Plumer

It is not wise equally to press upon young converts and newly formed churches all the truths of Scripture. There is an order of divine instruction; milk for babes, strong meat for men. Let that order be observed. At all events, let us keep the unity of the Spirit in the bond of peace.[18]

Martin Luther

Here the apostle is speaking in a general way regarding faith . . . it is faith in God, faith in one's neighbor, faith in oneself. And by faith in God any person is made righteous, because he acknowledges that God is truthful, in whom he believes and puts his trust.[19]

Chapter Wrap-Up

- Acting as the judge of another in disputable matters is contrary to the Word of God. We are not to judge others when it comes to disputable matters. That is God's job. (Romans 14:1–3)

- God accepts both the weak and the strong and commands the strong not to look down on the brother who differs with him. Divergent behaviors exist in the Body of Christ. Whether it is food or drink, sacred days, or the eating of meat, we should all do as unto the Lord and not criticize those who disagree with us. (Romans 14:4–9)

- The strong ought not be a stumbling block to the weak. They should not practice their freedom at the expense of another's spiritual development. (Romans 14:10–18)

- Christians should remember that they are to be loyal to God, not their freedoms. God calls for whatever action will bring peace and mutual edification. (Romans 14:19–21)

- The strong are to be blessed by exercising their freedoms in private. The weak are to act as their consciences direct them. (Romans 14:22–23)

Study Questions

1. What does the term "doubtful things" mean throughout Romans 14?

2. What does Paul mean when he talks about the strong and the weak believer?

3. According to Paul, judging a fellow believer is wrong. Why?

4. What should we do if we disagree over disputable matters?

5. How might some believers be stumbling blocks to other believers?

6. What does Paul mean when he says, "Do not let your good be spoken of as evil" (Romans 14:16 NKJV)?

Romans 15 Come Together

Chapter Highlights:
- **Recipe for Unity**
- **Christ's Example**
- **Trailblazing**
- **Paul's Plans**
- **A Prayer Request**

Let's Get Started

The theme of unity looms large in the early part of this chapter with parallel themes of encouragement and endurance. The apostle demonstrates that unity between the strong and the weak, between Jewish converts and Gentile converts, can be achieved in and through the Lord Jesus Christ.

There can be no unity as long as Christians cling to attitudes that cause tension. Paul reminds the Roman Christians that Jesus was one who chose not to go his own way, though he could have, but to serve those around him. Christ is our example for how to nurture unity and peace.

Paul also lifts up the Scriptures as a source of encouragement and hope for the believing community.

The last part of the chapter focuses on personal matters that Paul believes are of interest to the church in Rome.

Burden Bearing

ROMANS 15:1–2 *We then who are strong ought to bear with the scruples of the weak, and not to please ourselves. Let each of us please his neighbor for his good, leading to edification. (NKJV)*

Paul's use of "we" (Romans 15:1 NKJV) indicates again that he counted himself among "the strong." The strong are the ones with the ability to resolve the differences between themselves and the weak. It is up to them. In one sentence the second verse of chapter 15 sums up a crucial precept for any body of believers. Paul is clear. Every Christian's life should be characterized by a refusal to be self-interested and a resolution to look after others in the fold.

apply it

If Christians were successful at doing what Paul says they should do in Romans 15:2, ponder the difference it would make in your church.

John Murray

The strong are to help the weak and promote their good to edification (verse 2). . . ."not to please ourselves," must not be interpreted to mean that we are always to defer to the whims and wishes of others, not even those of fellow–believers and thus always follow the course of action that pleases them. To please men is not a principle of the believer's life (cf. Gal. 1:10).[1]

Born to Serve

ROMANS 15:3 *For even Christ did not please Himself; but as it is written, "The reproaches of those who reproached You fell on Me." (NKJV)*

Paul's expression "for even Christ did not please Himself" (Romans 15:3 NKJV) sets the tone for this section, if not for the whole chapter. Christ is our chief example. The phrase "for even Christ" reveals that Christ was the only one who had the right, the godly right, to please himself. His motive would have been absolutely pure if he had chosen to look out for himself, but Christ chose to look out for other people, who were fallen. He chose to respect their obvious limitations and their vast needs.

Paul's spirit had been touched by Jesus on the road to Damascus. In an instant he knew the heart of his Savior. Now having fellowshipped with and served the risen Lord faithfully for years, Paul reminds the troubled church that they needed to change their perspective and listen to Christ their leader.

Jesus preached, "If anyone desires to come after Me, let him deny himself, and take up his cross, and follow Me" (Matthew 16:24 NKJV). This is the spirit of the apostle's heart as we enter Romans 15.

Everyone wants to be considered strong. Boys flex their muscles to see who has bigger biceps. We play sports to see who has the stronger team. We want to be strong. We often fail to remember, however, that the strong have a responsibility to be leaders, to act as models, and to show compassion.

As a boy, I was often the last to be picked for baseball teams. No one picked me because I could never get a hit. As a member of the weak in the sport of baseball, I keenly felt the power of the strong. As I stood in front of the two captains and the boys who had already been picked, I knew that they had the power to accept or reject me. Rejection was not a fun feeling. Similarly in the spiritual realm, God has called upon the strong to bear the failings of the weak and not to reject them. Strength is a privilege, and with privilege comes responsibility.

If we live only "to please ourselves," our lives will wither. Paul is not suggesting that personal pleasure is bad, but so often it's all people think about—the next meal, the next movie, the next trip to Europe, the next cruise, the next sports event.

There has to be room somewhere in our minds for Paul's direction: "Let each of us please his neighbor for his good, leading to edification" (Romans 15:2 NKJV). Being selfish leaves no room for fellowship, prayer, or worship. Self-centeredness blinds us to the needs of others.

If we fail to love others, we will seriously hinder the growth of the Body of Christ.

When we please ourselves we do what comes naturally, but that is not the way of <u>Christ</u>. This is the first time in his letter that Paul uses Christ as an example. Earlier Paul refers to Jesus as our Lord and Savior, as the Son of God, and as Christ. Now Paul wants to focus on Jesus' behavior, not his lordship.

We say we believe in Christ, but we often live the way we want, which means we abandon Christ. By contrast Christ calls us to suffer with him. That's why Paul quotes from Psalm 69:9 saying, "For even Christ did not please Himself; but as it is written, 'The reproaches of those who reproached You [God] fell on Me' " (Romans 15:3 NKJV).

Jesus went to great lengths to serve others. Despite insults, rejection, beatings, and death on the cross, Jesus remained focused on obeying his <u>Father</u> and acting for our good. We need to do the same. Make it your goal to give the world a daily glimpse of Jesus.

what others say

Matthew Henry

The self-denial of our Lord Jesus is the best argument against the selfishness of Christians. Christ pleased not himself. He did not consult his own worldly credit, ease, safety, nor pleasure; he emptied himself, and made himself of no reputation; and all this for our sakes, and to set us an example. His whole life was a self-denying, self-displeasing life.[2]

Christ
1 Peter 2:18–21

Father
John 8:29

road to Damascus
road north from
Jerusalem through
Galilee

**palisades of the
Torah**
protection of the law

what others say

John Chrysostom

What Paul says is this: If you are strong, then let the weak test
your strength.[3]

C. E. B. Cranfield

Paul appeals to the example of Christ Himself (cf. 2
Corinthians 8:9; Philippians 2:5 ff; also 1 Corinthians 11:1); the
statement "did not please Himself" sums up with eloquent
reticence both the meaning of the Incarnation and the character of Christ's earthly life. He most certainly did not seek to
please, but sought rather to please His Father and to please
men.[4]

The Role of the Scroll

ROMANS 15:4 *For whatever things were written before were
written for our learning, that we through the patience and comfort of the Scriptures might have hope.* (NKJV)

To the apostle Paul, the Scriptures were authoritative. He did not
take a mere Bible-as-literature approach to the Word of God. He discovered in them a source of wisdom, knowledge, encouragement,
and hope.

The apostle's mind and heart were saturated with its truth. Paul's
teaching flowed out of his study and research of the "whole counsel
of God" (Acts 20:27 NKJV), and out of his personal experience. What
he shared was a careful presentation of the passions in his heart and
life.

A key to understanding Paul is understanding his conversion
encounter with Christ on the **road to Damascus**. A bright light
shone from heaven, temporarily blinding him, and Jesus' voice called
to him from heaven, telling him to stop persecuting Christ. Paul's
spiritual eyes were opened.

From that moment on God's grace guided his path. God used his
years of professional study as a Pharisee in ways he never anticipated,
and he discovered new meaning in the writings he had studied.

Remember, as a Pharisee, Paul showed violent hostility toward
anyone, Jew or Gentile, who threatened to cause a breach in the **palisades of the Torah** given to safeguard and uphold his beloved
nation Israel.

After his conversion Paul saw the Scriptures not as containing theoretical or historical documents, but as a book filled with instructions from God, bringing encouragement and assurance to those who choose to follow Christ. Paul spent the rest of his days trying to pass this truth on to the world.

go to

counselor
John 14:26; 15:26;
Acts 1:4–5

> **what others say**
>
> **Craig S. Keener**
>
> Paul can say that Scripture ["were written for our learning" (NKJV)] because he believes, like his Jewish contemporaries, that it is God's Word and remains relevant to new situations. This statement does not mean that he thought it was intended only for his own generation.[5]

One Mind and One Mouth

ROMANS 15:5–6 *Now may the God of patience and comfort grant you to be like-minded toward one another, according to Christ Jesus, that you may with one mind and one mouth glorify the God and Father of our Lord Jesus Christ.* (NKJV)

Having elevated the Scriptures to their holy purpose, one of Paul's greatest contributions to the historical faith, he now offers a prayer on behalf of the church that expresses Paul's desire for a spirit of oneness.

This prayer is authentication of Paul's personal experience with God. What God had given to the apostle he would surely give to others who believed. There is a constant need for hope, strength, and assurance in a world that leeches our human and spiritual potential. Knowing our daily need, God has given the Body of Christ a teacher and <u>counselor</u> in the person of the Holy Spirit.

When Paul says, "that you may with one mind and one mouth glorify the God and Father of our Lord Jesus Christ" (Romans 15:6 NKJV), he is not expressing a hope that all Christians will be exactly the same. Rather, he is expressing his hope that Christians will with all their different gifts and talents come together in a harmonious unity, like that of many instruments in an impressive orchestra.

something to ponder

> **what others say**
>
> **John Murray**
>
> They [Romans 15:5–6] are in the form of a wish addressed to men that God would accomplish in them the implied exhor-

example of love
Romans 5:8;
1 John 3:16–18

tation, an eloquent way of doing two things at the same time, exhorting men and prayer to God. Without the enabling grace of God exhortation will not bear fruit. Hence the combination. No form of exhortation is more effective in address to men than this.[6]

Henri Nouwen

The authority of Christ is an authority based on humility and obedience and received by experiencing the human condition in a deeper, broader, and wider way than any person ever did or ever will do.[7]

As Christ, So You

ROMANS 15:7 *Therefore receive one another, just as Christ also received us, to the glory of God.* (NKJV)

Paul is not asking the Roman Christians to give anything more than what they themselves had received. They were recipients of Christ's unconditional love. Paul told them to show the same love to their fellow Christians. He hopes the message he has delivered will enable both the strong and the weak to put their differences behind them so they can follow the example of love set by Jesus.

It is good for us to reflect on all that we have received from Christ. We mocked Christ with our sins, and he accepted us. With our sins we slapped Christ in the face, and he turned to us his other cheek. Finally, our sins nailed Christ to the cross, and what did he do in response? He asked God to forgive us because we knew not what we were doing. Filled with such a bounty of love and forgiveness, have we any excuse for failing to show love and forgiveness to those around us?

A Model of Servanthood

ROMANS 15:8 *Now I say that Jesus Christ has become a servant to the circumcision for the truth of God, to confirm the promises made to the fathers,* (NKJV)

Paul begins to build on his discussion of the example of Christ by explaining that Christ was first and foremost a servant of the Jews. Jesus directed almost all of his earthly ministry toward the nation of Israel and limited the ministry of the original twelve disciples to their own people. This was to fulfill the promises made to the patriarchs.

Paul's words would have reminded the Gentiles not to look down on the Jews. Indeed, salvation was from the Jews!

He's God of the Gentiles, Too

ROMANS 15:9–12 *and that the Gentiles might glorify God for His mercy, as it is written:*
  "For this reason I will confess to You among the Gentiles,
  And sing to Your name."
And again he says:
  "Rejoice, O Gentiles, with His people!"
And again:
  "Praise the LORD, all you Gentiles!
  Laud Him, all you peoples!"
And again, Isaiah says:
  "There shall be a root of Jesse;
  And He who shall rise to reign over the Gentiles,
  In Him the Gentiles shall hope." (NKJV)

Having explained Christ's focus on the Jews, Paul is quick to point out that God always had the Gentiles in mind. He proves this point by quoting from three Old Testament passages that present the Gentiles as giving praise to a God who saved them.

Keep in mind the Gentile church was in its early stages. It began at **Pentecost**, and this letter was written only about twenty-two years later. A great deal of teaching and dialogue needed to take place so both the Jews and the Gentiles would appreciate what God had accomplished in sending Christ. With Christ two very different worlds were brought together. It's not surprising that the bulk of Paul's letter is an effort to iron out the wrinkles of a union that, before Christ, neither group dreamed possible.

Paul's call to be an apostle to the Gentiles involved giving the Gentiles a solid theological foundation. If we think of the early church as a ship floating aimlessly on the waters of ignorance and youth, Paul's job was to steer the vessel on a straight course to knowledge about God and about God's relationship to humans.

Pentecost
Acts 2:1–4

apostle to the Gentiles
Acts 9:15;
Romans 11:13;
Galatians 1:16–17;
2:8;
2 Timothy 4:17

Pentecost
during a Jewish celebration, the Holy Spirit came on believers, enabling them to speak foreign languages

go to

promise to Abraham
Genesis 12:1–3;
Numbers 14:2; 15:7;
Acts 7:1–8

nations
Zechariah 2:11–12;
Matthew 25:32;
Acts 10:35

glorious day
Romans 11:25–27

Paul's Scripture Quotes

Verse in Romans	Title of Selection	Quoted from	Words Quoted	Expected Result
Romans 15:9	A Song of David	2 Samuel 22:50	You among the Gentiles; and sing to Your name	Praise
Romans 15:10	The Song of Moses	Deuteronomy 32:43	Rejoice, O Gentiles, with His people!	Rejoice
Romans 15:11	Psalm of David	Psalm 117:1	Praise the LORD, all you Gentiles! Laud Him, all you peoples!	Praise
Romans 15:12	Isaiah: Song of Messiah	Isaiah 11:10	There shall be a root of Jesse	Rally for action

nations
the world's Gentiles

The God who made a Covenant of Promise with Abraham is the same God who chose Mary and Joseph to parent the Christ child. They were the instruments God used to begin the New Covenant. God's love for the world stretches over all of time.

Hope for All

ROMANS 15:13 *Now may the God of hope fill you with all joy and peace in believing, that you may abound in hope by the power of the Holy Spirit. (NKJV)*

All that God accomplished in sending the Messiah to the Jews was glorious in and of itself, but God had an additional purpose in mind. He was going to keep his <u>promise to Abraham</u> so that *all* the **nations** of the world would be blessed through him. This blessing would result in the Gentiles giving glory to God. The overflow of his mercy to the Gentile world would bring millions into his kingdom.

We should never trivialize or belittle our Jewish heritage. God has richly blessed the nations of the world because of his promises to Israel. We must always obey the Word and "pray for the peace of Jerusalem" (Psalm 122:6 NKJV). God still has a <u>glorious day</u> in store for the nation of Israel.

Both Jews and Gentiles should be eternally grateful that God chose to love us by giving us the gift of his Son. This is why the apostle closes this section of his discussion with a brief, but appropriate, benediction. Paul wants his readers to feel joyful and peaceful. In this way the apostle closes his discussion of the conflict in Rome and is ready to move on to other matters.

When we are involved in one of life's battles, it's easy to become pessimistic, unhappy, and anxious. By remembering all Christ has done for us on the cross, we will get our minds back on the right track. The Holy Spirit can give us the power to hope when we have no strength.

apply it

Kudos!

ROMANS 15:14 *Now I myself am confident concerning you, my brethren, that you also are full of goodness, filled with all knowledge, able also to admonish one another. (NKJV)*

Having finished his explanation for how the weak and the strong can live harmoniously, Paul now turns to encourage his readers. Much of what preceded this passage had to do with making right decisions so "goodness" (Romans 15:14 NKJV) is probably a reference to moral excellence here, but Paul doesn't stop there. He tells them he thinks they are "filled with all knowledge, able also to admonish one another" (15:14 NKJV). Paul may have wanted to

priestly duty
every believer is a
priest and is on duty
at all times

silence any doubts the relatively new converts had about whether they were wise or knowledgeable enough to continue their community. It would have been a big boost to hear the great apostle speak of them in this way.

While it's necessary to address problems that exist in a fellowship, we also need to appreciate the good things that are happening. We need to monitor the negative or it will devour whatever gets in its way.

Just Doing My Job

ROMANS 15:15–16 *Nevertheless, brethren, I have written more boldly to you on some points, as reminding you, because of the grace given to me by God, that I might be a minister of Jesus Christ to the Gentiles, ministering the gospel of God, that the offering of the Gentiles might be acceptable, sanctified by the Holy Spirit. (NKJV)*

Paul's letter is assertive and to the point. In this passage it sounds as though he wanted to prevent any hurt feelings on the part of his readers. He tells the Romans that though he has been bold in some places, he was bold only because being bold is part of his God-given calling as a minister to the Gentiles.

No doubt Paul hoped the Roman Christians would join him in his ardent pursuit to spread the good news of God's salvation through Christ.

The apostle was not just the church's first theologian; he was a passionate missionary. He showed heartfelt concern for the feelings of others and was blessed with effective communication skills. We know this from his actions and words that we read in the Book of Acts, as well as in the fourteen books he authored in the New Testament. He was faithful to his calling and impressive in his giftedness.

Paul had received God's saving grace, and he was continually receiving God's grace to enable him to do the work God wanted him to do. Paul's "**priestly duty**" was to proclaim "the gospel of God" (Romans 15:16 NKJV). Paul knew that for his ministry to be fruitful, he had to do his work in the power given to him by the Holy Spirit.

When Paul became a Christian, he understood for the first time that a person is saved by grace and not by works. Grace eliminated the need to work one's way to heaven. But Paul also saw his own sinfulness. He never claimed to be worthy of his high calling to minister to others. In fact, he called himself the chief of sinners.

So the World May Know

ROMANS 15:17–19 *Therefore I have reason to glory in Christ Jesus in the things which pertain to God. For I will not dare to speak of any of those things which Christ has not accomplished through me, in word and deed, to make the Gentiles obedient— in mighty signs and wonders, by the power of the Spirit of God, so that from Jerusalem and round about to Illyricum I have fully preached the gospel of Christ. (NKJV)*

Paul proved to be a useful servant for a very special reason. Professor James R. Edwards writes that both Paul's "usefulness to God and his greatness in history are due to the fact he did not confuse the servant of the mission with the Lord of the mission."[13] It's hard to talk about your successes without drawing too much attention to yourself and giving too little glory to God. The apostle was aware of this problem and handled it carefully.

Paul acknowledged that all credit must go to Christ. It was Christ who called him, ordained him, and equipped him for the work of ministry. A true servant knows that every success is simply a manifestation of the grace of God.

Paul is a humble man. Real humility was destroyed when sin entered into man's experience. With godly humility removed, godly restraints on man's behavior were also removed. Man's appetite for self-fulfillment had no limits. Good things were taken to the extreme and man's unbridled pleasures destroyed him. So Paul's refusal to take credit was due to God living in and through him.

Paul expresses the mystery of godliness this way: "I have been crucified with Christ; it is no longer I who live, but Christ lives in me; and the life which I now live in the flesh I live by faith in the Son of God" (Galatians 2:20 NKJV). The apostle shows that the believer's identity with Christ is the key to true spirituality. It is faith in Jesus as God's Son that opens our understanding and allows us to perceive God's work of grace in our lives.

Paul's glory was in Christ and in him alone. Understanding this, he was now at liberty to share the rest of his experience as a servant of Christ. The Spirit had empowered him to accomplish much in the Gentile world. He used both signs and miracles.

The apostle's only tool was the Gospel of Jesus Christ. He had no programs, no balloons, and no door prizes. What he did was done through the grace of the Holy Spirit and the power of the Gospel. You recall in the beginning of this epistle that Paul demonstrated perfect confidence in the Gospel and wrote, "For in it the righteousness of God is revealed" (Romans 1:17 NKJV). This is all Paul had, and it is all he needed.

Trailblazer

ROMANS 15:20–22 *And so I have made it my aim to preach the gospel, not where Christ was named, lest I should build on another man's foundation, but as it is written:*
"To whom He was not announced, they shall see;
And those who have not heard shall understand."
For this reason I also have been much hindered from coming to you. (NKJV)

hardship and persecution
2 Corinthians 4:7–18

The Gospel had transformed Paul, and he was confident it would transform others as well. The Spirit had placed in Paul's heart a desire to go to places where the Gospel had never been preached.

He wanted to be a trailblazer. He took his directive from Isaiah 52:15: "For what had not been told them they shall see, and what they had not heard they shall consider" (NKJV).

It was because of Paul's commitment to bring the Gospel to new places that he hadn't made it to Rome yet. Paul explained to the believers in Rome that because he had been faithful to the mission God placed in his heart, he had "been much hindered from coming to [them]" (Romans 15:22 NKJV). Rather than being with them, he was preaching the Gospel to those who didn't know Christ.

Paul loved serving the Lord in spite of the hardship and persecution he endured. As the apostle to the Gentiles, he championed the first great missionary movement. His approach to evangelism and church planting has been studied by students and scholars ever since his writings were circulated. Many of his principles are used today by missionary organizations all over the world.

what others say

Elizabeth O'Connor

If we are to accept the challenge of the crisis of our times, we, as Christians, must know that the world's deepest need is for saints. These are people who can give themselves in ways that seem fanatical to those who live by the usual ethical and moral norms. These are people who live normally by the second mile. It is not sporadic with them. They have thrown the familiar "duty" maps away. They are utter fools for Christ's sake. They are always finding some cruel little cross to climb up on.[15]

forced
Acts 9:26–30

scrolls and parchments
2 Timothy 4:9–18

Stephen
Acts 7:1–8:1

contribution
money gift

scrolls and parchments
papyrus copies of parts of the Old Testament

Leave the Light on for Me

*ROMANS 15:23–27 But now no longer having a place in these parts, and having a great desire these many years to come to you, whenever I journey to Spain, I shall come to you. For I hope to see you on my journey, and to be helped on my way there by you, if first I may enjoy your company for a while. But now I am going to Jerusalem to minister to the saints. For it pleased those from Macedonia and Achaia to make a certain **contribution** for the poor among the saints who are in Jerusalem. It pleased them indeed, and they are their debtors. For if the Gentiles have been partakers of their spiritual things, their duty is also to minister to them in material things. (NKJV)*

Paul was a gifted, pioneer-spirited servant of Christ. He believed that he had worked in the regions of the two Antiochs, Cappadocia, Galatia, Phrygia, Achaia, and Macedonia as long as was spiritually profitable. His years of labor in these territories that lay south and west of the Black Sea represent a life well lived for the Lord.

It was now time for him to move on. The Spirit of God was urging Paul to complete a number of other missions, to take an offering to assist the poor "among the saints who are in Jerusalem" (Romans 15:26 NKJV), and to travel to Rome where he would face the conclusion of his unique service to the church.

For many years Paul had wanted to visit the church in Rome. With a number of trained servants in place carrying out their ministerial duties faithfully, a trip to Rome now seemed possible. Of equal if not greater importance was Paul's burden for Spain, the frontier of the empire in the West. Spain was a Roman colony where many Jews had migrated. His heart was drawn both to his people and to a territory that did not have a Christian church.

Paul seeks the Roman believers' prayer support. He needs protection from the hostile, nonbelieving Jewish community. They had forced his departure from Jerusalem at an earlier time in his ministry. It is only "by the will of God" that he hopes to go to Rome and "be refreshed" in the fellowship of these dear brethren (Romans 15:32 NKJV).

At this point in Paul's life and service he had been traveling for a long time with very little except his **scrolls and parchments**. His journey had begun with the martyrdom of Stephen in AD 36 when he consented to this young evangelist's death. A year later he was

<u>converted</u>. Paul's first missionary tour (see Illustration #5) had been with **Barnabas**, sent out by the church at Antioch in AD 45–50.

Now some twenty years later, having completed two additional mission tours (see Illustration #10), he is writing the church at Rome, presenting them with a major document on the foundations of the Gospel and an explanation of the relationship between Jew and Gentile in God's overall plan of redemption.

converted
Acts 9:1–15

Barnabas
name means "son of encouragement"; a Jewish Christian

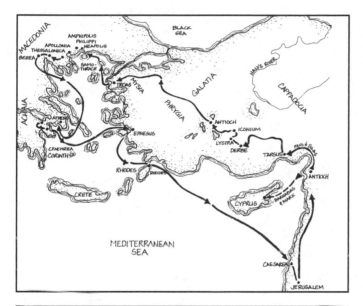

Illustration #10
Paul's Second and Third Missionary Journeys—The top map shows the route of Paul's second missionary journey. The bottom map shows his third trip through the area. He covered a wide territory and established many groups of believers throughout his lifetime. Often, he traveled with companions, training them to follow his example in teachings and lifestyle.

Remember, Paul is writing this letter from Corinth. He could have made a trip from Corinth to Rome in a relatively short amount of time, but instead he explains, "But now I am going to Jerusalem to minister to the saints" (Romans 15:25 NKJV). The purpose of the Jerusalem trip? "To make a certain contribution for the poor among the saints who are in Jerusalem" (15:26 NKJV). Paul puts duty before pleasure.

The financial gift Paul refers to was a collection made during Paul's third missionary journey. Paul mentions the churches are pleased to address this need, but he also points out that the Gentiles owe it to the Jews to share with them their material blessings, because the Jews shared with the Gentiles their spiritual ones. Here is a wonderful example of the strong bearing the burdens of the weak.

what others say

Saint Jerome

Mark well the swiftness of the Word. It is not satisfied with the East but desires to speed to the West as well![16]

James Montgomery Boice

Some Christians act as if believers should sail through life on automatic pilot, expecting God to direct their lives in a supernatural way apart from any direct involvement from them. . . . Paul did not think like that. He was open to God's special guidance, as we learn from the accounts of his missionary journeys in Acts. He obeyed God's leading. But he also made plans, and one of those plans, which was quite important in his thinking, was to carry the gospel to the far corners of the known Roman world—to Spain.[17]

Looking Forward to It

ROMANS 15:28–29 *Therefore, when I have performed this and have sealed to them **this fruit**, I shall go by way of you to Spain. But I know that when I come to you, I shall come in the fullness of the blessing of the gospel of Christ.* (NKJV)

"Work is work," Paul explained. He had to visit Jerusalem first, there was no getting around it, but as soon as his work was completed there, he would board the first ship to Rome. This is at least the third mention of his desire to visit the Roman believers. He knew that visiting them would be the occasion of one of Christ's more abundant blessings.

Like Paul, many of us long to do things that we know would enrich our lives extravagantly, but duty has a way of calling and often we must postpone the fulfillment of our heart's longings. Let's remember that God knows what we long for, and he is sovereign. The Lord of all will bring you the fulfillment of those longings, provided such would be the very best thing for you and the whole universe. Let us also remember that the final destination of our lives will be so glorious that no matter what we endure, all our suffering will seem like nothing in the end.

mob
Acts 21:30–32

faithful
Acts 28:30–31

Let Us Pray

> ROMANS 15:30–33 *Now I beg you, brethren, through the Lord Jesus Christ, and through the love of the Spirit, that you strive together with me in prayers to God for me, that I may be delivered from those in Judea who do not believe, and that my service for Jerusalem may be acceptable to the saints, that I may come to you with joy by the will of God, and may be refreshed together with you. Now the God of peace be with you all. Amen. (NKJV)*

Paul is realistic about the dangers he faces, but his obedience to the Spirit's leading must have kept his natural fears in check. He asks the Romans to pray for his safety from those who don't believe and that what he does in Jerusalem will go well with everyone. This is a wonderful example of courage and humility that is frequently apparent in Paul's writings.

From a purely human perspective, the events in Jerusalem went from bad to worse. In Acts 21–27 Luke offers a full account (see Illustration #11). Paul was nearly beaten to death by an out-of-control mob. Then he languished for two years in a Caesarean jail, which may have been worse than the beating. Paul arrived in Rome not as a pioneer missionary, but as a prisoner of the Roman government.

Paul died in Rome during the latter years of Nero's reign, about AD 68. According to Scripture, Paul never experienced the sense of joy and intimacy with the Roman church that he longed for, but God's servant, Paul the apostle, was nevertheless faithful until the Lord called him home.

He closes the chapter with his third benediction: "The God of peace be with you all. Amen" (Romans 15:33 NKJV). Paul wishes that all the believers in Rome would live together in a spirit of peace.

Illustration #11
Paul's Final Journey—This map shows the route of Paul's last journey from his capture in Jerusalem to his imprisonment in Caesarea and his final imprisonment and death in Rome.

God intends for our lives to be **benedictions**, regardless of the trials and tests we are called to bear. The God of peace guided the path that his servant Paul walked. The same God will guide the paths of our lives if we, like Paul, "present [our] bodies a living sacrifices, holy, acceptable to God" (Romans 12:1 NKJV). Paul's life was so deeply touched by God that his benedictions overflowed with references to God's grace and love. Our gratitude to God ought to manifest itself in similar expressions of praise, in worship, and in communion with other believers.

benedictions
blessings

benedictions
Acts 15:5, 13, 33

what others say

Theodoret of Cyr

Paul called God the God of peace here for a reason, because he was concerned about those at Rome who were battling one another or at least who were suspicious of one another. He wanted them to be at peace with each other because of the controversy which they were having over the observance of the law.[18]

Chapter Wrap-Up

- Unity is a significant part of the Gospel message. We are called to bear the burdens of the weak. (Romans 15:1–2)

- Christ Jesus is the way to perfect unity. We should follow the example of Christ. He will give us power to control our mouths and believe with our hearts. (Romans 15:3–6)

- If Christ could accept us while we were still in our sin, then we too must accept sinners in a like manner. Whether we are Jews or Gentiles, God's mercy has made a way for us. (Romans 15:7–13)

- Paul longs to visit Rome but must first journey to Jerusalem to deliver a relief offering to the poor there. (Romans 15:14–22)

- Paul commends the Romans and attributes the boldness of his letter to his calling as Christ's ambassador. He has been about the business of trailblazing for the sake of Christ. (Romans 15:23–29)

- In closing, Paul asked the Romans to pray for him, that he would persevere through the trials before him. (Romans 15:30–33)

Study Questions

1. Why should the strong bear the shortcomings of the weak? Whose is the example to follow?

2. The Gentiles were always a part of God's plan. How do the quotes from verses 9–12 prove this point?

3. Paul's guiding precept was, "I have reason to glory in Christ Jesus in the things which pertain to God" (Romans 15:17 NKJV). How did that help him to be a profitable servant?

4. Paul had a longing to visit Rome, but his trip there had to be postponed. What are some good things to keep in mind when it comes to the postponed fulfillment of deep longings?

5. Why did Paul say the Gentiles of Macedonia and Achaia owed an offering to the Jewish believers in Jerusalem?

Romans 16 A Fond Farewell

Chapter Highlights:
- **Appreciation**
- **Affirmations**
- **Affection**
- **A Gracious Warning**
- **Greetings from Friends**

Let's Get Started

Dr. Larry Richards writes, "In some circles it remains popular to portray Paul as a narrow, chauvinistic zealot, an ideologue more concerned with theology than with people. The image could hardly be more distorted . . . in fact, among the people Paul asked to be remembered to are many women—a rather strange thing if Paul were the confirmed chauvinist many suppose."[1]

ecclesiology
theological doctrine of the church

It is beyond question. Paul loved all people enough that he diligently worked to bring them the truth of God, regardless of what that mission cost him.

Romans 16, the concluding chapter in Paul's Epistle to the Romans, allows the reader to see his heart. We observe these:

- A heart for the church as people
- An appreciation for believers as fellow servants
- A concern for protection from false teachings and teachers
- Skills as a master teacher
- An understanding of spiritual warfare
- An understanding of community in the Body of Christ
- Thankfulness to God, who establishes all believers in the truth

The apostle's grasp of **ecclesiology** was both multifaceted and deep, as his letters to the churches demonstrate. Though the church is complex, Paul believed her to be at the core an embodiment of people who belong to God and to one another. Therefore, the church was a mosaic made up of faces reconciled to God through Jesus Christ.

Paul greets people by name, acknowledging their giftedness and service in Christ's name. This was more than doctrinal theory to the apostle; it was reality. Paul had been shoulder to shoulder in the trenches with a number of these folks and, directly or indirectly, he knew each one. Together they had served the Lord Christ. Together they had worked to advance the Gospel.

go to

hospitable
1 Peter 4:8–10

servant
Greek word means
"deaconess"

emissary
personal representa-
tive

deaconess
female officer in the
church who cared
for the needs of
women

Paul, their brother and friend, was immeasurably grateful for their prayers, their teamwork, and their fellowship. He highly valued each person. Each had become special to him, and he wanted them to be recognized and received by their brethren in Rome.

Meet Phoebe

ROMANS 16:1–2 *I commend to you Phoebe our sister, who is a **servant** of the church in Cenchrea, that you may receive her in the Lord in a manner worthy of the saints, and assist her in whatever business she has need of you; for indeed she has been a helper of many and of myself also. (NKJV)*

The first on Paul's list of people to greet is a woman by the name of Phoebe, a Gentile Christian. She lived in Cenchrea, a little port town just southwest of Corinth. Since Paul wrote this letter from Corinth, most believe Phoebe was Paul's **emissary** to deliver the letter.

There is sufficient information to support the idea that Phoebe was accustomed to serving. She was a **deaconess** in her church in Cenchrea. Paul refers to her as "sister" and "servant" and asks the Roman believers to "receive her in the Lord in a manner worthy of the saints" (Romans 16:1–2 NKJV). This is a woman of high standing. She has been "a helper of many and of myself also," concludes Paul (16:2 NKJV).

Paul asked the church, the entire body, to "receive her [Phoebe] in the Lord" (Romans 16:2 NKJV). Just as we show honor and deference to the Lord, so he was asking the brethren to please exercise graciousness to this valuable servant of Christ. It was an appeal to be <u>hospitable</u>, a common grace among believers.

Once we have experienced Christ's kindness to us, we are to show the same to fellow believers. Our unity in Christ binds us all together.

apply it

conveyed the epistle there would be an additional reason. Besides, as will become apparent, Phoebe was a woman who had performed distinguished service to the church and the commendation had to be commensurate with her character and devotion.[2]

Priscilla and Aquila
Acts 18:1–4

Hi, Priscilla and Aquila

ROMANS 16:3–5A *Greet Priscilla and Aquila, my fellow workers in Christ Jesus, who risked their own necks for my life, to whom not only I give thanks, but also all the churches of the Gentiles. Likewise greet the church that is in their house.* (NKJV)

house church
group of believers who gathered regularly in a home to worship

Having introduced Phoebe, Paul turns his attention to greeting a number of old friends. First, he sends special greeting to <u>Priscilla and Aquila</u>, a couple who were fellow workers in the ministry of the Gospel. His friendship with them had been a long and appreciated relationship. They first met in Corinth where Paul teamed up with them. They were fellow tentmakers who had been driven out of Rome by Claudius in AD 49 when he expelled the Jews.

Priscilla and Aquila, like Phoebe, were people of a deep, consistent faith. Paul tells the church in Rome "all the churches of the Gentiles" give thanks to them.

Priscilla and Aquila also had a **house church** (see Illustration #12). Paul wanted to send his greetings to all of the people that gathered there. This gives you a sense of Paul's love for the church. Paul had been involved in planting many fellowships of believers, but here was a church that had been started by his dear friends, a Jewish couple.

Hi, Y'all

ROMANS 16:5B–7 *Greet my beloved Epaenetus, who is the firstfruits of Achaia to Christ. Greet Mary, who labored much for us. Greet Andronicus and Junia, my countrymen and my fellow prisoners, who are of note among the apostles, who also were in Christ before me.* (NKJV)

Illustration #12
House Church—
Priscilla and Aquila
may have been
wealthy and may
have lived in a
house such as this
one with an inner
courtyard suitable
for holding large
gatherings.

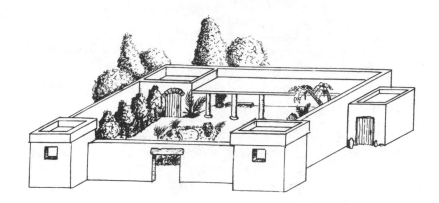

Paul sends a special word of greeting to Mary, "who labored much" for the Roman believers (Romans 16:6 NKJV). Paul saw her work as significant. There are six persons known as Mary in the New Testament, and this one is unknown apart from this text. But God knows who she is. And God knows each one of us—all of us whose names are "written in the Lamb's Book of Life" (Revelation 21:27 NKJV).

Four of the first seven names in Paul's list belong to women, and of the twenty-nine names in the total collection, one-third are women. This is evidence that Paul was not a chauvinist. In fact, he shows great respect for the women he knew and with whom he served.

Paul asks the believers in Rome to "greet Andronicus and Junia, my countrymen and my fellow prisoners, who are of note among the apostles" (Romans 16:7 NKJV). Andronicus and Junia were another husband and wife team who were highly respected as leaders among the apostles. (Paul is using the word *apostles* here in the general sense, meaning "those who are sent," as with missionaries.) Since Adronicus and Junia were brought to Christ before Paul, it is likely they were among the Roman visitors who had come to Jerusalem and were a part of the Pentecost experience. To be well known by the apostles suggests they had spent time in Israel.

The Mary that Paul mentions serves as a reminder of God's grace in all who believe. For most of us, stardom comes after this life, not during it. And that was the case for this Mary too. She lived for Jesus. Paul was led to shine a spotlight on her efforts, and now her name and her hard work live on in the pages of Scripture.

James Montgomery Boice

One fascinating thing about Romans 16 is what it reveals about Paul. Some have the idea that people who are interested in ideas—in this case those who study Christian theology—are not interested in people. They are supposed to immerse themselves in books. They are not "relational," as we say. There are people like this, of course. But Paul is a refutation of the idea that those who are interested in doctrine cannot be interested in those for whom the doctrine has been given.[3]

John Chrysostom

I think there are many, even some apparently good commentators, who hurry over this part of the epistle because they think it is superfluous and of little importance. They probably think much the same about the genealogies in the Gospels. Because it is a catalog of names, they think they can get nothing good out of it. People who mine gold are careful even about the smallest fragments, but these commentators ignore even huge bars of gold.[4]

John Murray

It was necessary and appropriate in apostolic times, as on some occasions today, for Christians to make their homes available for the congregations of the saints. It is not without significance that in our totally different present-day situation the practice of the house church is being restored and recognized as indispensable to the propagation of the gospel. In a city like Rome or Ephesus (cf. I Cor. 16:19) there would be more than one such congregation. The fact that the church in the house of Aquila and Prisca is particularly mentioned in this list of greetings shows that it did not comprise the whole church at Rome.[5]

Good Job, Friends!

ROMANS 16:8–12 *Greet Amplias, my beloved in the Lord. Greet Urbanus, our fellow worker in Christ, and Stachys, my beloved. Greet Apelles, approved in Christ. Greet those who are of the household of Aristobulus. Greet Herodion, my countryman. Greet those who are of the household of Narcissus who are in the Lord. Greet Tryphena and Tryphosa, who have labored in the Lord. Greet the beloved Persis, who labored much in the Lord.* (NKJV)

In this next group of people, Paul shifts gears from expressions of appreciation to expressions of affirmation. Paul expresses a personal attachment to Amplias, a converted Roman slave. Amplias as well as Urbanus are common slave names according to historical research.

Paul's expression of love to Amplias is a clear demonstration of how honest Paul was in his relationships. Paul was a man who was free in Christ to give himself to the people he served. We also see Paul was more intimate with some than with others, as was Jesus when he was on earth, and it wasn't a problem. It is never a problem when all parties are mature.

Urbanus had assisted the apostle sometime in the past and was also a blessing to others. Paul calls him "our fellow worker in Christ" (Romans 16:9 NKJV). Urbanus was no sloth.

Paul uses the loving expression "my beloved" when mentioning Stachys (16:9 NKJV). This suggests a bond of affection between them. Stachys was also a common slave name during that period of history. Paul had a special love for those who had a hard life in that pagan society.

Apelles was a fairly common name in the middle of the first century; it was even known among the imperial household. His name was common, but he was a man with an uncommon soul for God. Paul says Apelles was "approved in Christ" (16:10 NKJV). This indicates what God takes note of in the lives of his children. God never overlooks righteousness.

The next group that Paul greets seems to be more distant, but not less important. Aristobulus is a name that was common among the **Herodian** dynasty. Paul's greeting is to the Christians within the household. Most things scholars say about Aristobulus are still conjecture, but the believers—most likely slaves—within the household were on Paul's heart and no doubt in his prayers. Herodion was a Hebrew Christian. Beyond that we know nothing about him. Paul's greeting was surely brief, but Herodion was probably a distant relative. Paul may not have known him well. Once he remembered him, Paul felt compelled to mention his name.

It is suggested that those in the Narcissus household were probably the Christian slaves of the well-known Tiberius Claudius Narcissus, a wealthy **freeman** of the Roman Emperor Tiberius. We cannot be absolutely sure they are the same person. Nevertheless,

Paul was concerned about those in this household who were believers.

It is significant to note that Paul greets three women—Tryphena, Tryphosa, and Persis—who "labored much" (Romans 16:12 NKJV). Paul knows that God honors hard work, and he wants to give honor to these dear sisters in Christ. In Romans 13:7, Paul says, "Render therefore to all their due . . . customs to whom customs, fear to whom fear, honor to whom honor" (NKJV). Paul is practicing what he preached.

what others say

Craig S. Keener

"Tryphaena" and "Tryphosa" are Greek names sometimes used by Jewish as well as Greek women. One scholar, noting that both names come from the same root meaning "delicate," thinks that Paul may be playing on their names ironically when he says they "labor hard."[6]

Francis Davidson

It may be thought strange that Paul, who had never been to Rome, should yet have so many friends there. But the Jews of the first century (as of every century afterwards) were a commercial and migratory people. They moved along the trade routes and followed the markets. The commendations and salutations were to saints either going to, or living at, Rome.[7]

Say Hi to the Whole Gang

ROMANS 16:13–16 *Greet Rufus, chosen in the Lord, and his mother and mine. Greet Asyncritus, Phlegon, Hermas, Patrobas, Hermes, and the brethren who are with them. Greet Philologus and Julia, Nereus and his sister, and Olympas, and all the saints who are with them. Greet one another with a holy kiss. The churches of Christ greet you.* (NKJV)

Paul continues his greetings. It's as if he wants to make certain he doesn't overlook anyone who has touched his life in a significant way. His love isn't self-promoting, but thoughtful, genuine, and Christ-oriented.

All of those whom Paul mentions are ambassadors for Christ. Their history is our history. They carried the flag in their generation. They fulfilled the admonitions of their teacher and friend, Paul, who taught: "Let love be without hypocrisy. Abhor what is evil. Cling to

in Jerusalem
Mark 15:21

what is good. Be kindly affectionate to one another with brotherly love, in honor giving preference to one another; not lagging in diligence, fervent in spirit, serving the Lord" (Romans 12:9–1 NKJV).

The church in Rome represented a number of house churches. There were many slaves finding their freedom in Jesus Christ, while still in bondage to the imperial authority. A few Christians came from nobility and the ruling classes, but the majority were the world's outcasts, and they grew and became healthy, profitable servants of the Lord.

Paul greets Asyncritus, Phlegon, Hermas, Patrobas, Hermes, and the brethren with them; he greets Philologus, Julia, Nereus and his sister, and Olympas and all the saints with them. Paul concludes his greetings by telling them to "Greet one another with a holy kiss" (Romans 16:16 NKJV).

Kissing was a cultural act that signified acceptance and heartfelt brotherly love. As Paul suggests, a holy kiss is a formal, godly greeting.

Paul says to "Greet Rufus, chosen in the Lord, and his mother and mine" (Romans 16:13 NKJV). A man with the name Rufus is reported to have been <u>in Jerusalem</u> on the day of the Lord's crucifixion. He was with his father, Simon, and his brother Alexander. They were a Jewish family from Cyrene, an important city of Libya in North Africa. They were in the Holy City celebrating the Passover.

Many theologians and historians believe that this Rufus in Romans 16 is likely to have been the young lad that was in Jerusalem on that fateful day. The expression, "chosen in the Lord," surely lends itself to this speculation.

When Paul thinks of Rufus, he is also reminded of his mother, who has a special place in his heart. For Paul to address her as "mother" suggests a close friendship.

We have observed the apostle's demeanor toward his relatives and friends. Paul refers to them as "my beloved," "countrymen and . . . fellow prisoners," "approved," "hard workers," "fellow workers in Christ," and "chosen." These were men and women who were obedient in planting seeds of the faith that have been passed along one person at a time to the present day. If this is but a sampling of the early church, we can conclude that this church was distinguished by its faithful workers and their brotherly love.

false teachers
those who pretend to be Christians and teach falsehoods rather than God's truth

what others say

Brennan Manning

What makes authentic disciples is not visions, ecstasies, biblical mastery of chapter and verse, or spectacular success in the ministry, but a capacity for faithfulness. Buffeted by the fickle winds of failure, battered by their own unruly emotions, and bruised by rejection and ridicule, authentic disciples may have stumbled and frequently fallen, endured lapses and relapses, gotten handcuffed to the fleshpots and wandered into a far country. Yet, they kept coming back to Jesus. . . . I am still a ragamuffin, but I'm different . . . where sin abounded, grace has more abounded.[8]

James R. Edwards

First, despite the uncertainty about many of them, the names reveal a remarkable diversity in early Christianity. Paul mentions twenty-nine persons, twenty-seven of them by name, a full third of whom are women. There are Jewish, Greek, and Latin names. A few stem from the nobility and ruling classes, but the majority are names of slaves or freed persons. The Roman churches appear to have been cross-class churches, with membership predominantly from the lower strata of society.[9]

Watch Out for Troublemakers

ROMANS 16:17–20 *Now I urge you, brethren, note those who cause divisions and offenses, contrary to the doctrine which you learned, and avoid them. For those who are such do not serve our Lord Jesus Christ, but their own belly, and by smooth words and flattering speech deceive the hearts of the simple. For your obedience has become known to all. Therefore I am glad on your behalf; but I want you to be wise in what is good, and simple concerning evil. And the God of peace will crush Satan under your feet shortly. The grace of our Lord Jesus Christ be with you. Amen.* (NKJV)

Paul had a good eye. He had worshiped Jesus so long that he had gained wisdom. As a church planter, he had the heart and gifts of a pastor and teacher. Beyond the obvious expression of love and appreciation, Paul is rightly concerned for the believers' protection from **false teachers** who introduce division and pollute biblical teaching on the grace of God.

spiritual warfare
1 Peter 5:5–11

armor of God
Ephesians 6:10–19

division
Matthew 24:3–25;
2 Timothy 3:1–9;
Titus 1:10–16

stay away
1 Timothy 2:2

The apostle never loses sight of the fact that believers are engaged in spiritual warfare. In other epistles, he gives instruction on how to prepare for battle. In Romans 16, Paul is simply sounding the alarm and reminding these servants to be on the alert, not to tolerate anything that pollutes the faith.

We cannot escape doing spiritual battle, but if we put on the full armor of God, we can win, and in this way serve our Savior. There will be peace in the battle, if we are fighting with the right weapons. This is why Paul says, "The God of peace will crush Satan under your feet shortly" (Romans 16:20 NKJV). If he is going to be crushed under the feet of believers, that means we are to get in the fight now.

God, for Paul, was not some abstract, impersonal concept, nor was he some absentee clockmaker who designed life and expected it to work automatically on its own. Rather, Paul discovered God was ever present and personally involved in the life of each believer.

Paul closes this section with a blessing, "The grace of our Lord Jesus Christ be with you" (Romans 16:20 NKJV). The apostle of the grace of God focuses our attention back where the power of our faith rests—on the Gospel of God's grace in Christ Jesus.

What Paul was concerned about in his day, we are still concerned about today. Times have changed. Cultures are different. But the attacks on God's truth are the same. Paul warns the church in Rome to be alert for people who want to cause division. He tells the Romans to stay away from them.

In spite of the warnings, the apostle affirms his confidence in them. He says, "Your obedience has become known to all. Therefore I am glad on your behalf" (Romans 16:19 NKJV). Obedience is faith in action and it keeps the enemy on the defensive.

In other letters he discussed the spiritual battle must be fought with spiritual weapons. Paul told the Corinthians, "The weapons of our warfare are not carnal but mighty in God for pulling down strongholds, casting down arguments and every high thing that exalts itself against the knowledge of God, bringing every thought into captivity to the obedience of Christ" (2 Corinthians 10:4–5 NKJV).

Craig S. Keener

Genesis 3:15 promised that the serpent who deceived Adam and Eve to partake of the fruit (cf. Romans 5:12–21) would ultimately be crushed beneath the feet of Eve's seed. . . . Here Paul applies it more broadly to the Messiah's followers as well. His point is that they should persevere to the end, and their opposition will be defeated.[10]

go to

spiritual son
Philippians 2:20–22;
1 Timothy 1:2, 18

amanuensis
one who transcribes from another's dictation

So Long, Farewell, Auf Wiedersehen, Good-Bye

ROMANS 16:21–24 *Timothy, my fellow worker, and Lucius, Jason, and Sosipater, my countrymen, greet you. I, Tertius, who wrote this epistle, greet you in the Lord. Gaius, my host and the host of the whole church, greets you. Erastus, the treasurer of the city, greets you, and Quartus, a brother. The grace of our Lord Jesus Christ be with you all. Amen.* (NKJV)

Paul has a number of other greetings he wants to share with these dear friends. He wants them to know that they are in the hearts and prayers of the people with whom he has spent years serving the kingdom of God.

Paul writes, "Timothy, my fellow worker, . . . [greets] you" (Romans 16:21 NKJV). Timothy and Paul were companions on the second and third missionary journeys (see Illustration #10). Paul viewed Timothy as his spiritual son, so it makes sense that Paul would include his greeting.

Tertius, mentioned in verse 22, is Paul's faithful **amanuensis** who transcribed this letter. Paul often used the services of a secretary. Tertius would have done this duty for Paul as though he were doing it for the Lord himself. He would have asked Paul to be allowed to include his own greeting.

Finally, three others send their best wishes to the Romans.

As we look at the list of Paul's ministry partners, Timothy, Lucius, Jason, Sosipater, Gaius, Erastus, and Quartus, it's amazing to observe how God surrounded Paul with great men and women. They helped, through their good service, to enlarge on the use of Paul's gifts and expand the kingdom of God.

Silas, Titus, Barnabas, and Sosthenes, who are not mentioned in this letter, were among the other faithful workers with whom Paul had frequent contact and fellowship. Paul was a team player; he didn't try to reach the world for Jesus alone. He learned the art of receiving others whom the Spirit of God called. By observing Paul and those around him, we see how valuable it can be to offer our humble support wherever a need surfaces and our talents coincide.

These brethren who preceded us by nearly two millennia sent their greetings to people they had never met. Yet in the mystery of godliness, they experienced love in their hearts for the believers in Rome.

"To God Be the Glory," and Then Some

ROMANS 16:25–27 *Now to Him who is able to establish you according to my gospel and the preaching of Jesus Christ, according to the revelation of the mystery kept secret since the world began but now made manifest, and by the prophetic Scriptures made known to all nations, according to the commandment of the everlasting God, for obedience to the faith—to God, alone wise, be glory through Jesus Christ forever. Amen.* (NKJV)

Paul ends this theological treatise with a flourish. In its simplest form this doxology says, "To God, alone wise, be glory" (Romans 16:27 NKJV), but Paul packs a lot more into it than that.

He points out that what had long been a mystery—God's plan for saving humankind—had finally been revealed in Jesus Christ. Why? "For obedience to the faith" (Romans 16:26 NKJV). This is a reference to the Great Commission, the responsibility of all Christians to preach the Gospel.

Last, Paul describes God by using two adjectives. The first is "alone" (16:27 NKJV), meaning there is but one God, for Jew and Gentile alike. The second adjective is "wise" (16:27 NKJV), meaning

God's ways are not our ways, that if we are faithful in looking to him for guidance, he will make us the people he wants us to be. Glory be to God!

What Lay Ahead?

A fire raged throughout the city of Rome in AD 64, seven years after Paul's epistle was written. People saw how quickly Paul's letter to the Romans would prove to have very practical value in the years following its composition.

When Emperor Nero rebuilt the city in his honor, many blamed him for setting the fire. Needing a scapegoat, Nero blamed Christians and initiated widespread execution of them. Christians were torn to death by dogs and used as torches to light Nero's gardens and parties.

Although Nero's reign ended in 68, the persecution of Christians continued. The great colosseum (see Illustration #13) was built between 75 and 80. Built for sportive entertainment, the colosseum showcased gladiatorial combats, but was also where many Christians were thrown to beasts. Paul's letter to the Romans would prove to have very practical value in the years following its composition.

Illustration #13
Colosseum—Ruins of the great Roman colosseum are still standing, a present-day reminder of the brave faith of Christians who were willing to give up their lives for the sake of Christ.

There is little doubt the Christians in Rome looked to Paul's letter as a source of continual instruction and solace. "Bless those who persecute you," he wrote (Romans 12:14 NKJV), and, "Who shall separate us from the love of Christ? Shall tribulation, or distress, or persecution, or famine, or nakedness, or peril, or sword? . . . Yet in all these things we are more than conquerors through Him who loved us. For I am persuaded that neither death nor life, nor angels nor principalities nor powers, nor things present nor things to come, nor height nor depth, nor any other created thing, shall be able to separate us from the love of God which is in Christ Jesus our Lord" (Romans 8:35, 37–39 NKJV).

Likewise, Paul's assurance that all Christians were saved by grace through faith would have comforted those who suspected death was near. It is likely this epistle helped many Christians resist the temptation to turn away from Christ in the face of persecution and rather to press on toward the goal for which God called them.

what others say

Craig S. Keener

Synagogues, however, closed prayers, readings and services with benedictions, and Paul anticipated that his letter would be publicly read in house churches' worship services . . . Here Paul offers the sort of standard Jewish doxology used to close Hellenistic Jewish religious works (except, of course, for "through Jesus Christ"). "Amen" was the standard closing at the end of prayers and a number of Jewish books.[12]

J. Vernon McGee

"The mystery" means that it had not been revealed in the Old Testament. It refers to the present age when God is taking both Jew and Gentile and fashioning them into one body, the church. Here we see the obedience of faith. When you trust Christ, you will obey Him, my friend.[13]

Chapter Wrap-Up

- Paul commends Phoebe to the Romans and asks that they welcome her. (Romans 16:1–2)

- Paul sends a special greeting to Priscilla and Aquila, his fellow workers and a highly respected husband and wife team. Even though they were Jewish Christians, all the Gentile churches were grateful for their service. In addition, Paul sends greetings to twenty-nine people, twenty-seven by name, and also greetings to house churches. (Romans 16:3–15)

- Paul was God's ambassador of the grace of God in his generation. He sought to encourage godly and affectionate relationships. (Romans 16:16)

- Paul issues a warning about those who teach what is contrary to truth. He knows they have power over certain people, and this weakens the whole church by creating divisions. (Romans 16:17–20)

- Paul's team members, like their leader, want to greet the believers in Rome, so Paul includes their greetings at the end of his letter. (Romans 16:21–24)

- Paul concludes his writing with a beautiful doxology. His faith is bold and far reaching. He wants all nations to come to faith in the Lord Jesus Christ. (Romans 16:25–27)

Study Questions

1. How did Phoebe come to know the apostle at a level as personal as the text reveals?

2. How were Priscilla and Aquila involved in the church at Rome?

3. Paul extended sixteen special greetings to individuals and groups of Christians. How might a greeting from Paul have encouraged them?

4. How do false teachers create divisions in the church?

5. How does the church go about crushing Satan under its feet?

The Book of Romans Overview

Let's Get Started

In the four brief decades following the resurrection of Jesus, the Gospel burst out of tiny Palestine and spread across the Roman world. The story of the love of God expressed in Jesus Christ, and the promise of salvation for all who believe, shook the foundations of both Jewish and pagan belief. Christianity was truly a revolutionary faith, welcomed by millions.

While Christianity was firmly rooted in God's Old Testament revelation to the Jewish people, it seemed to Jew and Gentile alike to be a radical departure. In the first century some 10 percent of the population of the Roman Empire was Jewish. While that people was commonly misunderstood and ridiculed, there was still a significant group of Gentiles who were drawn to the Old Testament's high moral vision and its revelation of one God who created all things. The first Christian converts were drawn from this pool of Jewish believers and Gentile "god fearers" who were familiar with the Old Testament, and who acknowledged Jesus as the Messiah promised by the Old Testament prophets.

Yet how were these early Christians to reconcile their faith with the older revelation? What, really, was Christianity all about?

More than any book in the New Testament, the Book of Romans clearly defines the core teachings of Christianity, and shows the harmony of the new faith with God's revelation of himself in the Old Testament. And the key to understanding both the link between old and new and the stunning impact of the Gospel is to understand that Romans universalizes the message of the Old Testament.

Everybody's Gospel

When we look at the Old Testament we notice a striking fact. The first eleven chapters of the Old Testament are about God's dealings with the whole human race. The next 905 chapters focus on God's

treatise
a speech or written
work including facts
and principles that
lead to conclusions

special relationship with a single family—that of Abraham and his descendants, the Jewish people. The new focus begins in Genesis 12, as God chooses a man named Abram and makes him a series of promises. The Old Testament then traces the expansion and fulfillment of these promises through some two thousand years of history, up to the birth of Jesus Christ. It's no wonder then that first-century Jews saw themselves as God's chosen people, uniquely his, with little or nothing in common with the Gentiles all around them.

As the story of a crucified and risen Savior spread across the empire, thousands upon thousands of Gentiles became worshipers of the Jewish Messiah. Suddenly and unexpectedly the faith that had just been birthed in the Holy Land had become a universal faith, good news for all!

At first neither Jewish nor Gentile Christians grasped what was happening nor how to explain it. Then the apostle Paul, who had been largely responsible for stimulating the missionary movement that carried the Gospel message to the first-century Roman world, wrote a letter to the Christians in Rome. In this letter Paul carefully explained the universal Gospel of Jesus Christ—God's good news for all human beings—and showed that it is in complete harmony with the basic teachings of the earlier revelation.

There can be no doubt that the Book of Romans, this letter that Paul wrote to Christians living in Rome, is the key document in our New Testament. When we understand its teachings, we truly understand what Christianity is all about. The book of Romans defines Christianity.

Romans the Short Way

Paul's letter to the Romans is a carefully reasoned **treatise**. Each chapter flows logically and naturally into the next. Let's look at Romans section by section and follow Paul's reasoning.

Romans 1–3. The theme of Romans is righteousness, not as mere human goodness, but as absolute moral perfection. In the first three chapters of Romans Paul shows that Jew and Gentile alike lack this absolute righteousness. In fact both Jews and Gentiles are sinners. They are all under the wrath of God, and are doomed. But at the end of chapter 3 there's good news. Christ's death satisfied justice's demand that God punish sin. The death of Jesus as mankind's substitute revealed how God could be righteous and still offer forgiveness to Old Testament sinners, as well as to contemporary believers in Jesus.

Romans 4–5. In chapters 4 and 5 Paul goes on to show that God has always accepted faith in his promises in place of that perfect righteousness that no human being possesses. God accepted Abraham's faith in place of the righteousness Abraham lacked, and God accepts a believer's faith in Jesus in place of the righteousness he or she lacks. The principle of faith, so deeply rooted in the Old Testament, has been universalized, and applies to Jew and Gentile alike. And why did God choose to give his Son for us? God acted because he loves all human beings, despite the fact that all have made themselves his enemies. If we were to be saved, God had to act, because by nature all human beings are spiritually dead and thus we are unable to help ourselves.

Romans 6–8. Then in chapters 6 to 8 Paul unveils a stunning truth. God isn't satisfied to forgive sinners and credit them with righteousness. God intends to actually make righteous those who believe in Jesus! Paul explains that the Holy Spirit unites those who believe in Jesus to the Savior. This means when Jesus died on the cross, those who believe died with him. It also means that when Jesus was raised from the dead, believers were raised too and infused with spiritual life! Salvation involves an inner transformation so that, empowered by God's Holy Spirit, Christians can actually live a righteous life here and now! And our union with Jesus also means that in the resurrection we will become perfectly righteous, through and through, as Jesus himself is!

Romans 9–11. In chapters 9 to 11 Paul answers troubling questions that might be raised by those steeped in the Old Testament. Does the universalizing of the Gospel mean that God has abandoned the Jewish people? Is what God has done for all fair to Israel? Paul's answer is, first, that God is free to act as he chooses, as God's initial choice of Israel illustrates. Second, Paul points out that thousands of Jews have become Christians, so one can hardly say the Jews have been abandoned. And finally, Paul states that God has always accepted faith in his promises as a substitute for the righteousness that no human possesses.

go to

biological
Psalm 88:3–5, 9–12

spiritual
Ephesians 2:1–3

eternal
Revelation 20:7–14

Romans 12–16. In the last chapters of Romans Paul returns to the theme of practical righteousness. But now, rather than focus on how individuals are enabled by God's Spirit to live righteous lives, Paul draws a powerful portrait of Christians living together as a righteous community—a community that demonstrates to all the world the blessings God has always desired for humankind.

Charting Righteousness in Romans

Reference	Theme
Romans 1–3	Righteousness needed
Romans 4–5	Righteousness given
Romans 6–8	Righteousness experienced
Romans 9–11	Righteousness of God's choices
Romans 12–16	Righteousness worked out in community

Critical Truths

Paul's argument in Romans rests on several critical truths, or beliefs, that are central to Christianity. When we understand these truths we'll not only better understand the significance of Romans, but we will also better understand our Christian faith. Let's look at these critical beliefs and track their implications as Paul develops them in the Book of Romans.

Romans on Being Human

Human Beings Are Spiritually Dead

Looking back to the fall of Adam described in Genesis 3, Paul writes, "Just as through one man sin entered the world, and death through sin, and thus death spread to all men, because all sinned" (Romans 5:12 NKJV).

In Scripture "death" can mean three different things. It can mean <u>biological</u> death, the end of a person's life on earth. It can mean <u>spiritual</u> death, the end of a living person's link with God. Or it can mean <u>eternal</u> death, separation from God throughout eternity. In Romans Paul is primarily concerned with spiritual death, the end of a living person's link with God.

The Book of Genesis reports that God warned Adam against eating fruit from one forbidden tree. God said, "In the day that you eat of it you shall surely die" (Genesis 2:17 NKJV). Adam ate, and in addition to dying biologically years later, he died spiritually the moment he disobeyed. Paul reminds us the state of spiritual death was passed on to Adam's offspring (Romans 5:12–21), Jew and Gentile alike. Even before going on in Romans to speak of sin, Paul establishes the fact that all human beings are spiritually dead. In Romans 1 Paul notes that God has revealed himself to every human being who has ever lived through his creation. "What may be known of God is manifest in them," Paul says. "For since the creation of the world [God's] invisible attributes are clearly seen, being understood by the things that are made" (Romans 1:19–20 NKJV; see also Psalm 19:1–4). Man's reaction to God's revelation of himself has been to "suppress the truth in unrighteousness" (Romans 1:18 NKJV). Rather than thank and worship the Creator, human beings have invented their own deities and refused to acknowledge him. This, Paul argues, is clear evidence of the spiritual deadness of humankind.

Human Beings Are Sinners

The Old Testament uses three different words for "sin." The principal Hebrew word for sin is *hata*, meaning "to miss the mark" or "to fall short of the standard" that God sets for humankind. This implies that a moral standard established by God exists, and that it is known by human beings. In Romans 2 Paul universalizes this principle. He notes that the Jews have been given a special revelation of the divine standard of right and wrong in Old Testament law (2:17–28). But the Gentiles possess an internal, general revelation of the divine standard! Paul points out that all people have a moral sense. This is shown by the fact that when any individual, Jew or Gentile, violates his own standards his conscience accuses him. And Paul goes on to point out that no human being has ever lived up to his or her convictions about what is right, whether that conviction was shaped by God's revealed law or by the standards of his or her society. All have fallen short of their own standards of right and wrong, and in the sense of *hata*, all are sinners.

But mankind's condition as sinners is far more serious than "missing the mark" might suggest. Another basic word for sin in Hebrew is *pesa*, a word that describes a rebellion or revolt against the standard. Human beings not only fall short of doing what they know is

none
Romans 3:9–20

right, they consciously choose to reject and rebel against known moral standards.

A third word in the biblical vocabulary of sin is *'awon*, which is often rendered "iniquity" and which implies a twisting of the standard. Whether or not a person rebels against known standards of right and wrong, twists and distorts them, or simply falls short of them, he or she is guilty of sin. And this is the universal condition of humankind.

What is significant in Romans is that Paul shifts the focus from acts of sin to the fact that fallen human beings are sinners by nature. We do fall short of God's revelation of righteousness, and moreover we rebel against what we believe is right and we twist and distort God's standards for our own selfish ends. The fault is rooted in the fact that we are spiritually dead, unresponsive to God and, indeed, in rebellion against him.

The consequences of being sinners are traced in Romans 1:21–32. There Paul shows that sin has an impact on interpersonal morality and on individual personalities as well. As sinners human beings are vulnerable to "all unrighteousness, sexual immorality, wickedness, covetousness, maliciousness" (1:29 NKJV). Sin's grip on us is shown in our gossip, slander, envy, insolence, and arrogance. It is shown in our faithlessness, heartlessness, and ruthlessness. And while some human beings are "better" than others, there is <u>none</u> that is righteous as God calls us to be righteous.

Human Beings Are Under God's Wrath

Paul also argues that as spiritually dead sinners, all human beings are under the wrath of God. In fact, Paul indicates that the devastating effects that sin has on individuals, families, and society are evidence of God's wrath. The fact that God hates sin and will not let it go unpunished is underlined by our everyday experience!

The anguish caused by divorce, the violation felt by victims of crime, the hurt that even an unkind word can cause, are constant reminders that sin has terrible consequences. Thus, Paul tells us, "*the wrath of God* is revealed *from heaven against all ungodliness and unrighteousness of men*" (Romans 1:18 NKJV, emphasis added). The message of Scripture and experience is that sin will not go unpunished. Every human being stands guilty before God, already judged by him to be a sinner deserving of eternal punishment. This is the terrible condition of all humankind, Jew and Gentile alike.

Human Beings Need a Righteousness That Comes from God

righteous
Psalm 4:1;
Psalm 71:24
Isaiah 45:23

By the first century the concept of righteousness had been distorted in Judaism. The Old Testament calls God "righteous," and says that whatever God does is "righteous." Simply put, righteousness is defined by God's character, and ultimately his character is the standard by which all are measured. While the Old Testament speaks of righteous men and women, it also makes it clear that "in Your sight no one living is righteous" (Psalm 143:2 NKJV). In a relative sense those who trusted in God and sought to obey his law were identified as righteous. But in an absolute sense no human being is righteous as God is righteous. Yet God did command Israel to "be holy; for I am holy" (Leviticus 11:44 NKJV), thus establishing perfection as the ultimate standard by which all human beings would be judged.

Paul points out that the Jews had lost sight of this reality and were attempting to establish their own righteousness by trying to keep Old Testament law. Yet only a righteousness which came from God could be as perfect as the righteousness of God. Rather than being acceptable to God based on their efforts to be good, all human beings have fallen short of perfection and as such are subject to the wrath of God.

Nor is there one thing that a human being can do to make a difference! Even the law, which the Jews mistakenly viewed as a guide to perfection, condemned them. For "we know that whatever the law says, it says to those who are under the law, that every mouth may be stopped, and all the world may become guilty before God. Therefore by the deeds of the law no flesh will be justified in His sight, for by the law is the knowledge of sin" (Romans 3:19–20 NKJV).

This dark and pessimistic view of human nature has universal application to all, Jew and Gentile alike. Yet in Romans Paul sees this as good rather than bad news! If salvation depended on human effort, all would be lost. But salvation is offered to lost human beings as a free gift by a loving deity. Humankind has hope because our deliv-

his voice
Romans 1:19–20

erance from the power of sin and death does not depend on what we can do for God, but rather on what God has done for us!

Origen

Let us see in what way knowledge of sin comes through the law. It comes insofar as we learn through the law what to do and what not to do, what is sin and what is not sin. The law is like medicine through which we perceive the true nature of our disease. . . . The medicine itself is good, not least because it enables us to isolate the disease and seek to cure it.[1]

Paul's dark view of humanity reflected in Romans is good news, for those who take it to heart and who abandon all hope in themselves may choose to throw themselves entirely on the mercy of God.

Romans on God

The Jews thought of themselves as the unique people of God. In Romans Paul draws on Old Testament teachings to show that all human beings, Jews and Gentiles alike, share the same spiritual condition and have the same desperate need of God. In Romans Paul also counters the view that God is God of the Jews only, to show that he is the God of all.

God Speaks to All

One of the things that set the Jewish people apart was possession of the Old Testament Scriptures. God had revealed himself to the Jews! But Paul shows in Romans 1 that God has always spoken to all people, and while the revelation to Israel is far more clear and definitive, all people everywhere have heard his voice. Thus the fact the Gospel is for everyone, "for the Jew first and also for the Greek" (Romans 1:16 NKJV), is not new. God is the God of all, and from the beginning God has revealed himself to all.

God Gives Righteousness to All Who Believe

Paul has shown that all human beings are sinners, spiritually dead and under God's wrath. In Romans 4 Paul looks back into the Old Testament and demonstrates that God has always accepted faith in his promises in place of the righteousness that no human being possesses. In a key verse in Romans 4 Paul introduces several critical theological concepts. Paul writes that "to him who does not work but believes on Him who justifies the ungodly, his faith is accounted for righteousness" (Romans 4:5 NKJV). Let's look at some very important phrases in this verse.

go to

Old Testament
Isaiah 53:11–12

Believes on Him. In the New Testament a single Greek word group communicates the idea of faith, belief, and trust. The range of meanings carried by this word group are illustrated by English terms that are used to translate its various forms: to *rely on, to commit oneself to, to trust, believe, faithful, reliable, trust,* and *faith.*

In the New Testament Jesus Christ is set forward as the object of this kind of trust. There is a great gap here between biblical faith and intellectual assent or agreement. We may believe that George Washington was the first president of the United States, or that the earth is round rather than flat. We may believe that God exists, and that Jesus Christ was a real person who lived in the first century. But we do not have faith in the biblical sense until we have put our trust in Jesus and claimed the promise that God will forgive our sins for Jesus' sake. The person who trusts God does not rely for salvation on his or her own efforts to do good, but has come to rely completely on Jesus' sacrifice of himself on the cross to establish and maintain a personal relationship with God.

Justifies the ungodly. The Hebrew root translated "justify" has important judicial meaning. In law a person's actions are called into question and examined. If found innocent the person is "justified"; he or she is vindicated.

The Old Testament presents God as the judge who evaluates human actions. Because he is righteous, he does not clear the guilty. Yet in Psalm 51 David calls on God to justify him—to declare him innocent—despite the fact that he is guilty of sin! The Old Testament hints at how God can do this. But it is the New Testament that unveils the plan God intended to put into effect from before the creation of the material universe. As Romans 3:21–26 explains, Jesus died as an atoning sacrifice. That is, Jesus took our sins upon himself and paid the penalty that sin requires. With the penalty paid God justifies—declares innocent—all who believe in Jesus. These words recorded in Romans are undoubtedly some of the most significant in the entire Bible.

Abraham
Genesis 15:6

ROMANS 3:23–26 *For all have sinned and fall short of the glory of God, being justified freely by His grace through the redemption that is in Christ Jesus, whom God set forth as a propitiation by His blood, through faith, to demonstrate His righteousness, because in His forbearance God had passed over the sins that were previously committed, to demonstrate at the present time His righteousness, that He might be just and the justifier of the one who has faith in Jesus. (NKJV)*

Faith accounted for righteousness. Paul points out God has shown from the beginning that he will accept faith in place of that perfect righteousness which no person possesses. He did this for <u>Abraham</u>, the forefather of the Jewish people, before there was a Jewish people. In fact, God pronounced Abraham innocent and credited him with righteousness because of his trust in God before Abraham was circumcised. As circumcision was the sign that marked an individual off as a Jew, Paul argues that Abraham was declared righteous as a Gentile!

It follows that the principle of justification by faith—being declared innocent by God on the basis of trust in God rather than on the basis of what a person has actually done—is a universal principle, not a truth for Israel alone. Thus Paul concludes in Romans 4, "Now it was not written for [Abraham's] sake alone that it was imputed to him, but also for us. It shall be imputed to us who believe in Him who raised up Jesus our Lord from the dead, who was delivered up because of our offenses, and was raised because of our justification" (verses 23–25 NKJV).

> **what others say**
>
> **John Chrysostom**
>
> Whoever has become righteous through faith will live, not just in this life but in the one to come as well. This righteousness is not ours but belongs to God, and in saying this Paul hints to us that it is abundantly available and easy to obtain. For we do not get it by toil and labor but by believing.[2]

God Has Shown Love for All

In Romans the apostle has shown all human beings are helpless in the grip of sin and death. But then Paul presents the good news. God has chosen to freely forgive human beings! God in the person of Jesus Christ stepped into history to pay the penalty justice demands. In a great and stunning transaction Jesus took on himself the sins of the world, and Christ's own righteousness is credited to anyone who trusts in him.

The great mystery here is not what God has done for us in Christ, but why? Paul's answer is simple. "God demonstrates His own love toward us, in that while we were still sinners, Christ died for us" (Romans 5:8 NKJV).

Romans on Believers

In the first chapters of Romans the apostle Paul has described the universal condition of humankind, and the universal offer of salvation to all who will trust in Jesus Christ. In chapter 6 of Romans the focus shifts to believers. Here again, however, the message is universal in one vital respect. While the Old Testament made a distinction between Jew and non-Jew, Paul no longer makes that distinction. All Christians, whatever their ethnicity, race, gender or other differences are one now in Christ. What God intends to do for and in those who have come to him through Jesus is for all, without any of the old distinctions.

What then are the great contributions of Romans to our understanding of what God does for all believers?

God Enables Believers to Live Righteous Lives

Romans 6 introduces the stunning truth that Christians are "united with" Jesus Christ. God not only forgives the sins of those who believe in Jesus but also pronounces them innocent. God establishes a living link—a bond—between the individual believer and the Lord. Because of this bond we were, spiritually speaking, present at the cross and died with Jesus. We were also present at Jesus' resurrection and were raised to new life with him. Through this union that God established when we believed, Jesus' own power flows to us and enables us to live the righteous life that is impossible for sinners to achieve!

Paul is very careful to distinguish what we are able to do by our own efforts from what God is able to do in and through us. We do not achieve a righteous life. We are enabled as Christ's life is lived

go to

Jesus
John 1:1–14;
Philippians 2:5–11;
Colossians 1:15–20

Holy Spirit
John 14:15–17

Father, Son, and Holy Spirit
Ephesians 1:1–14

out through us. And here the apostle identifies clearly a truth implied but not defined in the Old Testament. For in Romans Paul speaks not only of "God," but also of "Jesus Christ," and of "the Holy Spirit." Christians are united with Christ in his death and resurrection, enabling us to live righteously by the power of the Holy Spirit.

what others say

Cyril of Alexandria

As we have died a death like his, so we shall also be conformed to his resurrection, because we shall live in Christ. It is true that the flesh will come to life again, but still we shall live in another way, by dedicating our souls to him and by being transformed into holiness and a kind of glorious life in the Holy Spirit.[3]

The Trinity in Scripture

The word *trinity* isn't found in the Bible. It's an invented theological term, used to express the conviction that the Bible's one God exists in three Persons. We see hints of this in Genesis 1:1, where the Hebrew name of God, Elohim, is a plural rather than singular noun. We see it in Genesis 1:26, which reports that God said, "Let Us make man in Our image" (NKJV). And we see it in frequent references to the "Spirit of God." Even the great affirmation of faith recited by Jews from ancient times, "the LORD our God, the LORD is one!" (Deuteronomy 6:4 NKJV), hints at trinity, for the word *one* is a Hebrew term that emphasizes plurality in unity, as in referring to one bunch made up of many grapes.

It is not until the New Testament however that a clear image is drawn of Scripture's one God existing in three persons. We see Jesus speak of the Father as "the only true God," and yet affirm that "I and My Father are one" (John 17:3; 10:30 NKJV). The Bible clearly speaks of Jesus as God come in the flesh, one with and yet distinct from God the Father. In the same way Jesus identifies the Holy Spirit as one exactly like himself, and in other passages the Spirit is unmistakably identified as God. In another of Paul's letters, Ephesians, the apostle defines the roles of Father, Son, and Holy Spirit in our salvation, acknowledging each as God.

The Role of Spirit in Romans

Understanding the fact that God exists in three Persons is important background for Romans. As we reach Romans 7 and especially Romans 8, we are introduced to the Holy Spirit as the person who is himself our living link with Jesus, and through whom flows the power that enables us to live godly and holy lives.

down payment
Romans 8:23

Romans teaches us that all Christians are linked individually to Jesus by the Holy Spirit. It is because of our union with Jesus that God can lift us beyond ourselves, enabling us to live righteous lives that it would be impossible for us to live on our own. God not only declares us to be righteous because of what Jesus did for us, but he also intends to actually make us righteous people here and now! And the key to living righteous lives is the fact that we are united to Jesus, so that his power can flow into and through us.

God Will Ultimately Make All Believers Like Jesus

As long as we live here on earth we will be torn between the pull of our old, sinful selves and the new creations we've become in Jesus. At times we'll respond to God's inner promptings and, in Paul's words, find that "the righteous requirements of the law" are being fully met in us. We'll freely, gladly, and spontaneously do the right thing, lifted up and enabled by the Holy Spirit within us. All too often, however, we'll give in to the pull of sin, or try to do right in our own strength and fail. But a day is coming when God will make us totally righteous, purging from us the last vestiges of sin and making us like Jesus himself. Paul looks forward to this day, the day of our resurrection, and says that the Spirit who now lives within us is the <u>down payment</u> that guarantees our ultimate deliverance. In Paul's words, we have been "called according to [God's] purpose," and this means that we have been "predestined to be conformed to the image of His Son, that He might be the firstborn among many brethren" (Romans 8.28 29 NKJV).

God guarantees that those who have trusted Jesus as Savior, who have been united with Jesus by faith, and who are linked to Jesus even now by the Holy Spirit, will be completely saved from sin. We will not only be declared innocent on the basis of Jesus' death, but we will also become truly innocent and pure, transformed by the very power of God that raised Jesus from the dead!

God Intends to Create a Loving Faith Community

In Romans 9–11 Paul pauses to answer objections that might be raised by Jewish critics or by uncertain Jewish believers. Again in these chapters Paul returns to the Old Testament to show that in universalizing the Gospel God has not acted inconsistently or unfairly. God has always been Sovereign, free to act as his nature dictates. With this established, Paul shares a vision of what God has for believers here and now.

Paul's focus in chapters 12–15 shifts from what God has for individual believers, to explore what the new relationship with Jesus means to believers living together as a community of faith. Again we need to remember that in the first century serious tensions existed between Jew and non-Jew, between members of different social classes, between men and women, between rich and poor. These same kinds of tensions exist today. There are racial tensions, radical differences between the generations, gender differences, and differences between rich and poor, the educated and the uneducated. Yet in Romans Paul gives us a vision of what God intends, and how it can be achieved. For God intends to create a healing community of love that will be a powerful witness to the world.

The principles of our life together as Jesus' own are again universal. They are intended to apply to all Christians, everywhere. They are especially intended to apply to us today, in our own churches and communities.

We are all to use our gifts to serve each other (Romans 12:1–8). God has equipped each believer with a spiritual gift—a special God-given ability to contribute to the growth and well being of others. As we accept our roles as servants of God's people and use our gifts for their benefit, we help to build the loving community of faith that Christians are to establish here and now.

We are to humbly love one another (Romans 12:9–21). A spirit of selflessness and a genuine concern for others is to characterize the Christian community. In a series of brief exhortations Paul gives us a picture of a people who are filled with God's Spirit living together as God intends.

We are to be good citizens and act in love toward all (Romans 13:1–14). God's people are to be responsive to secular authorities, and to use love as the standard by which we measure how to relate to our fellow citizens.

We are to maintain harmony within the community of faith (Romans 14:1–15:13). Disputable matters—matters about which the Bible remains silent and about which believers have differing convictions—are not to disrupt the harmony of the Christian community. We maintain harmony by acknowledging that Christ is Lord, and each individual believer is responsible to him. We maintain harmony by refraining from judging others whose convictions on disputable matters may differ from our own. And we maintain harmony by quietly living by our own convictions, not flaunting them, yet remaining sensitive to the feelings of others about them. Our goal is to welcome all who trust Jesus into our fellowship, to encourage them as they seek to grow in the faith, and "with one mind and one mouth" to glorify the God and Father of our Lord Jesus Christ (Romans 15:6 NKJV).

what others say

Saint Augustine

Paul says that we should receive the weak man in order that we might support his weakness by our strength. Neither should we criticize his opinions by daring to pass judgment on someone else's heart, which we do not see.[4]

Romans Packs a Punch

From the very beginning the Book of Romans has had an unmatched impact on Christianity. In the first century it defined the relationship between Jew and non-Jew, showing the universal application of the Gospel to all humankind.

Nearly every Christian writer before AD 200 alludes in his writings to the Book of Romans. The theologian Origen (AD 185–AD 254) wrote no fewer than fifteen books on this one epistle! In the course of following centuries other significant commentaries on Romans were written in both Greek and in Latin, the languages of the eastern and western churches. John Chrysostom (AD 347–AD 407), the famous preacher who became patriarch of Constantinople, left thirty-two homilies that constitute a verse-by-verse exposition of Romans. Perhaps most significant, the thought of Saint Augustine, the greatest of the Latin church fathers, was shaped by his reading of Romans.

The greatest impact of Romans on Christianity today can be traced to its role in the conversion of Martin Luther. Luther was a Catholic monk who struggled with a sense of his own sinfulness. Luther desperately tried to live up to the standard of righteousness that he found in Scripture. Driven to despair by the awareness of his failures, Luther found peace when he was gripped by the message of Romans 1:17: the just live by faith. Suddenly Luther realized that God freely gave his own righteousness to those who trust Jesus as Savior. Luther became the catalyst for the rediscovery of the doctrine of justification by faith alone, out of which the Protestant Reformation grew along with most Protestant churches existing today.

Romans had a major impact on such central figures in Christian history as Origen, John Chrysostom, Saint Augustine, Martin Luther, and John Wesley. One of the best-known examples of the impact of Luther's rediscovery of Romans' teachings happened in London, England. There one evening a failed missionary to American Indians sat and listened as Luther's commentary on Romans 1:17 was read aloud. Later the missionary wrote that he felt his heart "strangely warmed." Transformed by the message of justification by faith alone, that man, John Wesley, began preaching in the villages and fields of England. Wesley stimulated a great revival, which historians credit for saving England from the anarchy and horrors that accompanied the French Revolution. During his fifty years of active ministry Wesley also founded societies of believers from which our Methodist and Wesleyan Methodist churches grew.

what others say

Warren Wiersbe

Imagine! You and I can read and study the same inspired letter that brought life and power to Luther and Wesley! And the same Holy Spirit who taught them can teach us.[5]

Of all the books of the Bible, and of all books ever written, the Book of Romans is arguably the most influential book in the Christian world. Most wonderful of all, Romans has opened the eyes of untold millions to the love and grace of a God who cares for sinners, and who invites all to find forgiveness and new life in Jesus Christ.

Chapter Wrap-Up

- God's offer of salvation by grace through faith in Jesus Christ is universal. No one is left out.

- All humans fall short of their own standards for perfection, let alone God's. We are all sinners.

- God is not God of the Jews only. He is God of all, and he has always revealed himself to everyone.

- Every human who puts his or her faith in Christ is one of God's own and will one day enjoy the full presence of God for eternity. Furthermore, God grants believers the Holy Spirit whose instruction and strength will make righteousness not only a future promise but a present reality.

- The book of Romans is very likely the most influential book in all of Christian history. It has inspired such spiritual notables as Luther and Augustine.

Study Questions

1. What two groups made up the Christian church shortly after Jesus' resurrection?

2. What are the three types of death in Scripture, and which one is Paul concerned with in Romans?

3. What has God always accepted as a substitute for the righteousness no human possesses?

4. What is the basis for our salvation?

5. Is righteousness something that we will enjoy only in heaven?

Appendix A - The Answers

ROMANS 1: A SERVANT'S LONGING

1. Paul's confirmation began with his encounter with Christ on the road to Damascus. God sent a disciple by the name of Ananias to confirm both Paul's salvation and his call as an apostle to take God's message of love to the Gentile world (Acts 9:3–16). We find him taking his first mission assignment in Acts 13. (Romans 1:1)

2. Paul built his identity on being a servant of Christ. (Romans 1:1)

3. Jesus' resurrection from the dead was the ultimate confirmation of the Lord's divinity. He was declared by the Holy Spirit to be the Son of God. (Romans 1:4)

4. The key to the greatness of Paul's powerful worldview and the authority with which he ministered was his belief in the Scriptures and his understanding of God's grace through the Gospel of Jesus Christ. (Romans 1:2–5)

5. Paul was not ashamed because he knew the Gospel was the power of God giving life to all who believe. It was the Gospel that brought transformation in his life, and so he was not ashamed of the truth it brought to him and to the whole world. (Romans 1:16–17)

6. It was the Fall in Genesis 3 that introduced man to sin. In Romans 1–3, Paul writes of God's indictment of the world, demonstrating why man needs the righteousness of God. The truth was given to men, but since the Fall they have continued to "suppress the truth in unrighteousness." (Romans 1:18–23; Revelation 20:11–15)

ROMANS 2: JUDGMENTALISM AND HYPOCRISY

1. God is concerned about judgmentalism because humankind's judgment is always based on partial truth. God is the only one who has all the facts all the time. So God says that when we continue pointing the finger at each other we are bringing more condemnation upon our own heads. (Romans 2:1–4)

2. God's kindness buys us time. If God were not as kind as he is, he might pour out his wrath on us as soon as we sinned, but he doesn't. He gives us time to come to repentance. (Romans 2:3–4)

3. Paul meant that though people weren't experiencing God's wrath at that moment, they shouldn't therefore sit back and think all is well. As long as they continued to look down on people and ignore their own faults, the lake of God's wrath was getting bigger and bigger. (Romans 2:5–7)

4. God has declared everyone a sinner regardless of race. Then he offers his hand of love to all who will receive it. To receive God's grace is an expression of faith on the part of humans. (Romans 2:9–11; John 1:10–14; Ephesians 2:8–10)

5. Man (male and female), who is created in the image of God, has been given the gift of conscience. We are aware of our sinfulness. We are conscious of our rebellion. We are internally aware that we do not meet the requirements of the law. (Romans 2:12–16)

ROMANS 3: IN SEARCH OF RIGHTEOUSNESS

1. The Jews had an advantage in the sense that God entrusted the Jews with his Word. They had a direct source of righteousness from the perspective of the Creator. In addition, the Word given to the Jews was validated by a multitude of miracles, interventions, and special revelations. (Romans 3:1–4)

2. Our unrighteousness causes God to judge us because of how serious God is about sin. Our God is a holy God and cannot allow any sin to go unpunished. God restored our righteousness through Jesus Christ, thereby making salvation a free gift to all who receive Jesus as Savior and Lord. (Romans 3:5–8)

3. God, through Paul, points out, "There is no difference; for all have sinned and fall short of the glory of God." The sin of Adam has polluted every generation since Adam, and the sin of humankind throughout history is evidence of this truth. (Romans 3:22–23; 5:12–19)

4. The law defines righteousness and thereby exposes unrighteousness. It is this simple fact that makes a consciousness of sin universal. (Romans 3:19–20)

5. There can be no boasting in our accomplishments, in our works, in our gifts, for God is the author of our salvation, which is through grace and by faith. No one but Christ Jesus has ever kept the law completely. (Romans 3:27–28)

ROMANS 4: ABE'S FAITH

1. Faith. When God spoke to him, a totally new experience for Abraham, he believed God and the proof of his faith was his obedience. He did what God told him to do. (Romans 4:1–3; Genesis 12–22)

2. Circumcision followed the promise given to Abraham. Getting circumcised did not make Abraham righteous. He had faith when he was still uncircumcised. Circumcision was a mark of God's ownership and man's commitment to his God. It became a ritual under Mosaic law. (Romans 4:9–12)

3. Abraham believed he would have a son because God promised him that he would. (Romans 4:13–17)

4. Because God is holy, he cannot allow unrighteousness into his presence. Without righteousness, no one would see God, ever! Righteousness is our bridge back to God. (Romans 4:3, 22–25)

ROMANS 5: THE BENEFITS OF BELONGING TO CHRIST

1. Peace comes from justification by faith through Jesus Christ. (Romans 5:1–2)

2. We can rejoice in suffering because we know that suffering has meaning and purpose. Suffering produces perseverance, perseverance produces character, and character produces hope. (Romans 5:3–5)

3. The proof of God's love is that while we were sinners, Christ died for us. Our experience of God's love may be subjective, but this historical fact gives us unmistakable proof that God's love is not imagined. It is real. (Romans 5:6–8)

4. God's grace is bigger than sin, and the final results of grace will be far beyond the results of sin. (Romans 5:17).

5. God added the law to magnify the reality of the trespass. It gave definition to man's sin and thereby increased sin's transgression. (Romans 5:15, 20–21)

ROMANS 6: A LIFE-OR-DEATH SITUATION

1. It is true that where sin increased, "grace abounded much more" (Romans 5:20 NKJV), but sin does not cause grace to abound! It is simply the nature of grace to abound. In reality, it is God acting on behalf of sinful man showing us over and over that Satan is a defeated foe and we have been set free to follow God. (Romans 6:1–2)

2. When Paul speaks of believers being baptized "into [Christ's] death," he is referring to the end of the believer's old life as governed by association with Adam. Water baptism that follows conversion is an outward symbol of an inward reality. (Romans 6:3–4)

3. "To be united with Christ in resurrection" is to be united with Christ in his victory over death. Christians begin experiencing this victory as soon as they become Christians, and the consummation of the victory comes when we die and go to heaven. (Romans 6:5–7; 1 Corinthians 15:51–58)

4. Our union with Christ Jesus assures us that the old self, our sin nature, has been crucified. That's good news! Now we are called to listen to the Holy Spirit and not the cravings of the flesh. In truth, we are no longer slaves to sin, even though we are still tempted by sin. The same power that raised Jesus is available to raise us out of our sinful ways. (Romans 6:6–12)

5. We're still getting used to our new captain. Evil habits often take years to overcome, so while God is doing the work of sanctification the tendency to sin still raises its ugly head. If we don't repent and get right with God, we will continue in our former sin habits. (Romans 6:19–23)

ROMANS 7: THE TENSION OF TWO NATURES

1. The law was fulfilled in the life and the work of Jesus Christ. We are no longer in bondage to the law because we "died to the law through the body of Christ." We belong to Jesus Christ, who teaches us the spirit of the law, not just the letter. (Romans 7:6–7)

2. The new nature is freed from obligation to the law whereas the old nature is slave to it. The old nature is stimulated by the law while the new nature is prompted by the Holy Spirit. The old nature produces sin, acts unto death, whereas the new nature produces fruit unto God.

3. Because the law sets the standard for what's right

and what's wrong, it shows us where we have failed. (Romans 7:7–12)

4. The law is spiritual in that it comes from God, who is Spirit. The law is a direct revelation sent from God through Moses. To be unspiritual means to be a slave to sin. (Romans 7:14–20)

5. He means he is caught between the tension of two forces within him. One part desperately wants to follow God, but the old nature is a slave to sin. He is trying to fulfill the law as a Christian, and the result is failure and anguish. (Romans 7:24–25).

ROMANS 8: THE TRIUMPH OF SPIRIT-GUIDED LIVING

1. For a person to be "saved by the law," that person must keep the law perfectly. It is impossible, however, for a fallen human to keep the law no matter how sincerely s/he may seek to keep it, and therefore, the law is powerless to save people. The law can only show us our need for salvation in Christ, who (1) kept the law perfectly, and (2) paid the just penalty for our failure to keep the law. (Romans 8:1–4)

2. The mind has significant control in the spiritual journey. If the mind is following the desires of the sinful nature, then pollution enters our journey with God, but if the mind is set on the desires of the Spirit—God's righteousness—then life is filled with contentment and freedom. (Romans 8:5–8)

3. When we are controlled by the Holy Spirit, we are then liberated from the limitations that sin puts on life. The Spirit's control brings us into God's joy and freedom. (Roman 8:9–11; Galatians 5:1)

4. We know that everything belongs to Christ, but because of the grace of God we share in what is his. By the sovereign will of God, we are coheirs with his Son, Jesus. (Romans 8:12–17; 1 John 3:1–3)

5. Two of the most immediate and significant matters to which the Holy Spirit attends are helping us to pray and supporting us in our weakness. (Romans 8:26–27)

ROMANS 9: GOD IS IN CHARGE

1. Paul knew the Romans might be tempted to think he was exaggerating, so he stresses that he is telling the truth. (Romans 9:1–3)

2. God had given the Jewish nation a rich heritage. He lists the following:

a. Theirs is the adoption as sons.

b. Theirs is the divine glory.

c. Theirs are the covenants.

d. Theirs is the receiving of the law.

e. Theirs is the temple worship.

f. Theirs are the promises.

g. Theirs are the patriarchs. (Romans 9:4–5)

3. People are offended by the concept of election because from a finite perspective they think it makes God out to be unjust or unfair. But in fact, election is a demonstration of God's mercy and compassion. (Romans 9:6–16)

4. Paul chooses two very significant historical events to illustrate the doctrine of election: the first is the birth of Isaac as the child of promise and the second is the choice of Jacob over Esau. This had nothing at all to do with the character of the children, but it was such to establish "that the purpose of God according to election might stand" (Romans 9:11 NKJV).

5. Paul speaks of a "remnant according to the election of grace" (Roman 11:5 NKJV), of which he was a part. A remnant is a portion of a larger group, so out of all the Israelites, the remnant to which Paul referred was the people who because of grace chose to follow Christ as the Son of God. (Romans 9:27–28)

ROMANS 10: FAITH AVENUE

1. The Jews were zealous for God in the sense that they were focused on following the law and their Rabbinic traditions. They knew little if anything about the righteousness that comes through faith in Christ, and thus they refused God's open invitation. Their traditions and their polluted leadership prevented them from receiving Jesus, the Christ of Israel, their long-awaited Messiah! He offered them the righteousness that comes from faith in God and his promises, but they failed as a nation to receive their king. (Romans 10:1–5)

2. The Jews were stuck in a mode of thinking, impure and incomplete, that gave them a sense of righteousness that came from keeping the law, a "righteousness by law." The "righteousness by faith" is by grace through faith. This righteousness is a gift of God to all who receive his Son as Savior. (Romans 10:3–8; Ephesians 2:8–10; Titus 2:11–14)

3. Paul repeats the way of salvation again and again in his epistles. It is grace that makes salvation available—the grace of God in the life, death,

and resurrection of Jesus Christ as Lord. It is faith that enables fallen man to appropriate that grace and love into his heart and therein receive Jesus as Lord and Savior. It is by faith plus nothing. That is the nature of God's saving grace. (Romans 10:9–11)

4. When Paul says, "There is no distinction between Jew and Greek," he is saying there is only one way to God, regardless of one's ethnic or religious convictions. "The same Lord over all is rich to all who call upon Him" (Romans 10:12 NKJV). So no one can improve on God's free gift in Jesus Christ. We are all sinners. (Romans 10:11–13)

5. The expression "How beautiful are the feet of those who preach the gospel of peace" is in reference to those who respond to the call and will of God to go forth in faith proclaiming the message of the gospel, regardless of difficulties and insults. (Romans 10:14–15)

ROMANS 11: ISRAEL'S DESTINY

1. Paul clearly understood there is only one way for men and women to be saved from the eternal wrath of a holy, righteous God, and Jesus, the Messiah of Israel, is that way. Because Israel had officially rejected Jesus, Paul knew that many would be eternally lost. This was a great and ongoing grief in the heart of this faithful servant of God. (Romans 11:1–6)

2. Because of Israel's stand against Jesus, the spiritual dullness of the Jews, which had continued from the days of Isaiah the prophet, was now upon this generation also. Because they refused the way of faith (Romans 9:31–32), God made them impervious to his ministry of grace. This was the "spirit of stupor" to which Paul referred. (Romans 11:7–10)

3. Israel's fall was not permanent. God's love for this people had not diminished, but his discipline had increased due to their rebellion against, and rejection of, his Son, Jesus. Here we see God's sovereign power in full display. His righteous nature is inviolable. (Romans 11:11–12)

4. The "mystery" to which Paul referred was the salvation of the nation of Israel. Paul said, "all Israel will be saved." (Romans 11:25–32)

5. The unbelieving Israelites were God's enemies in the sense that they had rejected God's gift of righteousness by faith. They were still loved by God in the sense that ever since the faith of Abraham, God has loved his covenant people.

6. We should see mercy against the dark background of our sin because mercy is not necessary without sin. We must understand that our sin is what brought about our need for God's mercy.

ROMANS 12: HOW TO DO CHURCH

1. The ritual work of the Old Covenant had come to a complete end. Christ is the fulfillment of the law (Romans 10:5)! We are now "living sacrifices" in contrast to dead animal sacrifices. (Romans 12:1)

2. The health of our spirits is directly related to the health of our minds. When we renew our minds by reading scripture and praying, we are building healthy spirits. (Romans 12:2; Philippians 2:5; 2 Corinthians 10:5)

3. Because man is saved by grace, salvation is exclusively the work of our Creator. To elevate ourselves is to diminish the grace of God that brought us the gift of salvation. (Romans 12:3)

4. God has given the Body of Christ multiple gifts and callings. Each gift has a specific purpose in building up Christ's church to do the work of ministry and to exercise the practice of worship. No gift is insignificant and no gift is greater than another. All are given to exalt and bring glory to God. When this is happening, the church will grow in grace and in the knowledge of God. (Romans 12:6–8)

5. The tests of life are what prove your love sincere or false. If your love for someone falters and fails during difficult times, your love was never sincere. If your love continues through both thick and thin, your love is sincere. (Romans 12:9–13)

ROMANS 13: GOD AND COUNTRY

1. The Scriptures are very clear on the matter of submitting to governing authorities. Earthly authorities have been established by God and must be obeyed by everyone. There are no special exemptions. (Romans 13:1)

2. Some examples are family, politics, work, and church. (Romans 13:2–7)

3. By doing what is right, we will not need to fear those who rule over us. If their leadership transgresses our righteousness, we must do what is right and trust God to be our defender and hope. (Romans 13:3)

4. One's conscience is a very important part of one's spirituality. The conscience acts as an administrator who distinguishes between right and wrong as we do our best to make good decisions in a complicated world. The Holy Spirit will draw upon the conscience in order to guide us toward righteousness. If one ignores one's conscience, one might be ignoring the work of

the Holy Spirit. Regardless, the conscience is a gracious part of God's protection to assist believers in their walk. (Romans 13:5)

5. Taxes are always a test, especially when we are being overtaxed. Yet, we are to pay taxes to support those who engage in the work of governing full-time. (Romans 13:6–7)

6. God paid a "debt of love" when he sent Jesus to redeem a lost humanity. In like manner, we have a debt of love. As a part of God's redeemed, we are to extend love to one another; "love is the fulfillment of the law" (Romans 13:10 NKJV).

7. To do away with darkness, we must "put on the Lord Jesus Christ, and make no provision for the flesh, to fulfill its lusts" (Romans 13:14 NKJV). This is what Paul calls putting on the "armor of light" (13:12 NKJV). (Romans 13:11–14)

ROMANS 14: KEEPING PEACE

1. The term *doubtful things* refers to issues about which well-meaning, God-fearing Christians may differ because Scripture is unclear. In Romans 14, the doubtful things Paul addresses specifically are the matters of (1) clean and unclean foods, and (2) the observance of certain days. (Romans 14:1–4)

2. The "strong" believer is a person who has a grasp of his full liberty in Christ. Paul pointed out as an example that a strong believer's conscience is not plagued by doubts about whether it's morally right to eat meat. The strong believer knows, as Paul did, that "there is nothing unclean of itself" (Romans 14:14 NKJV), whereas the "weak" believer's conscience may not allow him or her to eat meat. The "weak" believer is weak in the sense that's s/he does not have a grasp of his or her full liberty in Christ. The "weak" believer is burdened by doubts about whether it's right to do things which the "strong" can do without any guilt at all. (Romans 14:5–8)

3. Judgment is a serious matter because it creates wounds in the Body of Christ that in turn create a spirit of separation and disunity. It creates a spirit of rejection while we are called to love and share the light of our Lord. (Matthew 7:1–6; Luke 6:27–31; 37–42; Romans 14.9–18)

4. We are to keep in mind that one day we will have to give an account to God for our own behavior. We are to remember that the "kingdom of God is not eating and drinking, but righteousness and peace and joy in the Holy Spirit" (Romans 14:17 NKJV). This is God's divine leverage against our tendency to judge instead of being a brother or friend. It should be mentioned, however, that this does not preclude godly discussion about issues. (Romans 14:16–18)

5. One would prove to be a stumbling block to another if one chose to exercise one's freedom at the expense of another person's spiritual growth. (Romans 14:19–21)

6. The "good" referred to here is the liberty to eat because all foods are clean. This liberty, however, may be regarded as evil if it is flaunted in the face of those who do not feel free to eat certain foods. Paul is encouraging his listeners to use the liberty lovingly, not arrogantly. (Romans 14:16, 22–23)

ROMANS 15: COME TOGETHER

1. The strong should bear the shortcomings of the weak because though Christ was the only person with the right to serve himself, he served others. The strong ought to follow his example. (Romans 15:1–4)

2. Paul selects a group of Old Covenant Scriptures that elevate the place of the Gentile in the plan and purpose of God. These Scriptures picture the Gentiles praising the God who saved them. (Romans 15:7–13)

3. The apostle Paul gloried in Christ Jesus. The Messiah was his focus in life and because of this, he was never distracted in his service to God. The immediacy of Christ's presence, both in Spirit and in power, helped to make Paul's service a glory to God and a blessing to the many churches he served. The same help is available to every succeeding generation. (Romans 15:17–22)

4. First we should remember that God knows our longings and will fulfill them if it is the best thing for us and the whole universe. Secondly, we ought to remember that no matter what suffering unfulfilled longings cause us here on earth, heaven will more than make up for it. (Romans 15:23–24)

5. Paul said that because the Gentiles were recipients of spiritual blessings from the Jews, it was appropriate for them to respond by giving back a material blessing. (Romans 15:25–29)

ROMANS 16: A FOND FAREWELL

1. Paul was a servant to the servants. He valued every person who gave of him- or herself for the work of God's Kingdom. Phoebe was that kind of person. She had helped many and had been "a helper" to Paul as well. It was by serving Paul and receiving service from Paul that Phoebe knew Paul on such a personal level. (Romans 16:1–2)

2. Priscilla and Aquila were in the city of Corinth where they practiced the trade of tentmaking.

Paul was proficient in this skill as well, and in God's providence the three of them partnered in tentmaking and sharing the gospel (see Acts 18:1–4). In this context they forged a fruitful friendship and ministry. (Romans 16:33–34)

3. It is beautiful to read Paul's greeting to his many friends and fellow workers. He held them all in high esteem in the Lord. His fellow servants loved him deeply and to have heard a word from him that was affirming would no doubt have brought joy to their hearts. (Romans 16:5–16)

4. False teachers create division and competition in the Body of Christ by being insincere and using "smooth words and flattering speech" to deceive the minds of the faithful. They teach what is contrary to the Word of God. They follow their own passions. (Romans 16:17–19)

5. The gospel renders Satan powerless so he seeks to confuse, clutter, and create tension in the church. But the gospel brings peace, and God's peace is a crushing blow to the work of our Enemy. God promises that if we resist Satan, he will flee! We are also to put on the full armor of God mentioned in Ephesians 6:10–19. (Romans 16:20; James 4:7)

THE BOOK OF ROMANS OVERVIEW

1. The two groups that made up the first Christians were Jews and Gentile God-fearers. The latter group was Gentiles who went to Jewish synagogue because they were interested in the Jewish God and in Jewish moral teachings.

2. The three types of death in Scripture are biological death, spiritual death, and eternal death. Biological death is when our bodies die, spiritual death is the state of being spiritually separated from God because of sin, and eternal death is the state of being spiritually separated from God forever. Paul is mainly concerned with spiritual death in Romans.

3. From Old Testament times until now God has always accepted faith in his promises as a substitute for the righteousness no human possesses.

4. The basis for salvation is the death and resurrection of Jesus Christ, the atoning sacrifice that God made for the sins of humans.

5. God starts the process of developing righteousness within believers as soon as they believe. He does this by giving us his spirit, the Holy Spirit, which resides in the hearts of all Christians.

Appendix B—The Experts

Anderson, Sir Robert (1841–1918)—Foremost British barrister and extensive world traveler, head of the Criminal Investigation Department of Scotland Yard, Political Crime Advisor to the British Home Office, and author of numerous books on prophecy.

Apollinaris of Laodicea (circa 310–390)—Syrian prelate and theologian, bishop of Laodicea (Syria), and Greek biblical commentator.

Augustine, Saint (354–430)—Early Christian church father and philosopher, also known as Saint Augustine of Hippo.

Barclay, William—Internationally recognized scholar, teacher, author, and pastor, and the editor of the *Daily Study* Bible series of books.

Barker, Kenneth L.—Executive Director of the NIV Translation Center of the International Bible Society, member of the NIV Translation Committee, and editor of the NIV Study Bible.

Barth, Karl—Honorary professor of Reformed Theology, Gettingen, Germany, 1921–25; professor of Dogmatics and New Testament Exegesis, Munster, 1925–30; professor of Systematic Theology in Bonn, 1930–35; and author of more than a dozen books.

Benson, Robert—Freelance writer. Author of *Between the Dreaming and the Coming True* and *Living Prayer*. Leads retreats and workshops on spirituality and writing.

Boice, James Montgomery—Pastor of historic Tenth Presbyterian Church, Philadelphia; speaker on *The Bible Study Hour*; president of Evangelical Ministries; editor of *Eternity Magazine*; and author of more than a dozen books.

Bonhoeffer, Dietrich—Author, teacher, and theologian, executed by the Nazis for his role in the German Resistance Movement.

Buechner, Frederick—Presbyterian minister and author of over twenty fiction and nonfiction books.

Calvin, John—French theologian, author, pastor, and reformer; founder of the Reformed church and a theocratic government in Geneva, Switzerland, which served as a focal point for defense of Protestantism throughout Europe. His famous *Institutes of the Christian Religion* were published in 1536.

Chambers, Oswald (1874–1917)—A Bible teacher, conference leader, and YMCA chaplain. His writing, compiled after his death by his widow, is available in devotional books, including the popular *My Utmost for His Highest*.

Chrysostom, John (347–407)—Syrian prelate, preacher, and archbishop of Constantinople, exiled and banished for his boldness.

Coleridge, Samuel Taylor (1772–1834)—English poet and critic, coauthor with William Wordsworth of the *Lyrical Ballads*.

Driscoll, Mark—Founder and pastor of Mars Hill Fellowship, Seattle, Washington, and church planting coordinator with Acts 29, headquartered in Boca Raton, Florida.

Dunn, James D. G.—Professor of Divinity, University of Durham, England, and author of many publications, including *The Evidence for Jesus* and *The Living Word*.

Edwards, James R.—Professor of Religion, Whitworth College; frequent contributor to scholarly journals; and coauthor of *The Layman's Overview of the Bible*.

Eusebius of Emesa (circa 300–359)—Greek prelate, theologian, and ecclesiastic writer of the Alexandrian school.

Godet, F. L. (1812–1900)—Influential Swiss Protestant Reformed scholar and professor of biblical exegesis and critical theology, Theological School of the National Swiss Church of the Canton.

Graham, Billy—World famous evangelist and author. (Billy Graham Evangelistic Association, 1300 Harmon Place, P.O. Box 779, Minneapolis, MN 56440–0779)

Haldane, Robert (1764–1842)—Evangelist, writer, founder of Society for Propagating the Gospel at Home (1797), and instigator of Haldane's Revival in Geneva, Switzerland, and southern France.

Henry, Matthew (1662–1714)—English scholar, pastor, and Bible expositor, best known for his 1704 detailed commentary on the Bible.

Hodge, Charles—Author, lecturer, theologian, professor of Original Languages of Scripture at Princeton Theological Seminary in 1820, and also professor of Oriental and Biblical Literatures.

Jerome, Saint (circa 347–420)—Latin church father who published the Latin version of the Bible, known as the Vulgate.

Keener, Craig S.—Professor of New Testament, Hood Theological Seminary, Salisbury, North Carolina; ordained minister in the National Baptist Convention USA; contributor to such journals as *The Expositor Times* and *Christianity Today*; and author of *Paul, Woman and Wives*.

Kohlenberger III, John R.—Author of the *NIV Interlinear Hebrew-English Old Testament* and the *NRSV Unabridged Concordance*.

Lewis, C. S. (1898–1963)—English scholar and writer, fellow and tutor at Oxford (1925–54), professor of English at Cambridge (1954–63), and author of literary studies, fantasy tales for children, and many works of Christian apologetics.

Lloyd-Jones, D. Martyn—Author, physician, and Presbyterian minister.

Luther, Martin (1483–1546)—German religious reformer and founder of Protestantism and the Reformation; professor of biblical exegesis, Wittenberg (1512–46); known for his Ninety-five Theses nailed to the church door at Wittenberg; translator of the Old and New Testaments from Greek into German; and author of many commentaries, catechisms, sermons, and hymns.

Manning, Brennan—Speaker, lecturer, and spiritual retreat facilitator.

Moo, Douglas J.—Professor at Trinity Evangelical Divinity School, Deerfield, Illinois, and editor of *Trinity Journal*.

Murray, John (1898–1975)—Professor of Systematic Theology at Westminster Theological Seminary, Philadelphia, Pennsylvania, and author of several books, including *Principles of Conduct: Aspects of Biblical Ethics and Redemption—Accomplished and Applied*.

Nouwen, Henri—Netherlands born and educated author, priest, psychologist, and theologian; former professor at Notre Dame, Yale Divinity School, and Harvard; and pastor of Daybreak, a worldwide ministry for the mentally and physically handicapped.

O'Connor, Elizabeth—Teacher, consultant, counselor, author, and support minister at The Church of the Saviour, Washington, D.C.

Origen (circa 185–254)—Christian writer and teacher, one of the Greek fathers of the church and author of fifteen books on Romans.

Pelagius (circa 354–418)—British monk, theologian, and author.

Piper, John—Pastor of Bethlehem Baptist Church, Minneapolis, Minnesota, and author of several books, including *Desiring God* and *The Pleasures of God*.

Plumer, William S. (1802–1880)—Professor of Didactic and Pastoral Theology, Western Theological Seminary; founder and editor of *Watchman of the South*; and author of several books, including *Commentary on Romans* (1870).

Richards, Larry—Author of over 175 books and general editor of *The Smart Guide to the Bible*™ Series.

Schaeffer, Francis A.—Philosopher, theologian, author of more than twenty books, and founder of L'Abri Fellowship international study and discipleship centers.

Schlatter, Adolf (1852–1938)—Professor at Tubingen University, author of more than a hundred books, and arguably one of the most brilliant New Testament interpreters of the twentieth century.

Stowers, Stanley K.—Professor of Religious Studies, Brown University, and author of several books.

Stuhlmacher, Peter—Professor of New Testament, University of Tubingen, Germany, and author of several books on Paul.

Swindoll, Charles R.—Popular Christian author of more than twenty best-selling books, featured daily on his worldwide broadcast *Insight for Living*, and president of Dallas Theological Seminary, Dallas, Texas.

Teresa, Mother (1910–1997)—Nobel Peace Prize recipient in 1979, noted for helping the dying, the destitute, lepers, AIDS victims, orphans, and society's outcasts around the world.

Theodoret of Cyr (393–458)—Greek theologian at the school in Antioch, Bishop of Cyrrhus, affirmed by the Council of Chalcedon, and author of church history, commentaries, exegesis, and biographies.

Tozer, A. W. (1897–1963)—Pastor with the Christian Missionary Alliance. Author of many books including *The Pursuit of God*.

Walvoord, John F.—Chancellor and professor emeritus of Systematic Theology, Dallas Theological Seminary; author or editor of twenty-six books and dozens of articles for magazines and scholarly journals.

Wiersbe, Warren—One of the evangelical world's most-respected Bible teachers, and author of more than one hundred books.

Yancey, Philip—Editor-at-large for *Christianity Today* magazine and author of eight Gold Medallion award-winning books.

Zacharias, Ravi—President of Ravi Zacharias International Ministries, internationally known lecturer, debater, author, Christian apologist, and host of the weekly radio program *Let My People Think*.

Zuck, Roy B.—Department chair and professor of Bible Exposition, Dallas Theological Seminary; author or editor of numerous books and magazine and journal articles.

Endnotes

Romans 1: A Servant's Longing

1. D. Martyn Lloyd-Jones, *Romans: An Exposition of Chapter One, The Gospel of God* (Edinburgh: The Banner of Truth Trust, 1985), 1.

2. Samuel Taylor Coleridge, quoted in *Man's Ruin* by Donald G. Barnhouse (Grand Rapids, MI: Eerdmans, 1955), 2.

3. Martin Luther, quoted in *Man's Ruin* by Donald G. Barnhouse (Grand Rapids, MI: Eerdmans, 1955), 2.

4. F. L. Godet, quoted in *Man's Ruin* by Donald G. Barnhouse (Grand Rapids, MI: Eerdmans, 1955), 2.

5. Francis A. Schaeffer, *The Finished Work of Christ* (Wheaton: Crossway Books, 1998), 16.

6. W. E. Vine, *An Expositionary Dictionary of New Testament Words* (London: Oliphants, 1959), 318.

7. Schaeffer, *The Finished Work of Christ*, 19.

8. Saint Augustine, *Ancient Christian Commentary on Scripture* (Downers Grove, IL: InterVarsity, 1998), 15.

9. Adolf Schlatter, *Romans: The Righteousness of God* (Peabody, MA: Hendrickson Publishers, 1995), 12.

10. Dietrich Bonhoeffer, *Letters and Papers from Prison* (Macmillan Company, 1953: New York), 13.

11. John F. Walvoord and Roy B. Zuck, eds., *The Bible Knowledge Commentary* (Colorado Springs, CO: Chariot Victor, 1985), 440.

12. Pelagius, *Ancient Christian Commentary on Scripture* (Downers Grove, IL: InterVarsity, 1998), 22.

13. William S. Plumer, *Commentary on Romans* (Grand Rapids, MI: Kregel, 1971), 57–58.

14. Joseph Shulam with Hillary Lecornu, *A Commentary on the Jewish Roots of Romans* (Baltimore, MD: Messianic Jewish Publishers, a division of The Lederer Foundation, 1997), 38.

15. Mother Teresa, quoted from "Mother Teresa Memorial Page," http://home.pacbell.net/mandmcc/motherteresa.htm.

16. Schaeffer, *The Finished Work of Christ*, 20.

17. Apollinaris of Laodicea, *Ancient Christian Commentary on Scripture* (Downers Grove, IL: InterVarsity, 1998), 29.

18. Karl Barth, *The Epistle to the Romans* (London: Oxford University Press, 1933), 35.

19. Lloyd-Jones, *Romans: An Exposition of Chapter One*, 311.

20. N. T. Wright, *What Saint Paul Really Said* (Grand Rapids, MI: William B. Eerdmans, 1997), 160.

21. Brendan Byrne, *Sacra Pagina—Romans* (Collegeville, MN: The Liturgical Press, 1996), 63.

22. Barth, *Epistle to the Romans*, 42.

23. J. Vernon McGee, *Thru the Bible Commentary Series, Romans Chapters 1–8* (Nashville, TN: Thomas Nelson, Inc., 1991), 36–37.

24. Barth, *Epistle to the Romans*, 49.

25. Schlatter, *Romans*, 42.

26. Pelagius, *Ancient Christian Commentary on Scripture*, 48.

27. Schaeffer, *The Finished Work of Christ*, 43.

Romans 2: Judgmentalism and Hypocrisy

1. Matthew Henry, *Commentary on the Whole Bible* (Grand Rapids, MI: Zondervan, 1961), 1757.

2. Henry, *Commentary on the Whole Body*, 1757.

3. Martin Luther, *Luther: Lectures on Romans*, vol. 25 of *The Library of Christian Classics*, ed. Wilhelm Pauck (Philadelphia: Westminster Press, 1961), 3.

4. Schaeffer, *The Finished Work of Christ*, 62–63.

Romans 3: In Search of Righteousness

1. Eusebius of Emesa, *Ancient Christian Commentary on Scripture* (Downers Grove, IL: InterVarsity, 1998), 81.

2. James R. Edwards, *New International Biblical Commentary: Romans* (Peabody, MA: Hendrickson, 1992), 84–85.

3. Lloyd-Jones, *Romans: An Exposition of Chapter One*, 305.

4. Apollinaris of Laodicea, *Ancient Christian Commentary on Scripture* (Downers Grove, IL: InterVarsity, 1998), 83.

5. Robert Anderson, *Redemption Truths* (Grand Rapids, MI: Kregel, 1980), 152.

6. Augustine, *Ancient Christian Commentary on Scripture*, 96.

7. Barth, *The Epistle to the Romans*, 85–86.

8. Brennan Manning, *The Ragamuffin Gospel* (Sisters, OR: Multnomah Publishers, 1990), 23.

9. Henry, *Commentary on the Whole Bible*, 1761.

10. Schaeffer, *The Finished Work of Christ*, 79–80.

11. Lawrence O. Richards, *The Victor Bible Background Commentary* (Wheaton, IL: Victor Books, 1994), 326.

Romans 4: Abe's Faith

1. James D. G. Dunn, *Romans 1–8*, vol. 38 of *Word Biblical Commentary* (Dallas: Word Books, 1988), 219.

2. Henry, *Commentary on the Whole Bible*, 1761.

3. Augustine, *Ancient Christian Commentary on Scripture*, 110.

4. Charles R. Swindoll, *The Grace Awakening* (Dallas: Word Publishing, 1990), 24.

5. Ibid., 25.

6. Schaeffer, *The Finished Work of Christ*, 92.

7. Augustine, *Ancient Christian Commentary on Scripture*, 112.

8. Lawrence O. Richards, *Complete Bible Handbook* (Waco, TX: Word Books, 1982), 611.

9. Luther, *Lectures on Romans*, 266.

10. John Piper, *Future Grace* (Sisters, OR: Multnomah Books, 1995), 190.

11. Henry, *Commentary on the Whole Bible*, 1762.

12. Edwards, *New International Biblical Commentary*, 118.

13. Piper, *Future Grace*, 189.

14. John Calvin, *Calvin's Commentaries* (Grand Rapids, MI: Eerdmans, 1973), 100.

15. Theodoret of Cyr, *Ancient Christian Commentary on Scripture* (Downers Grove, IL: InterVarsity, 1998), 122.

16. John Chrysostom, *Ancient Christian Commentary on Scripture*, 123.

Romans 5: The Benefits of Belonging to Christ

1. Calvin, *Calvin's Commentaries*, 104.

2. Joni Eareckson Tada, quoted in Dave Goetz, "Thriving with Limitations," *Leadership Magazine*, Winter 1996, 62–63.

3. Charles R. Swindoll, *Laugh Again* (Dallas: Word Publishing, 1991), 53.

4. Schaeffer, *The Finished Work of Christ*, 133.

5. Bonhoeffer, *Life Together*, 17–18.

6. Yancey, *The Bible Jesus Read*, 27–28.

7. Frederick Buechner, *Wishful Thinking* (New York: Harper & Row, 1973), 53–54.

8. Yancey, *The Bible Jesus Read*, 205.

9. Calvin, *Calvin's Commentaries*, 109–110.

10. Origen, *Ancient Christian Commentary on Scripture*, 135–136.

11. Mark Driscoll, "The Power of Grace: Revealing Our Slavery" (Seattle: Mars Hill Church sermon notes, December 13, 1998), 30.

12. Schaeffer, *The Finished Work of Christ*, 142.

13. Chrysostom, quoted in Luther, *Lectures on Romans*, 173.

14. Luther, *Lectures on Romans*, 310.

Romans 6: A Life-or-Death Situation

1. Edwards, *New International Biblical Commentary*, 158.

2. Chrysostom, *Ancient Christian Commentary on Scripture*, 153.

3. N. T. Wright, *What Saint Paul Really Said* (Grand Rapids, MI: William B. Eerdmans, 1997:), 136.

4. Oswald Chambers, *My Utmost for His Highest*, ed. James Reimann (Grand Rapids, MI: Discovery House, 1992), March 8 and January 15.

5. Schaeffer, *The Finished Work of Christ*, 161–162.

6. Luther, *Lectures on Romans*, 315.

7. Dietrich Bonhoeffer, *The Cost of Discipleship* (New York: Macmillan, 1963), 258.

8. Luther, *Lectures on Romans*, 319.

9. Calvin, *Calvin's Commentaries*, 133.

10. Charles Hodge, *Commentary on the Epistle to the Romans* (Grand Rapids, MI: Eerdmans, 1977), 211.

Romans 7: The Tension of Two Natures

1. William Barclay, quoted in Mark Driscoll, "The Power of Marriage: Revealing Our Union with Jesus" (Seattle: Mars Hill Church sermon notes, January 3, 1999), 32.

2. Matthew Henry, *Commentary on the Whole Bible*, 1768.

3. Schlatter, *Romans*, 154.

4. Plumer, *Commentary on Romans*, 318.

5. Schlatter, *Romans*, 158.

6. John Murray, *The Epistle to the Romans* (Grand Rapids, MI: Wm. B. Eerdmans, 1965), 250.

7. Douglas J. Moo, *The Epistle to the Romans* (Grand Rapids, MI: Eerdmans, 1996), 469–470.

8. Augustine, *Ancient Christian Commentary on Scripture*, 187.

9. Plumer, *Commentary on Romans*, 326–327.

10. Joseph Shulam with Hillary Lecornu, *A Commentary on the Jewish Roots of Romans* (Baltimore, MD: Messianic Jewish Publishers, a division of The Lederer Foundation, 1997), 249–250.

11. Walvoord and Zuck, *The Bible Knowledge Commentary*, 467.

12. Lawrence O. Richards, *Illustrated Bible Handbook* (Nashville: Thomas Nelson, 1982), 616.

13. Martin Luther, *Lectures on Romans*, 339.

14. Plumer, *Commentary on Romans*, 338.

15. Richards, *Illustrated Bible Handbook*, 616.

16. Augustine, *Ancient Christian Commentary on Scripture*, 199.

Romans 8: The Triumph of Spirit-Guided Living

1. Edwards, *New International Biblical Commentary*, 203–204.

2. Douglas J. Moo, *The Epistle to the Romans* (Grand Rapids, MI: Wm. B. Eerdmans, 1996), 484.

3. Henry, *Commentary on the Whole Bible*, 1770.

4. J. Vernon McGee, *Thru The Bible Commentary Series, Romans Chapters 1–8* (Nashville, TN: Thomas Nelson, Inc., 1991), 145.

5. Schlatter, *Romans*, 180.

6. Edwards, *New International Biblical Commentary*, 205.

7. Philip Yancey, *What's So Amazing about Grace?* 282.

8. Moo, *The Epistle to the Romans*, 485.

9. Yancey, *What's So Amazing about Grace?* 157.

10. Esther K. Rusthoi, "When We See Christ," *Hymns for the Family of God* (Nashville: Paragon Associates, 1976), 129.

11. Chrysostom, *Ancient Christian Commentary on Scripture*, 221–222.

12. Saint Jerome, *Ancient Christian Commentary on Scripture* (Downers Grove, IL: InterVarsity, 1998), 225.

13. John Calvin, quoted in Plumer, *Commentary on Romans*, 420.

14. Bonhoeffer, *Life Together*, 86.

15. Philip Yancey, *Reaching for the Invisible God* (Grand Rapids, MI: Zondervan, 2000), quoted in "Living with Furious Opposites," *Christianity Today*, September 4, 2000, 73.

16. Chambers, *My Utmost for His Highest*, March 7.

Romans 9: God's in Charge

1. C. E. B. Cranfield, *The International Critical Commentary* (London: T & T Clark, 1975), 448.

2. Cranfield, *Critical Commentary*, 448.

3. Mark Driscoll, "The Power of Election: Revealing God's Compassion" (Seattle: Mars Hill Church sermon notes, February 14, 1999), 38.

4. James D. G. Dunn, *Word Biblical Commentary* (Dallas: Word Books, 1988), 531.

5. Augustine, *Ancient Christian Commentary on Scripture*, 255.

6. D. Martyn Lloyd-Jones, *Romans: An Exposition of Chapter 10, Saving Faith* (Edinburgh: The Banner of Truth Trust, 1997), 2.

7. Larry Richards, *The Bible Reader's Companion* (Wheaton, IL: Victor Books, 1991), 745.

8. Peter Stuhlmacher, *Paul's Letter to the Romans* (Louisville, KY: Westminster/John Knox Press, 1994), 147–148.

9. Edwards, *New International Biblical Commentary*, 237–238.

10. Luther, *Lectures on Romans*, 386.

11. Edwards, *New International Biblical Commentary*, 240–241.

12. F. F. Bruce, *The International Bible Commentary* (Carmel, New York: Guideposts, 1986), 1332.

13. W. Burrows, *The Preacher's Complete Homiletic Commentary* (New York: Funk & Wagnalls Company), 334.

Romans 10: Faith Avenue

1. Lloyd-Jones, *Romans: An Exposition of Chapter 10*, 20–21.

2. A. T. Robertson, *Word Pictures in The New Testament* (Nashville, TN: Broadman Press, 1931), 387.

3. D. Martyn Lloyd-Jones, in Robertson, *Word Pictures in The New Testament*, 270.

4. Cranfield, *Critical Commentary*, 517.

5. James Montgomery Boice, *Romans: Volume 3, God and History, Romans 9–11* (Grand Rapids, MI: Baker Books, 1993), 1159–1160.

6. Lloyd-Jones, *Romans: An Exposition of Chapter 10*, 87–88.

7. Edwards, *New International Biblical Commentary*, 253.

8. Hodge, *Commentary on the Epistle to the Romans*, 340.

9. Moo, *The Epistle to the Romans*, 644.

10. Schlatter, *Romans*, 215.

11. Lloyd-Jones, *Romans: An Exposition of Chapter 10*, 198.

12. John F. Walvoord and Roy B. Zuck, *The Bible Knowledge Commentary* (Colorado Springs, CO. Chariot Victor, 1983), 481.

13. Plumer, *Commentary on Romans*, 523.

14. Douglas J. Moo, *The Epistle to the Romans* (Eerdmans, 1996: Grand Rapids, MI), 663.

15. Augustine, *Ancient Christian Commentary on Scripture*, 279.

16. Hodge, *Commentary on the Epistle to the Romans*, 349.

Romans 11: Israel's Destiny

1. D. Martyn Lloyd-Jones, *Romans: An Exposition of Chapter 11, To God's Glory* (Edinburgh: The Banner of Truth Trust, 1998), 5.

2. Joseph Shulam with Hillary Lecornu, *A Commentary on the Jewish Roots of Romans* (Baltimore, MD: Messianic Jewish Publishers, a division of The Lederer Foundation, 1997), 363.

3. Calvin, *Calvin's Commentaries*, 242.

4. Billy Graham, *Storm Warning* (Minneapolis: Grason, 1992), 57.

5. Luther, *Lectures on Romans*, 425.

6. Cranfield, *Critical Commentary*, 547–548.

7. Francis Davidson, *The New Bible Commentary* (Grand Rapids, MI: Eerdmans, 1953), 958.

8. Schlatter, *Romans*, 220.

9. F. F. Bruce, *The International Bible Commentary* (Carmel, NY: Guideposts, 1986), 1337.

10. Lloyd-Jones, *Romans: An Exposition of Chapter 11*, 87.

11. A. T. Robertson, *Word Pictures in The New Testament* (Nashville, TN: Broadman Press, 1931), 396.

12. Jerome, *Ancient Christian Commentary on Scripture*, 294.

13. Frederick L. Godet, *Commentary on the Epistle to the Romans* (Grand Rapids, MI: Zondervan Publishing House, 1956), 408.

14. Cranfield, *Critical Commentary*, 573.

15. Peter Stuhlmacher, *Paul's Letter to the Romans* (Westminster/John Knox Press, 1994: Louisville, KY), 173.

16. Boice, *Romans: Volume 3*, 1402.

17. Edwards, *New International Biblical Commentary*, 277–278.

18. Boice, *Romans: Volume 3*, 1476.

Romans 12: How to Do Church

1. A. W. Tozer, *The Pursuit of God* (Camp Hill, PA and Bloomington, MN: Christian Publications and Garborg's Heart 'n Home, 1993), April 26.

2. Haldane, *Exposition of the Epistle of the Romans*, 557.

3. Schlatter, *Romans*, 230.

4. Chrysostom, (Edited by Gerald Bray), *Ancient Christian Commentary on Scripture* (Downers Grove, IL: InterVarsity Press, 1998), 306.

5. John F. Walvoord and Roy B. Zuck, *The Bible Knowledge Commentary* (Colorado Springs, CO: Chariot Victor, 1983), 488.

6. Chrysostom, *Ancient Christian Commentary on Scripture*, 310.

7. Lawrence O. Richards and Gib Martin, *A Theology of Personal Ministry* (Grand Rapids, MI: Zondervan, 1981), 119.

8. Mark Driscoll, "Romans: The Mission Heart of God" (Seattle: Mars Hill Church sermon notes, April 18, 1999), 47.

9. Edwards, *New International Biblical Commentary*, 287.

10. Cranfield, *Critical Commentary*, 630.

11. Bonhoeffer, *Life Together*, 97.

12. Billy Graham, quoted by William Griffin and Ruth Graham Dienert, *The Faithful Christian* (Minneapolis: Grason, 1994), 93.

13. Swindoll, *The Grace Awakening*, 303.

14. Ambrosiaster, Gerald Bray, ed., *Ancient Christian Commentary on Scripture* (Downers Grove, IL: InterVarsity Press, 1998), 317.

15. Frederick L.Godet, *Commentary on the Epistle to the Romans* (Grand Rapids, MI: Zondervan Publishing House, 1956), 437.

16. Joseph Shulam with Hillary Lecornu, *A Commentary on the Jewish Roots of Romans* (Baltimore, MD: Messianic Jewish Publishers, a division of The Lederer Foundation, 1997), 419.

17. Richards, *The Bible Reader's Companion*, 748.

18. Edwards, *New International Biblical Commentary*, 298.

19. Luther, *Lectures on Romans*, 466.

20. Augustine, *Ancient Christian Commentary on Scripture*, 323.

Romans 13: God and Country

1. F. F. Bruce, *The International Bible Commentary* (Carmel, NY: Guideposts, 1986), 1340.

2. Charles Hodge, *Commentary on the Epistle to the Romans* (Wm. B. Eerdmans, 1968: Grand Rapids, MI), 406.

3. James Montgomery Boice, *Romans, vol. 4* (Grand Rapids, MI: Baker Books, 1995), 1643.

4. Pelagius, *Ancient Christian Commentary on Scripture*, 325.

5. Edwards, *New International Biblical Commentary*, 308.

6. Calvin, *Commentaries on the Epistle of Paul*, 483.

7. Ravi Zacharias, *Can Man Live Without God?* (Dallas: Word Publishing, 1994), 134.

8. Graham, *Storm Warning*, 84–85.

9. Origen, *Ancient Christian Commentary on Scripture* (Downers Grove, IL: InterVarsity, 1998), 330.

10. Augustine, *Ancient Christian Commentary on Scripture*, 331.

11. W. Burrows, *The Preacher's Complete Homiletic Commentary* (New York: Funk & Wagnalls Company), 426.

12. Calvin, *Commentaries on the Epistle of Paul*, 490.

13. Robert Benson, *Living Prayer* (New York: Tarcher/Putnam, 1998), 191.

14. Augustine, *Ancient Christian Commentary on Scripture*, 336.

Romans 14: Keeping Peace

1. Charles Hodge, *Commentary on the Epistle to the Romans* (Grand Rapids, MI: Wm. B. Eerdmans, 1968), 417.

2. Lawrence O. Richards, *The Teachers Commentary* (Wheaton: Victor Books, 1987), 836.

3. John Calvin, quoted by William S. Plumer, *Commentary on Romans* (Grand Rapids, MI: Kregel, 1971), 604.

4. Plumer, *Commentary on Romans*, 606.

5. Stuhlmacher, *Paul's Letter to the Romans*, 223.

6. Chrysostom, *Ancient Christian Commentary on Scripture*, 345.

7. Swindoll, *The Grace Awakening*, 299.

8. Stanley K. Stowers, *A Re-Reading of Romans* (New Haven: Yale University Press, 1994), 323.

9. F. F. Bruce, *The International Bible Commentary* (Carmel, NY: Guideposts, 1986), 1342.

10. Stuhlmacher, *Paul's Letter to the Romans*, 228.

11. Karl Barth, *The Epistle to the Romans* (London: Oxford University Press, 1933), 519.

12. Edwards, *New International Biblical Commentary*, 330.

13. Schlatter, *Romans*, 258.

14. Douglas J. Moo, *The Epistle to the Romans* (Grand Rapids, MI: Wm. B .Eerdmans, 1996), 856.

15. Leon Morris, *The Epistle to the Romans* (Grand Rapids, MI: Wm. B. Eerdmans, 1988), 489–490.

16. Charles Hodge, *Commentary on the Epistle to the Romans* (Grand Rapids, MI: Wm. B. Eerdmans, 1968), 427.

17. Pelagius, *Ancient Christian Commentary on Scripture*, 348.

18. Plumer, *Commentary on Romans*, 607.

19. Luther, *Lectures on Romans*, 506.

Romans 15: Come Together

1. John Murray, *The Epistle to the Romans* (Grand Rapids, MI: Wm. B. Eerdmans, 1968), 197–198.

2. Henry, *Commentary on the Whole Bible*, 1793.

3. Chrysostom, *Ancient Christian Commentary on Scripture*, 353.

4. C. E. B. Cranfield, *The Epistle to the Romans.* vol. II (New York: T & T Clark International, 1975) 732.

5. Craig S. Keener, *The IVP Bible Background Commentary , New Testament* (Downers Grove, IL: InterVarsity, 1993), 444.

6. John Murray, *The Epistle to the Romans* (Grand Rapids, MI: Eerdmans, 1965), 200.

7. Henri Nouwen, *The Genesee Diary* (Garden City: Doubleday, 1966), 162.

8. C. S. Lewis, *Mere Christianity* (New York: Macmillan, 1958), 158.

9. Elizabeth O'Connor, *Call to Commitment* (New York: Harper & Row, 1963), 139.

10. O'Connor, *Call to Commitment*, 162.

11. Nouwen, *The Genesee Diary*, 169.

12. Augustine, *Ancient Christian Commentary on Scripture*, 361.

13. Edwards, *New International Biblical Commentary*, 346.

14. Yancey, *What's So Amazing about Grace?* 280.

15. O'Connor, *Call to Commitment*, 158.

16. Jerome, *Ancient Christian Commentary on Scripture*, 366.

17. James Montgomery Boice, *Romans, vol. 4*, 1871.

18. Theodoret of Cyr, *Ancient Christian Commentary on Scripture*, 368.

Romans 16: A Fond Farewell

1. Lawrence O. Richards, *The Revell Bible Dictionary*, 764–765.

2. John Murray, *The Epistle to the Romans* (Grand Rapids, MI: Wm. B. Eerdmans, 1968), 226.

3. Boice, *Romans, vol. 4*, 1911.

4. Chrysostom, *Ancient Christian Commentary on Scripture*, 369.

5. John Murray, *The Epistle to the Romans* (Grand Rapids, MI: Wm. B. Eerdmans, 1965), 228–229.

6. Craig S. Keener, *The IVP Bible Background Commentary, New Testament* (Downers Grove, IL: InterVarsity, 1993), 448.

7. Francis Davidson, *The New Bible Commentary* (Grand Rapids, MI: Wm. B. Eerdmans, 1953), 964.

8. Manning, *The Ragamuffin Gospel*, 183.

9. Edwards, *New International Biblical Commentary*, 357.

10. Keener, *The IVP Bible Background Commentary*, 449.

11. John G. Mitchell, *Right with God* (Portland, OR: Multnomah Press, 1990), 282.

12. Craig S. Keener, *The IVP Bible Background Commentary*, New Testament, (Downers Grove, IL: InterVarsity, 1993), 449–450.

13. J. Vernon McGee, *Thru the Bible Commentary Series, Romans Chapters 1–8* (Nashville: Thomas Nelson, Inc., 1991), 758.

The Book of Romans Overview

1. Origen, quoted in *Ancient Christian Commentary on Scripture, Romans, vol. 6* (Downers Grove, IL: InterVarsity Press, 1998), 106.

2. Chrysostom, quoted in *Ancient Christian Commentary on Scripture, Romans, vol. 6* (Downers Grove, IL: InterVarsity Press, 1998), 31–32.

3. Cyril of Alexandria, quoted in *Ancient Christian Commentary on Scripture, Romans, vol. 6* (Downers Grove, IL: InterVarsity Press, 1998), 157.

4. Augustine, quoted in *Ancient Christian Commentary on Scripture, Romans, vol. 6* (Downers Grove, IL: InterVarsity Press, 1998), 340.

5. Warren Wiersbe, *The Bible Exposition Commentary* (Colorado Springs, CO: Chariot Victor, 1998), 514.

Index

suffering, 123
Burrows, W.
 on the laws of social life, 203
 on the stumbling stone, 143
Byrne, Brendan, 18

C

Calvin, John
 on Abraham's faith and God's
  grace, 61
 on authority, 199–200
 on believers and sin, 86
 on grace vs. works, 162
 on holiness, 206
 on hope, 118
 on judgmentalism, 212
 on justification and grace, 69
 on obedience to governing
 on peace, 65
captive, 103
Carmel, Mount
 Elijah's victory, 160
 illustration #6, 161
carnal, 99, 110, 146, 150, 254
 definition of, 150
Cenchrea, 246
Chambers, Oswald
 on tribulations, suffering, and
  persecution, 124
 on union with Jesus Christ, 83
character
 hope produced by, 65
 perseverance as producing, 65
childbirth
 laws surrounding, 91
 pain in, 117, 118
choices, 34, 40, 86, 102, 138,
  140, 150, 159, 263
Christendom
 definition of, 35
Christian body, the, 183
Christian community, 10, 176,
  196, 209, 235, 274
Christian faith, 40, 264
Christian fellowship, 119
Christian martyrs, 66
Christianity
 faith as key to, 261
 Old Testament roots of, 261
 significance of Romans (book
  of) to, 1, 262, 275
 as supplanting Judaism, 165
Christian(s)
 accountability to God, tips
  regarding, 274
 as believer-priests, 179
 as called to love and serve, 186,
  217, 230, 274
 challenges to, universal, 237
 characteristics of, ideal, 118

responsibility to all, 84, 256
 a righteous community, 264
 sons and daughters of Christ, 115
 are united with Christ, 271, 272
Chrysostom, John
 on Abraham's faith, 62
 on Christ as second Adam, 72
 on Christ vs. law, 215
 on death to sin, 81
 on gifts, individual, 183
 on glory, 117
 on good works, 182
 on righteousness through faith, 270
 on value of the epistle, 249
 on "strong" believers, responsibility
  of, 228
Cilicia, 2, 64
circumcised, 34, 57, 58, 141, 280
circumcision, 33, 35, 52, 58, 270,
  280
circumcision of the heart, 35
 definition of, 35
city of Jerusalem, the, 155
coheirs with Christ, believers as, 115,
  125, 281
coins, then and now
 illustration #8, 171, 201
Coleridge, Samuel Taylor, 4
Colosseum, 250
 illustration #13, 257
commitment
 of God to people, 135
 to God, 138
communication with God, 12
communion
 definition of, 34
compass, 18
 the gospel, 16
compassion of God, 136
compromise, 17, 145
condemnation, 31, 43, 51, 71, 97,
  107, 109, 130, 131, 213, 221
 definition of, 107
conduces
 definition of, 98
confess, 148, 150
conformed, 121, 125, 181, 199, 273
 definition of, 181
congregation, 13, 211, 249
conscience
 definition of, 31
consequences
 for disobedience, God has
  established, 18, 118
 of sin, 18, 51, 70, 72, 73, 84, 266
contentment, 112, 121, 281
context
 definition of, 96
contribution, 238, 240, 271
conversion, 53, 58, 97, 152, 154,
  166, 172

definition of, 53
counsel, 3, 64, 69, 190, 197
courage, 241
covenant
 Davidic, 5
 definition, 14
 new, 6, 7, 40, 47, 63, 129,
  150, 179, 180, 212
 old, 6, 7, 16, 30, 63, 69, 94, 115,
  129, 141, 179, 180, 193, 195,
  212, 217, 232
covetousness, 21, 95, 266
 definition of, 95
Cranfield, C. E. B.
 on Gentile Christians, 172
 on God's covenant people, 129
 on God's purpose, 164
 on incarnation, 228
 on a loving God, 186
 on Martin Luther, 148
created, 19, 70, 80, 95, 121, 124
creation, 16, 18, 61, 116, 117, 118,
  121, 137, 139, 161, 265
cross, the, 16, 18, 86, 191, 269
Cyrene, 252
Cyril of Alexanderia, 272

D

Damascus
 definition of, 2
 illustration #4, 42
 road to, 41, 42, 103, 226, 228
David
 definition of, 5, 55
Davidic Covenant
 definition of, 5
Davidson, Francis
 on apostasy of the Jews, 165
 on the saints, 251
deadness
 definition of, 60
death
 of Claudius, 1
 definition of, 69, 98
 fruit for, 93
 physical and spiritual, 98
 sin nature, 69
 sin as producing, 69
 spiritual, 69
 of Stephen, 2, 27
 "white funeral," 83
debauchery, 205, 206
debt of love, 202, 203
deceit, 21, 44
deceived, 84, 255
deception, 53
decree, 135, 195
demonic, the, 63
 definition of, 63

155, 175, 230, 270
God
  appreciation from, 113, 231, 234
  character of, 91, 136, 267
  and creation, 16, 17, 18, 161, 269
  dependence on, 169
  discipline by, 28
  divine nature of, 22
  expectations of us by, 94
  faithfulness of, 39, 49, 100, 161,
    164, 176
  faithfulness to Jews, 40
  free choice of (doctrine of
    divine election), 136, 138, 160,
    161, 162, 163, 164, 172, 173
  glory of, 14, 18, 25, 46, 55, 63, 64,
    78, 94, 100, 137, 151, 155, 175,
    230, 270
  invisible qualities of, 17, 256
  Jesus as Son of, 5, 6, 16, 29, 47,
    227
  as judge, 44, 269
  kindness of, 6, 25, 36
  as longsuffering, 26, 139
  as Lord, 17, 73, 150, 282
  love for, 120, 176, 193
  love for us, 187
  mercy of, 129, 168, 174, 268
  Messiah promised by, 261
  nature of, 129
  obedience to, 29, 120, 198
  our obligation to, 114
  as omniscient, 138
  patience of, 139
  peace with, 63, 64, 77, 220
  personal relationship with, 39, 269
  power of, 15, 96, 170, 273
  praising, 68
  promises of, 59, 142, 173
  recognizing, 18
  rejection of, 163
  righteousness of, 16, 18, 46, 55,
    134, 147, 148, 152, 264, 267
  serving, 154
  sovereignty of, 144, 197
  as superhuman, 174
  theophanies of, 132
  truth of, 42, 145, 230, 245
  unconditional love from, 230
  will of, 10, 11, 39, 84, 96, 100,
    102, 114, 119, 161, 181, 213,
    221, 238, 241
  wisdom of, 175
  wrath of, 17, 18, 19, 22, 28, 64,
    262, 266, 267
Godet, F. L.
  on grace, 171
  on manifestations of love, 190
  on Reformation, 5
God's ways are not man's ways, 257
Gomorrah, Sodom and, 141

good works, 29, 54, 55, 88, 94, 111,
  179, 198
gospel of Jesus Christ, 8, 23, 236, 262
gossip, 214, 266
grace of God
  access to, 64
  being born again, 152
  as bigger than sin, 71
  definition of, 6
  faith enabling man to receive, 230
  as gift from God, 29
  human effort and, 138, 267
  justification as by, 56
  and mercy, relationship between, 19,
    54, 120, 152
  reign of, through Christ, 70
  result of, 54
  salvation by, 56
  significance of, 86
grace and mercy, 78, 121, 146, 152
Graham, Billy
  on Christian responsibility, 187
  on Christianity as daily decision, 202
  on spiritual renewal, 164
gratitude, 9, 10, 138, 242
greed, 121
grief, 130, 131, 132, 165, 189, 210,
  282
growth, 1, 63, 166, 182, 184, 213,
  217, 227, 274
guilt, 18, 27, 31, 44, 46, 56, 68, 70,
  107, 153

H

Haldane, Robert, 181
handiwork, 18
happiness, 10, 69, 98
hardships, 237
harmony, 3, 14, 189, 212, 262, 275
hatred, 14, 86, 135, 188, 190
heart
  definition of, 27
Henry, Matthew
  on Abraham as spiritual father, 58
  on Abraham's faith, 52
  on God's grace, 48
  on God's wrath, 28
  on good works, 94
  on Jesus, self-denial of, 227
  on justification of believers, 109
  on repentance, 26
Herod, 188
high priest, 92, 179, 180
  illustration #3, 12
His will
  definition of, 101
Hodge, Charles
  on conscience, 221
  on God in nature, 157
  on grace and holiness, 88

on limitation of human
    authority, 198
  on salvation, 151
holiness, 5, 7, 18, 26, 42, 71, 87, 88,
  98, 206, 213, 272
  definition of, 87
Holy City, Jerusalem as, 155
holy kiss, 252
Holy Spirit
  compelled to listen to the voice of,
    114
  control by, 110
  empowered by God's, 263
  empowers the believer's prayer
    life, 112
  free from condemnation, 104
  free to minister, 219
  gifts of, 183
  gives us the power to hope, 233
  helps us in our weakness, 121
  his grace moves hearts, 154
  hope and the ministry of, 119
  indwells in our bodies, 93
  Jesus linked to believers through, 83
  joins a person to Christ, 80
  living link with Jesus, 273
  prays on our behalf, 119
  teaches us to have a faithful
    prayer life, 119
homosexuality, 20, 21
honesty, 141, 206
hope, 28, 60, 62, 65, 118, 170
hospitality, 187
house church, 10, 247, 248, 252, 258
  illustration #12, 238
human nature, 111, 138, 201, 267
humility, 3, 13, 183, 193, 230, 236,
  241
hypocrisy, 25, 27, 29, 31, 33, 35, 152,
  185, 193, 251

I

idols, 19, 32, 45, 198, 209, 210
illness, 43
immortality, 28
impenitent
  definition of, 27
imperfect and aorist
  definition of, 100
implication, 59, 200, 264
incarnation, the
  definition of, 6
incarnational
  definition of, 155
inheritance, 54, 60, 115, 116
innocent, 18, 34, 46, 57, 77, 111,
  138, 204, 269, 270, 271, 273
insignificant, 116
insults, 227
insurrection, 201

sincerity and, 185
unconditional, 230
undeserving, 47
the world, 15
Luther, Martin
on arrogant people, 164
on death and sin, 73
on destroying the flesh, 28
on evil, 192
on faith, 222
on the Epistle to the Romans, 4
on God being eternal, 85
on grace, 57
on mercy, 139
on sin, 101
on tempation, 86
lying, 130

M

Macedonia, 238
magnify, 94, 95, 166
makes intercession
definition of, 119
Manning, Brennan
on authentic disciples, 253
on the gospel of grace, 47
Mary and Martha, 189
Mary, mother of Jesus, 232
mediator, 12, 92
meditate, 97
mentor, 56, 155
mercy, 16, 17, 19, 47, 54, 78, 87,
120, 129, 136, 139, 173, 174,
268
definition of, 16
Messiah
Old Testament prophecies about, 1
rejected by God's chosen people,
130, 142, 166
savior of mankind, 5
a stumbling block, 142
through the Jewish race, 43
messianic mission
definition of, 35
metaphor
baptism as, 78
branch of an olive tree as, 168
God as a potter, 139
light as, 206
minister, 8, 164, 183
ministry
of the Holy Spirit, 119
of Jesus, 79, 230
of Paul, 2, 164, 166, 234, 238, 255
miracles, 236
mission from God, 237
mitigated
definition of, 118
mocked, 16, 230

money
coins then and now, 170, 171
contribution, 238
debt, 203
one hundred denarii, 170
taxes, 189, 195, 200, 201, 202, 207
ten thousand talents, 170
Moo, Douglas J.
on Christian behavior, 113
on Christians fulfilling the law, 109
on God overcoming law, 97
on the Reformers' teaching, 153
on the "strong," 219
on a universally applicable principle,
156
mortality, 20
Mosaic Law
definition of, 6
Moses
baptized into, 78
God made an agreement, 6
Old Covenant, 63, 129, 132
personal knowledge of God, 136
Ten Commandments, 30
tent meeting, 136
motives
wrong attitudes and, 101
Mount Calvary, 94
Mount Carmel, 160, 161
Mount Sinai, 94, 132
mystery
of godliness, 94, 236, 256
salvation of Israel as, 171, 172

N

Nathan, 6
Nero
definition of, 188
New Covenant
definition of, 63
New Testament, 3, 17, 41, 220,
234, 269, 286, 293
noble, 110, 151, 195
Nouwen, Henri
on Christ's authority, 230
on growing in grace, 235

O

O'Connor, Elizabeth
on Christian responsibility, 235
on need, church response to, 233
on saints, 237
obedience
of early Roman Christians, 6
"eternal life" looks like, 29
of faith, 17
faith in action, 254
to God, 120

to governing authority, 230
honors God's boundless love, 80
keeps the enemy on the defensive,
254
love for God, 120
of the law
definition of, 59
Old Covenant
definition of, 63
old man
definition of, 81
Old Testament, 3, 6, 17, 72, 130, 161,
261, 267, 269, 274
definition of, 6
omniscient
definition, 138
one man's
definition of, 71
ordained
definition of, 195
Origen
on death through sin, 71
on debt vs. sin, 203
on the knowledge of sin, 268

P

pagan
definition of, 13, 45
Palestine, 191, 261
parable
definition, 170
unmerciful servant, 170–171
paratoma
definition of, 166
partiality
definition of, 29
patience, 139, 146, 228, 229
Paul
built his identity as being a servant
of Jesus, 3
a committed Pharisee, 91
conversion of, 2
covenant responsibilities, 32
dead to sin, 78
debtor to both Jews and Greeks, 14
establishes a need for righteousness,
77
explains how the gospel manifests its
power, 152
Judgment Day is coming, 32
killed Christians, 2
mocked by the ignorant, 16
perseverance produces character, 65
the "secrets of men," 32
used Abraham as an example, 52
used Christ as an example, 227
used David as an example, 55
uses analogy of wages, 53
wanted to rescue the Romans from

their bondage, 9
wrote the book of Romans, 1
peace
  in battle, 254
  among Christians, 220
  eternal, 28
  with God, 77
  God's, 109, 220
  gospel for the sinner, 43
  internal political, 1
  from justification by faith, 64
  meaning of, 220
  with others, 191
  Paul's concern for, 219
  proclamation of, 155
  serenity of conscience, 65
Pelagius
  on our freedom, 221
  on judgment, 199
  on lust, 21
  on propitiousness, 11
pentecost, 231, 248
perfection, 42, 46, 66, 101, 113, 161,
  233, 262
persecution
  of Christians, 257
  comes in many different forms, 188
  in the face of, 258
  in Paul's time, 188
perspective
  biblical, 197
  Christlike, 181, 182, 216
  divine, 54
  God's, 96
  human, 60, 241
  Jewish, 104
  unbalanced, 3
pharaoh, 131, 136, 137, 139
Pharisees, 1, 11, 51, 59, 61, 65, 91,
  97, 145, 199, 219, 228
Phoebe, 246, 247, 259, 283
piety
  definition of, 9
Plumer, William
  on Christians, 101
  on divine instruction, 222
  on the enemy of the gospel, 94
  on the gift of preaching, 156
  on the law, 98
  on vouchsafes, 11
  we belong to God, 213
poor people being helped, 236, 238
power
  of God, 15, 96, 170, 273
  of Jesus, 155
praise
  Christian martyrs, 66
  gratitude to God, 242
  a way to honor and adore our
    Savior, 175

prayer
  in Bible, 119
  a difficult discipline, 119
  Holy Spirit empowers those who
    pray, 12, 119
  Jesus values, 9
  keep a priority, 173
  learned, like speaking, 12
  our method of communicating with
    God, 12
  Psalms is our prayer book, 12, 119
praying, 11, 95, 148
predestined
  definition of, 121
  pride, 13, 35, 40, 93, 101, 111,
    137, 143, 147, 182, 183, 184
Priscilla, 247, 248
problems, 31, 33, 77, 82, 129, 135,
  138
promises from God, 6, 59, 61
prophecy, 6, 118, 183
prophets, 5, 45, 46, 132, 150, 160,
  161, 163, 261
  definition of, 150
Prophets, the
  definition of, 46, 163
propitious
  definition of, 11
prostitutes, 30, 189
purpose
  God's, 3, 162, 273
  law's, 108
  of prayer, 12
put to death
  definition of, 114

R

reap, 11, 19, 84, 206
Rebekah, 134
reconciled
  definition of, 14, 68
recounts, 66
redemption
  adoption, 118
  blood, 47
  God's overall plan, 239
  is a costly matter, 47
  of our bodies, 113, 117, 118
Reformation, the
  definition of, 56
regulations, 111
reign
  definition of, 92
repent, 26, 36, 139, 141
repentance, 26, 36, 150
respect, 29, 33, 117, 153, 188, 195,
  200, 201, 226
resurrection, 5, 61, 68, 80, 89, 261
retribution

definition of, 19
revenge, 190, 191, 192
Richards, Larry
  on differences among Christians,
    211
  on Esau, 135
  focus on relationships, 184
  on Jesus, costly death of, 49
  on justification and righteousness,
    56
righteous, 21, 28, 43, 85, 108, 147,
  264, 267, 273
righteousness, 6, 16, 18, 21, 42, 46,
  57, 58, 77, 114, 142, 147, 149
road to Damascus, 103, 226, 228
Roman Empire, 1, 7, 8, 10, 15, 41,
  85, 188, 189, 261
Romans, book of
  as carefully reasoned treatise, 262
  as good news, 268
  historical context, 196
  impact on Christianity, 275
  Martin Luther's conversion, 276
  Paul as author, 1
  practical value of, 257
  significance of, 264
Rome
  Christians in, 3, 10, 16, 258, 262
  definition of, 1
  Jews expelled from, 247
  Nero as emperor of, 257
  Paul's imprisonment in, 242
  persecution of Christians in, 257
  Spain as colony of, 238
root, analogy of, 167
root of Jesse, 231, 232

S

sabbath, 147, 212
sacrifice
  of animals, 180, 193
  blood, 179
  living, Christians as, 179, 180, 181,
    193
  propitiation, 47, 49
saints
  definition of, 7
salvific
  definition of, 35
sanctification
  certainty of, 123
  conflicts during process of, 100
  definition of, 51, 100, 107, 190
  justification and, 51
  takes a lifetime, 190
Sanhedrin
  definition of, 41
Sarah
  Abraham's wife, 60

barrenness of, 58, 60

God's word to, 134

son, Isaac, 134

Satan, 8, 21, 43, 101, 114, 122, 124, 135, 145, 152, 192, 253, 254

Schaeffer, Dr. Francis A.

on blessings of Christian fellowship, 14

on Christ as kinsman-redeemer, 72

on Christians and sin, 84–85

on faith, grace, and salvation, 56

on God's grace, 48

on homosexuality, 21

on the incarnation, 6

on Paul's pride in the gospel, 67

on rituals of faith, 35

Schlatter, Adolf

on Christian character, 181

on Christian life, 111

on confession of faith, 153

on giving thanks, 9

on grace, 166

on salvation, 20

on union with Jesus Christ, 94

on upbuilding, 219

second coming, 204

self-centeredness, 227

self-interest, 192, 225

selfishness, 159, 216, 227, 266

self-righteousness, true righteousness vs., 42, 51, 87, 88

serpent, 101, 255

servant, servanthood, 1, 3, 4, 5, 7, 10, 15, 17, 19, 80, 154, 170, 211, 230, 243, 246

service, 55, 87, 131, 187, 200, 238, 255

sexual immorality, 20, 21

sexuality, 20, 21, 266

shadows, 142

shame, 16, 20, 87, 130, 142, 143, 144, 152, 197

shameful, 20

shepherd, 67

Shulam, Joseph

on God's law, 100

on non-retaliation, 190

on unfaithful people, 162

significance, 86, 161, 164, 249, 264

sin

as absence of God, 47

adultery as, 32, 33, 91, 202, 209

baptismal death and, 85

Christian struggle with, 86, 101

confessing, 152, 153

consequences of, 18, 72, 84

destructiveness of, 84

the Fall as beginning of, 16, 96, 121

forgiveness for, 85

forgiveness of, God's, 85

God as hating, 266

God as tolerating, 139

God's forgiveness of, 85

human, universality of, 280

Jesus' sacrificial atonement for, 179

justification from, 34, 63, 85

lying as, 130

original, 45, 70

overcoming, steps of, 83, 84

paratoma, 166

reality of, 21, 28

retribution for, 19

sin nature, 96, 103, 110, 182

sincerity, 193

sinless perfection

definition of, 101

sinned

definition of, 30

sinners, 22, 36, 43, 67, 73, 74, 150, 199, 265, 266

slavery, 83, 85, 86, 87, 117

Sodom and Gomorrah, 141

Solomon, 209

songs, 56, 62

sonship

definition of, 5

sovereign, 53, 55, 59, 115, 121, 135, 159, 161, 196, 197

sow, 84, 154, 165

spiritual war, 245, 254

stone on which people stumble, 142, 143

Stowers, Stanley K., 216

strength, 53, 60, 67, 86, 133, 206, 227

stress, 209

Stuhlmacher, Peter

on accepting other Christians, 213

on God's grace, 135

on God's mercy, 173

on helping fellow Christians, 217

submission, 84, 197, 201

Swindoll, Charles R.

on grace, 53

on Paul's circumstances, 67

on saints and grace, 187

on spiritual merit, 54

on the wonderful life of believers, 215

T

temple, 11, 32, 107, 132, 179, 180

temptation, 86, 169, 187, 216

Ten Commandments, 30, 33, 45, 91, 198

ten thousand talents, 170

tent meeting, 136

tentmakers, 247

testimonies, 2, 103

thanksgiving, 103

Theodoret of Cyr

on the God of peace, 242

on hope, 62

theophany, 132

threshold, 140

Timothy, 255, 256

Titus, 255

torah, 40, 100, 228

torture, 131

total depravity

definition of, 43

Tozer, A. W., 181

treatise

definition of, 262

tree of the knowledge of good and evil, 96

truth

attacks on, 254

focusing mind on, 60

God's, 21, 163, 253, 254

rejection of, 28

suppression of, 17, 18, 22, 265

Tryphena and Tryphosa

twin sisters, 249, 251

U

unbelievers

compassion for, 131

prepared for destruction, 139

unclean, 14, 19, 87, 209, 215

unconditional commitment, 135

unconditional condition, 171

unconditional love, 230

unconditional promise, 5, 6

unfaithful, 40, 42, 100, 162, 164

unity

between Old and New Testaments, 17

of the church, 166

upbuilding, 219

uphold, 199, 228

V

validity, 29

vile passions

definition of, 20

vindicated, 269

vouchsafes, 11

W

waiting

to be adopted, 118

fruitful, 204

hope, 118, 123

for redemption, 117

Walvoord, John F., and Roy B. Zuck

on God's heralds, 155

on how Paul's letters began, 10

on humility, 183

on sanctification, conflicts in, 100
water baptism, 78, 79
water communion, 34
Wesley, John, 4, 276
"white funeral," 83
whole counsel, 3, 22, 228
whole creation, the, 117
wickedness
    definition of, 21
Wiersbe, Warren, 276
wisdom
    God's infinite, 17
    God's peace and, 109
    trust in God's, 138
womb, 60
Word of God, 12, 23, 42, 61, 110,
    119, 130, 133, 156, 187, 212,
    223, 228
work of righteousness
    definition of, 80

works, 17, 18, 29, 51, 53, 54, 55, 94,
    134, 142, 162
world, the
    definition of, 15, 63
worrying, 206
worship, 47, 64, 117, 160, 175, 176,
    198, 214
wrath, 17, 18, 20, 27, 28, 36, 59, 139,
    200, 266
wrath of God, 17, 19, 28, 266
Wright, N. T.
    on being human, 82
    on justification, 17
Writings, the
    definition of, 163
wrongdoing, 19, 163

Y

Yahweh, 44, 136, 165

Yancey, Philip
    on God as father, 115
    on God as shepherd, 67
    on grace, 113
    on love for God, 120
    on loveworthiness, 236
    on our perception of God as a father,
    69
you will die, 114
you will live, 114

Z

Zacharias, Ravi, 201
zeal, false vs. real, 145–146
zealot, 199, 245
Zebedee, 188
Zion, 142, 143, 171, 172